# perspectives

## Management

# perspectives

## Management

Academic Editor
**F. William Brown**
*Montana State University–Bozeman*

coursewise
publishing
inc.

Bellevue • Boulder • Dubuque • Madison • St. Paul

Our mission at **Coursewise** is to help students make connections—linking theory to practice and the classroom to the outside world. Learners are motivated to synthesize ideas when course materials are placed in a context they recognize. By providing gateways to contemporary and enduring issues, **Coursewise** publications will expand students' awareness of and context for the course subject.

For more information on **Coursewise,** visit us at our web site: http://www.coursewise.com

To order an examination copy:
Houghton Mifflin Sixth Floor Media  800-565-6247 (voice) / 800-565-6236 (fax)

## Coursewise Publishing Editorial Staff

Thomas Doran, ceo/publisher: Environmental Science/Geography/Journalism/Marketing/Speech
Edgar Laube, publisher: Political Science/Psychology/Sociology
Linda Meehan Avenarius, publisher: **Courselinks™**
Sue Pulvermacher-Alt, publisher: Education/Health/Gender Studies
Victoria Putman, publisher: Anthropology/Philosophy/Religion
Tom Romaniak, publisher: Business/Criminal Justice/Economics
Kathleen Schmitt, publishing assistant
Gail Hodge, executive producer

## Coursewise Publishing Production Staff

Lori A. Blosch, permissions coordinator
Mary Monner, production coordinator
Victoria Putman, production manager

Library of Congress Catalog Card Number: 99-067634

ISBN 0-618-02577-4

Printed in the United States of America by Coursewise Publishing, Inc.
7 North Pinckney Street, Suite 346, Madison, WI 53703

10 9 8 7 6 5 4 3 2 1

# from the
# Publisher

## Tom Romaniak

*Coursewise Publishing*

I majored in accounting and finance when I went to college. In my mind, these were the toughest areas of the business curriculum, and I enjoyed the challenge that my accounting and finance courses presented. I viewed some of the other areas of the business curriculum as "soft." After all, how difficult could it be to manage and market? Instead of discussing management concepts and principles, I wanted to learn more about the time value of money, depreciation schedules, and debt instruments. At the time, I didn't appreciate the non-numbers-related courses.

These days, I realize how naïve and foolish my thinking was. Since college, I have worked in two different publishing companies and have been exposed to a variety of business situations. This experience has taught me a valuable lesson. To be successful, regardless of your position or department, you need some basic managing skills. But you don't necessarily need to be able to manipulate and massage numbers.

Pay attention! This is important stuff. The concepts and principles that you will learn in the management course you are now taking will benefit you for years to come—not only in your professional life, but also in your personal life. Everyone needs to know how to resolve conflicts, manage resources, motivate others, and make good decisions.

It doesn't matter if you are a secretary, a marketer, a sales rep, or even an accountant. You can be a brilliant accountant, but without some basic management skills, you will be of little value to your organization, and your opportunities for advancement will be limited.

Bill Brown has done a tremendous job of editing this reader. He has combed through the literature to select the articles that will be of most value to you. The readings presented in this volume will augment the management principles and concepts outlined in your text and enhanced by your professor. These readings will help you place the concepts into a context you can understand. Thanks, Bill, for your outstanding work.

I welcome your thoughts and opinions about this volume and the corresponding **Courselinks**™ site for Management, where you will find additional information and resources. Let us know what we did right and what we need to improve upon.

Tom Romaniak
tomr@coursewise.com

# from the
# Academic Editor

## F. William Brown

*Montana State University–Bozeman*

Welcome to the first edition of *Perspectives: Management,* a collection of readings designed to complement and supplement your management textbook. The readings in this volume have been selected from a variety of sources and will help you learn more about the fascinating field of managers and management. The readings are arranged in eight sections that correspond to the general organization of most contemporary management texts.

As the title of this collection suggests, there are multiple "perspectives" on management. Occasionally, students ask me for the rules or laws that govern the world of management and are at first skeptical when I say I can't do so. Although we know a lot about what effective managers do and what high-performing organizations are like, we really don't have any algorithmic solutions to the many challenges that confront people in responsible management positions. At its best, the world is probabilistic and contingent, and management is not some isolated, distinct part of it. At its heart, management is about influence, emanating from both the positions managers hold and the quality of their personalities and personas.

To understand management, we have to understand both the manager and the world of the manager. To put it another way, we have to understand ourselves and the world around us. As long as management is about people—and thank goodness it is—it will never have the predictability and replicability of, say, physics or chemistry. For some, this indeterminate nature is maddening and off-putting, but for most people, it is also the source of their attraction to and appreciation for the field.

One way to learn about management is to study managers and management in the world in which they operate. The readings in this collection should help you to both affirm the things you have learned and hold to be true about management, and to understand the limits and uniqueness of a given perspective. My hope for you, whether you are preparing for a career in management or just passing through a management course on the way to a different career, is that in some way this reader will help you gain a lifelong appreciation for the dynamism and the wonder of the messy, ambiguous, exciting, creative world of management.

*F. William "Bill" Brown is an associate professor of management in the College of Business at Montana State University in Bozeman, Montana. He teaches courses on leadership, management, and strategy, and consults with a variety of business and industry clients. Bill is a native of New Orleans. Before becoming an academic and consultant, he had a 20-year career as an Army officer, serving in a variety of leadership positions both in the United States and overseas.*

*Prior to coming to Montana State University, Bill was a faculty member at the University of Nebraska–Lincoln and at Baylor University. At those universities, he taught management and leadership courses and did university-sponsored consulting work with business, industry, academic, and governmental organizations.*

*In addition to his bachelor's degree in psychology, Bill has master's degrees in public administration and business administration. He received his Ph.D. in business administration from The George Washington University in Washington, D.C. Like his teaching and consulting, his research and writing interests center on leadership, management, and organizational development. In 1996, he co-authored* Interpersonal Skills for Leadership, *published by Prentice Hall. The recipient of several teaching awards and the author of numerous articles on management and leadership, his work has been published in* The Journal of Applied Psychology, The Journal of Business and Management, The Journal of Management Consulting, The Journal of Behavioral Decision Making, The Journal of Extension, *and* The Leadership and Organization Development Journal.

*When not working, Bill enjoys hiking and camping in the mountains with his wife and dogs, reading, and gardening. He considers himself a bad golfer and a pretty good cook.*

# Editorial Board

We wish to thank the following instructors for their assistance. Their many suggestions not only contributed to the construction of this volume, but also to the ongoing development of the Management web site.

# WiseGuide Introduction

## Critical Thinking and Bumper Stickers

The bumper sticker said: Question Authority. This is a simple directive that goes straight to the heart of critical thinking. The issue is not whether the authority is right or wrong; it's the questioning process that's important. Questioning helps you develop awareness and a clearer sense of what you think. That's critical thinking.

Critical thinking is a new label for an old approach to learning—that of challenging all ideas, hypotheses, and assumptions. In the physical and life sciences, systematic questioning and testing methods (known as the scientific method) help verify information, and objectivity is the benchmark on which all knowledge is pursued. In the social sciences, however, where the goal is to study people and their behavior, things get fuzzy. It's one thing for the chemistry experiment to work out as predicted, or for the petri dish to yield a certain result. It's quite another matter, however, in the social sciences, where the subject is ourselves. Objectivity is harder to achieve.

Although you'll hear critical thinking defined in many different ways, it really boils down to analyzing the ideas and messages that you receive. What are you being asked to think or believe? Does it make sense, objectively? Using the same facts and considerations, could you reasonably come up with a different conclusion? And, why does this matter in the first place? As the bumper sticker urged, question authority. Authority can be a textbook, a politician, a boss, a big sister, or an ad on television. Whatever the message, learning to question it appropriately is a habit that will serve you well for a lifetime. And in the meantime, thinking critically will certainly help you be course wise.

Question Authority

## Getting Connected

This reader is a tool for connected learning. This means that the readings and other learning aids explained here will help you to link classroom theory to real-world issues. They will help you to think critically and to make long-lasting learning connections. Feedback from both instructors and students has helped us to develop some suggestions on how you can wisely use this connected learning tool.

## WiseGuide Pedagogy

A wise reader is better able to be a critical reader. Therefore, we want to help you get wise about the articles in this reader. Each section of *Perspectives* has three tools to help you: the WiseGuide Intro, the WiseGuide Wrap-Up, and the Putting It in *Perspectives* review form.

## WiseGuide Intro

In the WiseGuide Intro, the Academic Editor introduces the section, gives you an overview of the topics covered, and explains why particular articles were selected and what's important about them.

Also in the WiseGuide Intro, you'll find several key points or learning objectives that highlight the most important things to remember from this section. These will help you to focus your study of section topics.

WiseGuide Intro

At the end of the WiseGuide Intro, you'll find questions designed to stimulate critical thinking. Wise students will keep these questions in mind as they read an article (we repeat the questions at the start of the articles as a reminder). When you finish each article, check your understanding. Can you answer the questions? If not, go back and reread the article. The Academic Editor has written sample responses for many of the questions, and you'll find these online at the **Courselinks**™ site for this course. More about **Courselinks** in a minute. . . .

## WiseGuide Wrap-Up

Be course wise and develop a thorough understanding of the topics covered in this course. The WiseGuide Wrap-Up at the end of each section will help you do just that with concluding comments or summary points that repeat what's most important to understand from the section you just read.

In addition, we try to get you wired up by providing a list of select Internet resources—what we call R.E.A.L. web sites because they're **R**elevant, **E**nhanced, **A**pproved, and **L**inked. The information at these web sites will enhance your understanding of a topic. (Remember to use your Passport and start at http://www.courselinks.com so that if any of these sites have changed, you'll have the latest link.)

## Putting It in *Perspectives* Review Form

At the end of the book is the Putting It in *Perspectives* review form. Your instructor may ask you to complete this form as an assignment or for extra credit. If nothing else, consider doing it on your own to help you critically think about the reading.

Prompts at the end of each article encourage you to complete this review form. Feel free to copy the form and use it as needed.

## The Courselinks™ Site

http://www.courselinks.com

The **Courselinks** Passport is your ticket to a wonderful world of integrated web resources designed to help you with your course work. These resources are found at the **Courselinks** site for your course area. This is where the readings in this book and the key topics of your course are linked to an exciting array of online learning tools. Here you will find carefully selected readings, web links, quizzes, worksheets, and more, tailored to your course and approved as connected learning tools. The ever-changing, always interesting **Courselinks** site features a number of carefully integrated resources designed to help you be course wise. These include:

- **R.E.A.L. Sites**  At the core of a **Courselinks** site is the list of R.E.A.L. sites. This is a select group of web sites for studying, not surfing. Like the readings in this book, these sites have been selected, reviewed, and approved by the Academic Editor and the Editorial Board. The R.E.A.L. sites are arranged by topic and are annotated with short descriptions and key words to make them easier for you to use for reference or research. With R.E.A.L. sites, you're studying approved resources within seconds—and not wasting precious time surfing unproven sites.

- **Editor's Choice**  Here you'll find updates on news related to your course, with links to the actual online sources. This is also where we'll tell you about changes to the site and about online events.

- **Course Overview** This is a general description of the typical course in this area of study. While your instructor will provide specific course objectives, this overview helps you place the course in a generic context and offers you an additional reference point.

- **www.orksheet** Focus your trip to a R.E.A.L. site with the www.orksheet. Each of the 10 to 15 questions will prompt you to take in the best that site has to offer. Use this tool for self-study, or if required, email it to your instructor.

- **Course Quiz** The questions on this self-scoring quiz are related to articles in the reader, information at R.E.A.L. sites, and other course topics, and will help you pinpoint areas you need to study. Only you will know your score—it's an easy, risk-free way to keep pace!

- **Topic Key** The online Topic Key is a listing of the main topics in your course, and it correlates with the Topic Key that appears in this reader. This handy reference tool also links directly to those R.E.A.L. sites that are especially appropriate to each topic, bringing you integrated online resources within seconds!

- **Message Center** Share your ideas with fellow students and instructors, in your class or in classes around the world, by using the Message Center. There are links to both a real-time chat room and a message forum, which are accessible all day, every day. Watch for scheduled CourseChat events throughout the semester.

- **Student Lounge** Drop by the Student Lounge, a virtual "hangout" with links to professional associations in your course area, online article review forms, and site feedback forms. Take a look around the Student Lounge and give us your feedback. We're open to remodeling the Lounge per your suggestions.

## Building Better Perspectives!

Please tell us what you think of this *Perspectives* volume so we can improve the next one. Here's how you can help:

1. Visit our **Coursewise** site at: http://www.coursewise.com

2. Click on *Perspectives*. Then select the Building Better *Perspectives* Form for your book.

3. Forms and instructions for submission are available online.

Tell us what you think—did the readings and online materials help you make some learning connections? Were some materials more helpful than others? Thanks in advance for helping us build better *Perspectives*.

## Student Internships

If you enjoy evaluating these articles or would like to help us evaluate the **Courselinks** site for this course, check out the **Coursewise** Student Internship Program. For more information, visit:

http://www.coursewise.com/intern.html

# Brief Contents

# Contents

At **Coursewise**, we're publishing connected learning tools. That means that the book you are holding is only a part of this publication. You'll also want to harness the integrated resources that **Coursewise** has developed at the fun and highly useful **Courselinks**™ web site for *Perspectives: Management*. If you purchased this book new, use the Passport that was shrink-wrapped to this volume to obtain site access. If you purchased a used copy of this book, then you need to buy a stand-alone Passport. If your bookstore doesn't stock Passports to **Courselinks** sites, visit http://www.courselinks.com for ordering information.

## section 1

### The Manager's Job: The Nature of Managerial Work

## section 2

### Where Managers Do Their Work: Organizations and Their Environments

# section 3

## Ethics, Diversity, and the Social Responsibility of Managers

# section 4

## Getting Organized to Accomplish Work

# section

# 5

## Planning and Decision Making

# section

# 6

## Leading and Motivating Others to Accomplish Work

# section
# 7

## Keeping the Focus: Maintaining Control and Managing Change

# section
# 8

## Managing in the Twenty-First Century

# Topic Key

This Topic Key is an important tool for learning. It will help you integrate this reader into your course studies. Listed below, in alphabetical order, are important topics covered in this volume. Below each topic, you'll find the reading numbers and titles, and R.E.A.L. web site addresses, relating to that topic. Note that the Topic Key might not include every topic your instructor chooses to emphasize. If you don't find the topic you're looking for in the Topic Key, check the index or the online topic key at the **Courselinks**™ site.

## Careers
5   Seeing the Fruit of One's Labor
9   Work and Life: The End of the Zero-Sum Game
38  Position Yourself to "Get a Life" in the 21st Century

Hoovers Online
http://www.hoovers.com/

American Psychological Association
http://www.apa.org/

Managing Your Boss
http://www.srg.co.uk/mgboss.html

Fortune.com
http://cgi.pathfinder.com/fortune/

## Case Studies
30  Case Study: Critical Success Factors for Creating Superb Self-Managing Teams at Xerox
34  After the Layoffs, What Next?

Mckinsey Quarterly
http://www.mckinseyquarterly.com/home.htm

Andersen Consulting
http://www.ac.com/

Fortune.com
http://cgi.pathfinder.com/fortune/

## Communication
28  Pillsbury's Recipe Is Candid Talk
29  The X Styles

Growing an Ownership Culture
http://www.nceo.org/columns/ci1.html

Managing Your Boss
http://www.srg.co.uk/mgboss.html

Supervising Others
http://www.morebusiness.com/running_your_business/management/d930234012.brc

American Society for Training and Development
http://www.astd.org/

Mediation and Dispute Resolution—The Basics
http://www.shpm.com/articles/divorce/mdlhbasx.html

## Decision Making
20  Black and White
21  Movers and Shakers
22  The Numbers Man
23  The 75 Greatest Management Decisions Ever Made

Logic and Feeling in Decision Analysis
http://rowlf.cc.wwu.edu:8080/~market/tj/logic.html

Enchanted Mind
http://www.enchantedmind.com/

Training Decision Making in Organizations: Dealing with Uncertainty, Complexity, and Conflict
http://www.workteams.unt.edu/reports/smiddltn.htm

Mind Tools—Problem Solving and Analytical Techniques
http://www.mindtools.com/page2.html

## Diversity
17  The Dark Side of Business Flexibility

American Psychological Association
http://www.apa.org/

Fortune.com
http://cgi.pathfinder.com/fortune/

Mckinsey Quarterly
http://www.mckinseyquarterly.com/home.htm

Andersen Consulting
http://www.ac.com/

Business Week Online
http://www.businessweek.com/

## Emotional Intelligence
27  What Makes a Leader?

## Employee Incentive Programs
26  What Money Makes You Do
33  At L.L. Bean, Quality Starts with People

Mckinsey Quarterly
http://www.mckinseyquarterly.com/home.htm

Andersen Consulting
http://www.ac.com/

Fortune.com
http://cgi.pathfinder.com/fortune/

The Society for Human Resource Management
http://www.shrm.org/

## Executive Management
31  The New Man inside Intel
32  Discounting Dynamo—Sam Walton

Mckinsey Quarterly
http://www.mckinseyquarterly.com/home.htm

Andersen Consulting
http://www.ac.com/

Fortune.com
http://cgi.pathfinder.com/fortune/

Business Week Online
http://www.businessweek.com/

## Future Management Trends
1   Musings on Management
16  Get Horizontal: Horizontal Firms Like Intel vs Vertically Integrated Firms Like General Motors
18  Organizational Design in the 21st Century
19  The Struggle to Create an Organization for the 21st Century
36  Catching the Third Wave: How to Succeed in Business When It's Changing at the Speed of Light
37  The Corporation of the Future
39  The Customized, Digitized, Have-It-Your-Way Economy

Mckinsey Quarterly
http://www.mckinseyquarterly.com/home.htm

Wharton: Center for Leadership and Change Management
http://www-management.wharton.upenn.edu/leadership/

Andersen Consulting
http://www.ac.com/

Fortune.com
http://cgi.pathfinder.com/fortune/

Business Week Online
http://www.businessweek.com/

# section

1

## Learning Objectives

- Explain the nature of managerial work.

- Describe the challenges facing contemporary managers.

- Comment on the application of managerial theory and practice in different situations.

- List the major stages in the development of management theory.

# The Manager's Job: The Nature of Managerial Work

Although management is defined in various ways, Peter Drucker, the great management theorist, suggests that "management is a process of accomplishing work through the efforts of others." If this is true, then people have been practicing the principles of management throughout history. The Bible, the annals of military endeavors, and all of recorded political history tell over and over again of the efforts of people to get themselves, their resources, and other people organized to accomplish some goal.

Despite this long and venerable legacy, management as a distinct social science discipline has a relatively short history. Although distinguished postsecondary institutions with schools specifically oriented to the management of business and commerce (such as Dartmouth, Stanford, Harvard, and the Wharton School of the University of Pennsylvania) have existed since the early 1900s, management has been recognized as a separate social science only since World War II. As commercial enterprises have become more complicated and the necessity for coordinated effort more important, the field of "management" has gained great attention, recognition, and importance. With its roots in psychology and sociology, management now has its own well-developed research base, and an enormous amount of both popular and research-based literature is published each year in an effort to better understand and assist in the process of managing.

Perhaps the most important questions for you to answer in your study of management are: "What is management?" and "What do managers do?" The answers to these questions can vary and sometimes reflect two competing perspectives. At one extreme are some superrational approaches to management, often expressed in mathematical and graphical terms, suggesting a singular "best" way for managers to approach their work. At the other extreme are the more intuitive approaches.

The first reading in this section comes from Henry Mintzberg, a scholar and frequent commentator on management. One of the most difficult tasks in management is to provide usable, coherent advice to those who are in charge of getting things done. Often, this advice takes the form of shorthand, quick-fix, axiomatic solutions to complex organizational problems. In this article, Professor Mintzberg provides his often contrarian views on much of this current business orthodoxy and points out the implications and unintended consequences of the conventional wisdom.

In Reading 2, Donna Shalala, Secretary of Health and Human Services in the Clinton administration and a former Chancellor of the University of Wisconsin, gives her perspective on the special challenges and methods needed to run large and complex public organizations. She specifically repudiates the logical-rational assumptions of scientific management, acknowledging management's chaotic nature, while offering her experience-based perspective on how to gain some control.

In the last few years, much attention has been paid to the spiritual aspects of management and leadership. Reading 3, an interview with modern-day business philosopher Tom Morris, provides managerial advice based on the teachings of Aristotle. Morris speculates that these ancient principles have special relevance for modern managers.

In Reading 4, Brian Dumaine reviews some of the most important ideas in management offered over the last 40 years. Prominent among them are those of Peter Drucker, one of the most prolific and respected management theorists, best known for his seminal book *The Practice of Management,* first published in 1954. Peter Drucker continues to provide commentary on the practice of management, and his most current thinking is highlighted in Reading 35 in Section 8.

## Questions

**Reading 1.** Why do you think that a leading management professor such as Henry Mintzberg would recommend the discontinuation of conventional MBA programs? How do you think your professor would feel about this recommendation?

**Reading 2.** Which do you feel is easier to manage—a governmental organization or a business? Why?

**Reading 3.** What relevance do truth, beauty, and unity have to a manager seeking to do a good job?

**Reading 4.** After looking at the history of significant events in the development of modern management, what do you feel will be the next important paradigm?

Why do you think that a leading management professor such as Henry Mintzberg would recommend the discontinuation of conventional MBA programs? How do you think your professor would feel about this recommendation?

# Musings on Management

Ten ideas designed to rile everyone who cares about management.

## Henry Mintzberg

*Henry Mintzberg is a professor of management at INSEAD in Fontainebleau, France, and at McGill University in Montreal, Canada. He is currently coordinating a venture of five business schools in Canada, England, France, India, and Japan that is seeking to create a master's program for the development of practicing managers.*

Management is a curious phenomenon. It is generously paid, enormously influential, and significantly devoid of common sense. At least, the hype about management lacks common sense, as does too much of the practice. I should really say *im*-practice, because the problems grow out of the disconnection between management and the managed. The disconnection occurs when management is treated as an end in itself instead of as a service to organizations and their customers.

These concerns had been building in my mind for years when a particular event caused them to gel. I had been asked to give a speech at the World Economic Forum in Davos, Switzerland, in 1995; so I visited managing director Maria Cattaui in her office near Geneva to discuss possible topics. I first proposed a presentation on government and suggested she allot me the better part of an hour to cover the topic properly. "I would really prefer you do something on management," she replied. "And besides, many chief executives tend to have an attention span of about 15 minutes."

I went home, thought about this, and decided to respond in kind. It was a perfect opportunity. I listed ten points on one sheet of paper under the label "Musings on Management" and faxed it to Maria Cattaui. Fortunately, she was open-minded—indeed, enthusiastic. So that was what I presented at Davos: ten points, by then reduced to ten minutes, one musing on management per minute.

The *Harvard Business Review* being even more open-minded, I can now develop my musings at somewhat greater length. Readers should be warned, however, that I will insult almost everyone in one way or another. I must apologize to those I miss, for the object of my exercise is to shake us all out of the complacency that surrounds too much of the practice of management today, a practice that I believe is undermining many of our organizations and hence our society. We had better take a good look at what is wrong with this hype called management.

**1. Organizations don't have tops and bottoms.** These are just misguided metaphors. What organizations really have are the *outer* people, connected to the world, and the *inner* ones, disconnected from it, as well as many so-called *middle* managers, who are desperately trying to connect the inner and outer people to each other.

The sooner we stop talking about top management (nobody dares to say *bottom* management), the better off we shall be. The metaphor distorts reality. After all, organizations are spread out geographically, so that even if the chief executive sits 100 stories up in New York, he is not nearly as high as a lowly clerk on the ground floor in Denver.

The only thing a chief executive sits atop is an organization chart. And all that silly document does is demonstrate how mesmerized we are with the abstraction called management. The next time you look at one of these charts, cover the name of the organization and try to figure out what it actually does for a living. This most prominent of all corporate artifacts never gets down to real products and real services, let alone the people who deal with them every day. It's as if the organization exists for the management.

Try this metaphor. Picture the organization as a circle. In the middle is the *central* management. And around the outer edges are those people who develop, produce, and deliver the products and services—the people with the knowledge of the daily operations. The latter see with complete clarity because they are closest to the action. But they do so only narrowly, for all they can see are their own little segments. The managers at the center see widely—all around the circle—but they don't see clearly because they are distant from the operations. The trick, therefore, is to connect the two groups. And for that, most organizations need informed managers in between, people who can see the outer edge and then swing around and talk about it to those at the center. You know—the people we used to call middle managers, the ones who are mostly gone.

**2. It is time to delayer the delayerers.** As organizations remove layers from their operations, they add them to the so-called top of their hierarchies—new levels that do nothing but exercise financial control and so drive everyone else crazy.

I used to write books for an independent publishing company called Prentice-Hall. It was big—very big—but well organized and absolutely dedicated to its craft.

Then it was bought by Simon & Schuster, which was bought by Paramount. Good old Prentice-Hall became a "Paramount Communications Company." It was at about this time that one of my editors quoted her new boss as saying, "We're in the business of filling the O.I. [operating income] bucket." Strange, because my editor and I both had thought the company was in the business of publishing books and enlightening readers. Next, publisher Robert Maxwell got involved, and not long ago the whole thing was bought yet again, so that now Prentice-Hall has become a "Viacom Company." After all this, will publishing books remain as important as satisfying bosses?

Take the metaphor of the circular organization and plunk a financial boss on top of the chief in the center. Then pile on another and perhaps another. The weight can become crushing. To use a favorite management expression, the new layers don't "add value" at all. By focusing on the numbers, they depreciate true value and reduce the richness of a business to the poverty of its financial performance. Listen to what *Fortune* wrote a few years ago: "What's truly amazing about P&G's historic restructuring is that it is a response to the consumer market, not the stock market" (November 6, 1989). What's truly amazing about this statement is the use of the phrase "truly amazing."

Nowhere does the harshness of such attitudes appear more starkly than in the delayering of all those middle managers. Delayering can be defined as the process by which people who barely know what's going on get rid of those who do. Delayering is done in the name of the "empowerment" of those who remain. But

too many of them, at the outer edges, become disconnected instead, while the real database of the organization, the key to what was its future, lines up at the unemployment office. Isn't it time that we began to delayer the delayerers?

**3. Lean is mean and doesn't even improve long-term profits.** There is nothing wonderful about firing people. True, stock market analysts seem to love companies that fire frontline workers and middle managers (while increasing the salaries of senior executives). Implicitly, employees are blamed for having been hired in the first place and are sentenced to suffer the consequences while the corporations cash in. Listen to this sample of contemporary management wisdom: "In the face of the dismaying results that began in 1985, just after John Akers became CEO, and that persisted, IBM failed to accept the reality that its so-called full-employment practice, in which it forswore layoffs, was no longer workable. A retired IBM manager who worked closely for years with IBM's top executives recalls the mystique that grew up around this practice: 'It was a religion. Every personnel director who came in lived and died on defending that practice. I tell you, this was like virginity.' Just recently, a day late and a dollar short, IBM at last gave it up" (*Fortune*, May 3, 1993).

You can almost feel the writer gloating and thinking, Isn't this wonderful—finally IBM has joined the club. The magazine article, about big companies in decline, was entitled "Dinosaurs?" But everyone knows that dinosaurs lasted a couple of hundred million years and, even then, probably succumbed to natural forces. With mass firings and other callous behaviors toward one another, we could well be getting rid of ourselves after barely a few hundred thousands years.

I did some work recently for a large U.S. insurance company, with no market analysts to worry about because it is a mutual. I was told a story about a woman there who was working energetically to convert a paper database to an electronic one. Someone said to her, "Don't you know you are working yourself out of a job?" "Sure," she retorted. "But I know they'll find something else for me. If I didn't, I'd sabotage the process." Imagine how much her feeling of security is worth to that company. Or imagine the case of no job security. A few years ago, some middle managers at one of the major Canadian banks formed what they called their 50/50 club. They were more than 50 years old and earning more than $50,000 per year, and it was clear to them that many members of the group were systematically being fired just before they qualified for their pensions. How much sabotage was going on at that bank?

Lean *is* mean. So why do we keep treating people in these ways? Presumably because we are not competitive. And just why aren't we competitive? To a large extent because we have been unable to meet Japanese competition. So how do we respond? By managing in exactly the opposite way from the Japanese. Will we never learn?

**4. The trouble with most strategies are chief executives who believe themselves to be strategists.** Great strategists are either creative or generous. We have too few of either type. We call the creative ones visionaries—they see a world that others have been

blind to. They are often difficult people, but they break new ground in their own ways. The generous ones, in contrast, bring strategy out in other people. They build organizations that foster thoughtful inquiry and creative action. (You can recognize these people by the huge salaries they don't pay themselves. Their salaries signal their people, We're all in this together. Salaries are not used to impress fellow CEOs.) The creative strategists reach out from the center of that circular organization to touch the edges, while the generous ones strengthen the whole circle by turning strategic thinking into a collective learning process.

Most so-called strategists, however, just sit on top and pretend to strategize. They formulate ever so clever strategies for everyone else to implement. They issue glossy strategic plans that look wonderful and take their organizations nowhere with great fanfare. Strategy becomes a game of chess in which the pieces—great blocks of businesses and companies—get moved around with a ferocity that dazzles the market analysts. All the pieces look like they fit neatly together—at least on the board. It's all very impressive, except that the pieces themselves, ignored as every eye focuses on the great moves, disintegrate. Imagine if we took all this energy spent on shuffling and used it instead to improve *real* businesses. I don't mean "financial services" or "communications," I mean banking or book publishing.

Consider how we train strategists in the M.B.A. classrooms. We take young people with little business experience—hardly selected for their creativity, let alone their generosity—and drill them in case after case in which they play the great strate-

gists sitting atop institutions they know nothing about. An hour or two the night before to read 20 pithy pages on Gargantuan Industries and its nuclear reactors and then off to 80 supercharged minutes in the classroom to decide what Gargantuan must do with itself into the next millennium. Is it any wonder that we end up with case studies in the executive suites—disguised as strategic thinking?

**5. Decentralization centralizes, empowerment disempowers, and measurement doesn't measure up.** The buzzwords are the problem, not the solution. The hot techniques dazzle us. Then they fizzle. *Total quality management* takes over and no one even remembers *quality of work life*— same word, similar idea, no less the craze, not very long ago. How come quality of work life died? Will TQM die a similar death? Will we learn anything? Will anyone even care?

The TQM concept has now magically metamorphosed into empowerment. What empowerment really means is stopping the disempowering of people. But that just brings us back to hierarchy, because hierarchy is precisely what empowerment reinforces. People don't get power because it is logically and intrinsically built into their jobs; they get it as a gift from the gods who sit atop those charts. Noblesse oblige. If you doubt this, then contrast empowerment with a situation in which the workers really do have control. Imagine a hospital director empowering the doctors. They are perfectly well empowered already, with no thanks to any hospital managers. Their power is built into their work. (Indeed, if anything, doctors could stand a little disempowering—but by nurses, not by managers.)

Better still, consider a truly advanced social system: the beehive. Queen bees don't empower worker bees. The worker bees are adults, so to speak, who know exactly what they have to do. Indeed, the queen bee has no role in the genuinely strategic decisions of the hive, such as the one to move to a new location. The bees decide collectively, responding to the informative dances of the scouts and then swarming off to the place they like best. The queen simply follows. How many of our organizations have attained that level of sophistication? What the queen bee does is exude a chemical substance that holds the system together. She is responsible for what has been called the "spirit of the hive." What a wonderful metaphor for good managers—not the managers on top but those in the center.

If empowering is about disempowerment, then is decentralization about centralizing? We have confounded our use of these words, too, ever since Alfred P. Sloan, Jr., centralized General Motors in the 1920s in the name of what came to be called decentralization. Recall that Sloan had to rein in a set of businesses that were out of control. There was no decentralization in that.

Part and parcel of this so-called decentralization effort has been the imposition of financial measures—control by the numbers. If division managers met their targets, they were ostensibly free to manage their businesses as they pleased. But the real effect of this decentralization *to* the division head has often been centralization *of* the division: the concentration of power at the level of the division chief, who is held personally responsible for the impersonal performance. No wonder that now, in reaction, we have

all this fuss about the need for empowerment and innovation.

Division chiefs—and headquarters controllers looking over their shoulders—get very fidgety about surprises and impatient for numerical results. And the best way to ensure quick, expected results is never to do anything interesting; always cut, never create. That is how the rationalization of costs has become to today's manager what bloodletting was to the medieval physician: the cure for every illness.

As a consequence of all this (de)centralizing and (de)layering, measurement has emerged as the religion of management. But how much sensible business behavior has been distorted as people have been pushed to meet the numbers instead of the customers?

"After all you've done for your customers, why are they still not happy?" asked the title of a recent article (*Fortune*, December 11, 1995). The answer: because business "has not yet figured out how to define customer satisfaction in a way that links it to financial results." Be quite clear what this means: customers will be satisfied and happy only when companies can put a dollar sign on them.

To explain its point, *Fortune* included a box labeled "What's a Loyal Customer Worth?" It offered several steps to answering that question: first, "decide on a meaningful period of time over which to do the calculations"; next "calculate the profit . . . customers generate each year"; after that, "it's simple to calculate net present value. . . The sum of years one through *n* is how much your customer is worth. . . "

Just a few easy steps to a happier customer. Because no article on management today can be without its list of easy steps, here

come my "Five Easy Steps to Destroying Real Value" (any step will do):

- *Step 1.* Manage the bottom line (as if companies make money by managing money).

- *Step 2.* Make a plan for every action. (No spontaneity please, definitely no learning.)

- *Step 3.* Move managers around to be certain they never get to know anything but management well, and let the boss kick himself upstairs so that he can manage a portfolio instead of a real business. (For *herself*, see Musing 9, below.)

- *Step 4.* When in trouble, rationalize, fire, and divest; when out of trouble, expand, acquire, and still fire (it keeps employees on their toes); above all, never create or invent anything (it takes too long).

- *Step 5.* Be sure to do everything in five easy steps.

If this sort of thing sounds familiar, it's because the analytical mentality has taken over the field of management. We march to the tune of the technocrat. Everything has to be calculated, explicated, and categorized. The trouble is that technocrats never get much beyond the present. They lack the wisdom to appreciate the past and the imagination to see the future. Everything is centered on what's "in," what's "hot." To plan, supposedly to take care of the future, they forecast, which really means they extrapolate current quantifiable trends. (The optimists extrapolate positive trends; the pessimists, negative ones.) And then, when an unexpected "discontinuity" occurs (meaning, most likely, that a creative competitor has invented something new), the technocrats run around like so many

Chicken Littles, crying, "The environment's turbulent! The environment's turbulent!"

Measurement is fine for figuring out when to flip a hamburger or how to fill the O.I. bucket at that "communications" company. But when used to estimate the market for a brand new product or to assess the worth of a complicated professional service, measurement often goes awry. Measurement mesmerizes no less than management. We had better start asking ourselves about the real costs of counting.

**6. Great organizations, once created, don't need great leaders.** Organizations that need to be turned around by such leaders will soon turn back again. Go to the popular business press and read just about any article on any company. The whole organization almost always gets reduced to a single individual, the chief at the "top." ABB exists in the persona of Percy Barnevik. And General Motors is not an incredibly complex web of three quarters of a million people. It's just one single hero: "CEO Jack Smith didn't just stop the bleeding. With a boost from rising auto sales, he made GM healthy again" (*Fortune*, October 17, 1994). All by himself!

Switzerland is an organization that really works. Yet hardly anybody even knows who's in charge, because seven people rotate in and out of the job of head of state on an annual basis. We may need great visionaries to create great organizations. But after the organizations are created, we don't need heroes, just competent, devoted, and generous leaders who know what's going on and exude that spirit of the hive. Heroes—or, more to the point, our hero worship—reflect nothing more than our own inadequacies. Such worship stops us from thinking for ourselves as adult human beings. Leadership becomes the great solution. Whatever is wrong, the great one will make it right.

Bill Agee was the great hero at Bendix. Out he went. Jim Robinson played the same role at American Express. Suddenly that flipped over, too. And on it goes. Who's next? The popular business press is amazing for its ability to turn on a dime. Every magazine issue is a whole new ball game—no responsibility for what was written just a few weeks earlier. Too bad the press has developed the technocrat's blindness to the past.

Part of this cult of leadership involves an emphasis on the "turning around" of old, sick companies. Just look what we invest in that! Think of all those consulting firms specializing in geriatrics, ready to help—hardly a pediatric, let alone an obstetric, practice to be found. Why don't we recognize when it's time for an old, sick organization to die? Would we say that it was one of the great wrongs of this century to have let a talent like Winston Churchill die? Of course not; it was a natural event, part of the life cycle. But when it comes to the great old companies, we feel compelled to keep them alive—even if it means we must resort to interventionist life-support systems.

What we really need, therefore, is a kind of Dr. Kevorkian for the world of business—someone to help with pulling the plug. Then young, vibrant companies would get the chance to replace the old, spent ones. Letting more big companies die—celebrating their contributions at grand funerals—would make our societies a lot healthier.

**7. Great organizations have souls; any word with a *de* or a *re* in front of it is likely to destroy those souls.** Well, there are still some healthy big organizations out there. You can tell them by their individuality. They stay off the bandwagon, away from the empty fads. Did you ever wonder why so many really interesting ones headquarter themselves far from the chic centers of New York and London, preferring places like Bentonville, Arkansas (Wal-Mart Stores), and Littlehampton, West Sussex (The Body Shop)?

If you really want to adopt a new technique, don't use its usual name, especially with a *de* or *re*. Call it something completely different. Then you will have to explain it, which means you will have to think about it. You see, techniques are not the problem; just the mindless application of them. Wouldn't it be wonderful if the editors of HBR printed a skull and crossbones next to the title of every article, like those on medicine bottles: an example might be "Warning! For high-technology companies only; not to be taken by mass-production manufacturers or government agencies."

Consider the mindless application of reengineering. I opened the popular book on the topic and at first thought, This is not a bad idea. But when I saw the claim on page 2 that the technique "is to the next revolution of business what specialization of labor was to the last," namely, the Industrial Revolution, I should have closed the book right there. Hype is the problem in management; the medium destroys the message. But I read on. Wasn't this what the Ford Motor Company did to automobile production at the turn of the century, what McDonald's did to fast food 30 years ago? Every once in a while, a smart operator comes along and improves a process. Companies like Ford and McDonald's did not need the book; quite the contrary. They needed imagination applied to an intimate knowledge of a business.

In other words, there is no reengineering in the idea of reengineering. Just reification, just the same old notion that the new system will do the job. But because of the hype that goes with any new management fad, everyone has to run around reengineering everything. We are supposed to get superinnovation on demand just because it is deemed necessary by a manager in some distant office who has read a book. Why don't we just stop reengineering and delayering and restructuring and decentralizing and instead start thinking?

**8. It is time to close down conventional M.B.A. programs.** We should be developing real managers, not pretending to create them in the classroom.

I have been doing a survey. I ask people who know a lot about U.S. business to name a few of the really good U.S. chief executives, the leaders who really made, or are making, a major *sustained* difference. I am not talking about the turnaround doctors but the real builders. (Stop here and make your own list.)

You know what? Almost never has anyone been named who has an M.B.A. No one ever seems to mention Bill Agee or measurement maven Robert McNamara, two of Harvard's best-known graduates. Many do name Jack Welch, Andy Grove, Bob Galvin, and Bill Gates. This is rather interesting because all these people have been either seriously educated (Welch and Grove both have doctorates in chemical engineering) or hardly formally educated at all (Galvin and Gates never finished bachelor's degrees).

Years ago, when things were going better in U.S. business, I used to think that the brilliance of the country's management lay in its action orientation. Managers didn't think a lot; they just got things done. But now I find that the best managers are very thoughtful people (whether or not they have Ph.D.s) who are also highly action oriented. Unfortunately, too many others have stopped thinking. They want quick, easy answers. There is an overwhelming need to be in the middle of whatever is popular. Getting an M.B.A. may be just another example of that need.

It is plain silly to take people who have never been managers—many of whom have not even worked full-time for more than a few years—and pretend to be turning them into managers in a classroom. The whole exercise is too detached from context. We need to stop dumping management theories and cases on people who have no basis even to judge the relevance.

Let's begin by recognizing today's M.B.A. for what it is: technical training for specialized jobs, such as marketing research and financial analysis. (And these are *not* management.) Then maybe we can recognize good management for what *it* is: not some technical profession, certainly not a science or even an applied science (although sometimes the application of science) but a practice, a craft. We have some good things to teach in management schools; let's teach them to people who know what's going on.

It used to be that the M.B.A. was a license to parachute into the middle of an organization, there to climb the proverbial ladder without ever having developed an intimate understanding of what lies below—in order to boss around the people who have.

That was bad enough. But now we have a new and more insidious track to the executive suite. After the M.B.A., you work as a consultant with some prestigious firm for a time, skipping from one client organization to another. And then you leap straight into the chief executive chair of some company, making judicious moves to others in the hope that you may one day end up running a company like IBM. That system might work on occasion. But it is no way to build a strong corporate sector in society.

I think of that approach as a cookie model of management because it was born in what might be called generic consumer-products companies—the ones that sell consumer goods that come out identically, like cookies, one after another. Certain critical skills in these businesses reside in marketing and can be carried from one company to another, but only within this narrow consumer-goods sphere. Cookie management just doesn't work for running nuclear reactors or conducting liver transplants. So there has to be a better way to select and develop managers. Maybe the Groves, Galvins, Gateses, and Welches of this world—who, incidentally, have devoted their careers to single companies—know of one.

**9. Organizations need continuous care, not interventionist cures.** That is why nursing is a better model for management than medicine and why women may ultimately make better managers than men. The French term for a medical operation is "intervention." Intervening is what all surgeons and too many managers do. Managers keep operating on their systems, radically altering them in the hope of fixing them, usually by cutting things out. Then they leave the consequences of their messy business to the nurses of the corporate world.

Maybe we should try nursing as a model for management. Organizations need to be nurtured—looked after and cared for, steadily and consistently. They don't need to be violated by some dramatic new strategic plan or some gross new reorganization every time a new chief executive happens to parachute in.

In a sense, caring is a more feminine approach to managing, although I have seen it practiced by some excellent male chief executive officers. Still, women do have an advantage, in which case the corporate world is wasting a great deal of talent. Let us, therefore, welcome more women into the executive suites as perhaps our greatest hope for coming to our senses.

A few years ago, I spent a day following around the head nurse of a surgical ward in a hospital. I say "following around" because she spent almost no time in her office; she was continually on the floor. (Bear in mind that, long ago, the partners of Morgan Stanley operated on the floor, too: their desks were right on the trading floor.)

But being on the floor has not been the favored style of management, in nursing or elsewhere. Two other styles have been preferred. One can be called the *boss* style, in which the man-

ager knows and controls everything personally, like Nurse Ratched in *One Flew Over the Cuckoo's Nest*. This style has gradually been replaced by the currently popular *professional* style, in which whoever knows management can manage anything, regardless of experience. Here credentials are what matter, and these, together with the absence of firsthand experience, help to keep managers in their offices reading performance reports and supposedly empowering their subordinates. Professional management is management by remote control.

At the first sign of trouble, empowerment becomes encroachment by senior managers, who, because they don't know what is going on, have no choice but to intervene. And so the organization gets turned into a patient to be cured, even if it was not really sick in the first place. It finds itself alternating between short bouts of radical surgery and long doses of studied inattention.

There is a third style, not nearly common enough but practiced by that head nurse I followed around and by other effective managers. Let's call it the *craft* style of managing. It is about inspiring, not empowering, about leadership based on mutual respect rooted in common experience and deep understanding. Craft managers get involved deeply enough to know when not to get involved. In contrast to professional managers who claim "hands off, brain on," the craft manager believes that if there is no laying on of hands (to extend our metaphor), the brain remains shut off.

Women complain about glass ceilings. They can see what goes on up there, at the so-called top; they just cannot easily get through. Well, glass ceilings apply to all sorts of people in all sorts of situations, and that includes the people above who cannot touch what is below, who cannot even be heard when they shout. But worse still may be the concrete floors. Too many managers can't even see what is going on at the ground level of their organizations, where the products are made and the customers served (presumably). This suggests that we need more than *transparency* in management. We need to smash up the ceilings and bust down the floors as well as break through the walls so that people can work together in that one big circle.

In her book, *Female Advantage: Women's Ways of Leadership* (Doubleday, 1990), Sally Helgesen found that women managers "usually referred to themselves as being in the middle of things. Not at the top, but in the center; not reaching down, but reaching out." Does that sound like our metaphor of the circle? I guess we have now come full circle, so it is time to conclude with our last musing—about which I will add nothing.

10. The trouble with today's management is the trouble with this article: everything has to come in short superficial doses.

 **Article Review Form at end of book.**

Which do you feel is easier to manage—a governmental organization or a business? Why?

# Are Large Public Organizations Manageable?

## Donna E. Shalala

Americans like many big things: cars, open spaces, movies. But we don't like big bureaucracies. Americans think that large government organizations are too complex, too impersonal, too inefficient, and cost too much. They are partly right. But at the same time that Americans express a dislike of bureaucracy, they also treasure many of the programs that government runs. The paradox is illustrated by the comment of one individual: "Keep your bureaucratic hands off of my Medicare."

This paradox was very much on my mind in 1993 when the president asked me to become the chief executive officer (CEO) of one of the largest government organizations in the world. This was not my first encounter with the federal government; I had already served in the Carter administration and had close contact with government in my jobs as the president of two leading public universities. But I knew that taking over the leadership of the Department of Health and Human Services (HHS), a department whose budget, at that time,

consumed 40 percent of federal spending—would be unlike anything I ever did before.[1]

The Department of Health and Human Services (HHS) includes more than 300 programs, covering a wide spectrum of activities in medical and social science research; food and drug safety; financial assistance and health care for low income, elderly, and disabled Americans; child support enforcement; maternal and infant health; substance abuse treatment and prevention; and services for older Americans. The $354 billion budget for Fiscal Year 1997 is implemented by 59,000 employees. The department is the largest grant-making agency in the federal government, providing some 60,000 grants per year. It is also the nation's largest health insurer, handling more than 800 million claims per year. The department's programs are administered by 11 operating divisions in both head-quarter locations as well as ten regional offices. The department has a vast array of constituencies that reflect its multiple programs. It works closely with state and local governments since many of the services funded by the de-

partment are provided by state or county agencies or through private sector grantees.

Because of its size and complexity, HHS is one of the most difficult jobs in the world for a public official. It is also a department whose policies touch the lives of every American. While HHS has many unique attributes, it shares a number of elements with other federal departments. I found, for example, that the reflections of Carter Administration Treasury Secretary Michael Blumenthal (1979) on his experience were very useful as I began my tenure in HHS. As I reflect on my experience over the years, I must acknowledge that we have not accomplished everything we wanted to. All of us have taken some wrong turns and endured the hard lessons of that great teacher: experience.

Let me start by knocking down two myths. The first, described by Hargrove and Glidewill (1990), is that my job—and others like it—are simply impossible. Too many difficult clients. Too many internal conflicts. Too little public confidence. But I found that it is not true. Managing a large organization is

"Are Large Public Organizations Manageable?" by Donna E. Shalala, *Public Administration Review,* July/August 1998. Reprinted with permission.

the art of the possible, the art of finding the possible within what might be viewed as impossible pressures.

The second myth goes back to the theories of Frederick Taylor (1967). He viewed organizations as essentially machines. He did not focus on the human dimensions of management, the personal challenges that any manager faces. His approach would lead a manager to believe that if you pull the right levers in the right way, you'll get the right result. Were it only that easy!

In complex organizations there will be failures for any number of reasons: poor communication, impractical or unclear goals, lack of public or congressional support, lack of sufficient expertise or resources, too much—or too little—oversight, and too much work. Between these two extremes—that nothing works or that everything can be made to work—lies some basic truths about large modern organizations. I offer you Donna Shalala's Top Ten Lessons for Managing a Large Complex Bureaucracy.

Some of these lessons are well established norms for administering large public and political organizations. They are found in the literature and in practice. Others are borrowed from recent scholarship, such as Doig and Hargrove's analysis of what makes an innovative and successful leader in government (1990). And some of the lessons are from two decades of my experience as a sub-cabinet official in the Carter administration, as a student of government and politics, and as a leader of large public universities. Finally, some of these lessons are well known but others are less so. But I believe they are all applicable to large public organizations. I offer these

lessons because I believe they might be useful to individuals in other top management roles in complex public organizations. My experience suggests that one does not have to revert to traditional hierarchies or employ command and control methods to manage an organization. Management doesn't mean micromanagement or tightly drawn control.

## Lesson Number One: Know the Cultures of Your Organization

I emphasize cultures, not culture. Organizations are usually made up of many smaller units—each with its own history, needs, culture, and constituencies,—but working toward a larger objective. As James Q. Wilson noted, "many government agencies have multiple, competing cultures. . . . A major responsibility of the executive is not only . . . to infuse the organization with value, it is also to discover a way by which different values (and the different cultures that espouse those values) can productively coexist" (1989, 105).

That is certainly the case at major research universities. The goal is the same: well educated students and quality research. But different colleges, schools, and departments often take very different roads to reach that goal. Levin and Sanger (1994) are right when they emphasize the importance of understanding these cultures and constituencies. The National Institutes of Health (NIH) is a good example of this situation. Have you ever tried to apply standard personnel rules to hiring scientists? I can tell you right now: They don't work. Scientists have their own language and traditions. And their own measures for assessing merit.

When I became Secretary of HHS, personnel managers in the Office of the Secretary had overall responsibility for hiring scientists for NIH. These personnel officers were highly skilled, but they weren't used to hiring first-rank scientists in a competitive market place. I thought the scientists at the NIH were best able to judge scientific competency and credentials. It is a good example of a larger problem: how to mesh uniform governmental rules with varying organizational cultures.

There are also times when it's actually helpful for an organization to have more than one identity. When NIH, the Centers for Disease Control (CDC), the Food and Drug Administration (FDA), and the Public Health Service all line up in favor of a particular policy, say, banning the marketing of tobacco to children, that policy will more likely be accepted by Congress, the public—and, we hope—the courts.

Unique cultures within a department can also increase credibility. That's why a cabinet secretary is not always the best salesperson for a departmental policy. In criminal investigations, the Federal Bureau of Investigation (FBI) is usually called on to speak on behalf of the Justice Department. If there's a major fire, the local fire commissioner may have more credibility than the mayor. At HHS, I like to let the experts—especially physicians and scientists—speak directly to the public, because the great scientific agencies—CDC, the FDA, NIH, the National Cancer Institute (NCI), and the Public Health Service—are institutions trusted by the American people. The physician-scientists who head them, while appointed by the president, have enormous credibility. They must be the reassuring voice—and face—explaining the Hanta virus outbreak, food borne illnesses, AIDS transmission, and the age at which women should start having annual mammograms. When they appear before the public in white lab coats, the scientists in HHS present a very convincing argument.

Finally, the press provides its own cultures and traditions. That's why there is no substitute for a public affairs staff with Washington experience. And I've had the best. I've tried to include the public affairs staff in policy discussions; their presence in the deliberations often sharpens the policy discussion.

## Lesson Number Two: Find Ways to Assure That Appropriate Coordination Takes Place

There's a scene in the movie Ben Hur, where Ben Hur is trying, without success, to get his four new chariot horses to run. The Bedouin who owns the horses tells him that each horse has its own personality, and they must be harnessed together in a way that allows them to run as a team. The same holds true for any large organization. The sum has to be greater than the parts.

The different agendas of smaller units have to be melded or modified—and a belief in the larger team built. When I first became Secretary of HHS, I encouraged my top appointees to distinguish the department's forest from their particular tree by asking each of them to participate in each other's budget hearings—and to prepare a budget for the entire department. In other words, to look at the department

from my perspective. When they took a look at the big picture, some senior administrators recommended cuts in their own budget requests. We are still using that process. There are, of course, other ways to share information, build cooperation, and keep an organization the size of HHS speaking with one voice. One, described by Roger Porter (1982) as "centralized planning," has been rejected by most leaders, even very forceful ones like Richard Darman.[2] A second, which Porter calls "multiple advocacy," lies between centralized planning and ad hoc decision-making, and generally uses existing systems, some of which, in the case of HHS, I've been fine tuning.

For almost any public organization, the primary system for melding a team and an agenda is the budget process—a process which is increasingly important when money is tight and budgets have to be balanced. In this new era, however, the budget process has the potential of being divisive and competitive—instead of a road to team building and unity.

But at HHS, and other public agencies, there are other ways to build a team. At HHS, the Executive-Secretariat controls the enormous paper flow. This office has been described in many ways—for example, as a traffic cop or a paper tracker. But more importantly, the Executive-Secretariat is the honest broker. It ensures that ideas are considered throughout the department—and that everyone is brought to the table. It also provides an opportunity for multiple sources of information and ideas to be raised. In this way, I get the benefit of every viewpoint. Moreover, when a decision is made, every participant has the opportunity

to comment on it and, as a result, each participant owns it.

The assistant secretary for policy and evaluation runs the numbers, evaluates the likely consequences of a proposed policy, and makes recommendations to the secretary (Radin, 1992). This office also has the ability to look at possible linkages between various parts of the department's activities as we consider policies that cross bureaucratic lines.

Some units within the Office of the Secretary, likewise, are designed to coordinate what the entire department does, especially in an emergency. When the Mad Cow Disease was discovered in England, we wanted to avoid panic by getting out accurate information about the steps that had been taken to protect American beef—years before. The assistant secretary for health did that. He was able to oversee the work and the public statements of the FDA, the NIH, CDC, and the Public Health Service, and to coordinate with the Department of Agriculture.

## Lesson Number Three: Don't Overlook the Needs and Abilities of the Career Public Service

My first day of work started with many top jobs in HHS unfilled. And it stayed that way for some time. So what did we do? We ran the department with the top civil servants—the people who are responsible for most of our day-to-day leadership. It was fun.

In his 1977 book, *A Government of Strangers*, Hugh Heclo wrote: "If democratic government did not require bureaucrats and political leaders to need each other, it might not matter so much when in practice they discover they do not." I don't agree. The two sides do need each other. I also don't share Heclo's belief that career civil servants resist the leadership and policy turns of political leaders.

I think the relationship is reciprocal. Both institutional and political guidance are needed. Trust can be built by using the experience and institutional memories of career civil servants. When I became secretary, I wanted to send a very strong message to the civil service that they were important, and that we were going to be a team. So my first appointment was from the Senior Executive Service, a career person of great competence and experience. We need to make sure we respect the integrity of the civil service in words and action. In fact, relying on career professionals is especially important in the age of downsizing.

Today, political staffs are doing more work, with less help and in less time.[3] This is an open invitation for policy mistakes and failure. Many of these potential mistakes and failures can however be avoided by using the career civil service to identify hidden minefields from the past and to help plan, not just implement, policies for the future.

## Lesson Number Four: Choose the Best and Let Them Do Their Jobs

The days of political appointments as a spoils system are over. A large organization is complex, its programs are difficult to manage, and its purpose is almost always vital to the well being of the American people. That's why political appointees must be experts in their fields and skillful leaders and managers. The individuals who became a part of the team of HHS are specialists who have the ability to become generalist managers. They must be adept at both policy and politics. Otherwise they will not get the respect and cooperation they need from career staff. So, while we've worked to create a team, I believe that the most important thing any public administrator can do is choose the right top management.

At HHS, the president nominated many leading experts in their field. They were Democrats and our party was ten deep in talent for each position. Some even compared our team to the incomparable 1927 Yankees. During the second term, the team is just as distinguished and a bit more operational with deeper state and local experience. This is because we are involved in full-scale implementation of major presidential policies (e.g., welfare reform, children's health, health reforms).

Each of these leaders had years of academic and/or professional experience in their areas of expertise, not to mention a deep sense of mission. But we are also worried about the next generation. I always try to remember that we will be replaced by those we recruit. I am very proud of our record of bringing presidential management interns into HHS; in fact, the department has hired the largest number of these interns within the federal government.

## Lesson Number Five: Stitch Together a Loyal Team

I've always thought that you need to instill loyalty in both professional and personal ways. We worked hard to make everyone feel that they are a part of a team and that they are listened to. I've tried to make sure that we have developed a corporate identity in the face of our very diverse responsibilities.

I talked about how proud I am of our appointments and their diversity of skills and experience. But that core team showed up with different agendas, different approaches to achieving their agendas, and often without knowing much about their new colleagues.

So I encouraged a healthy debate in private, but made it clear that I didn't want arguments in public. I can't say we were always successful, but for the most part we put together a loyal and cooperative team of very nice people who liked each other. And I encouraged that sense of togetherness by creating events for my top staff where they could get to know each other better.

## Lesson Number Six: Stand Up and Fight for the People Who Work for You

People behave in large organizations pretty much the way they behave outside of work. They are motivated by friendship, support, and loyalty. That's why showing the people who work for you that you really care about them pays dividends.

I had a unique opportunity to do that during the government shutdown. The shutdown actually strengthened HHS because it gave people a renewed sense of loyalty to each other and the department. I sent everyone a letter saying: We're fighting for you. Furthermore, to show my support, I was very visible—making the case in the media about the devastating impact of the shutdown.

Then we did something that almost no other agency thought of. During the shutdown, pay checks were supposed to be half the normal amount. We found a legal way not to cut pay so drastically. We put off taking out deductions in our employees' checks until after Christmas. So the checks were made whole—and the employees appreciated our caring.

We also managed our budget with considerable skill to avoid Reductions in Force (RIFs)—the entire department held vacancies and helped to absorb cutbacks.

## Lesson Number Seven: Set Firm Goals and Priorities and Stick with Them

The old saying is still true: To govern is to choose. But in a large organization, with a limitless number of decisions to make—and a very limited time with which to make them—how do you choose? Larry Lynn was correct when he wrote, "public executives need a frame of reference to aid them in skillfully allocating their time, attention, and political influence." But they also need a reality check. Managing is not the same as coming up with a wish list. If you try to do everything, you'll accomplish nothing. You need to set priorities.

I have six secretarial initiatives. Devised in consultation with officials throughout the department (in both headquarters and the regions), they include proposals for children's health, reducing tobacco use among teens and preteens, youth substance abuse prevention, health care quality improvement, efforts

to reduce fraud and abuse in Medicare and Medicaid, and increased support for single parents moving from welfare to work.

I have asked all the agencies within HHS not only to focus on those initiatives, but also to do cross-cuts, to share information, and to pool money and other resources. Each of these initiatives is the responsibility of an interagency team and we have attempted to make sure that we don't duplicate efforts within the department.

Setting priorities doesn't mean choosing only what's easily achievable. When the president first came to office, we set a goal of increasing child immunizations. We established targets, and as the president recently announced, we met them. Our work with the inspector general on health care fraud is recognized as a model for other agencies. But at least some of my six initiatives will be more difficult, such as reducing teen drug use.

The roots and solutions of social problems are often beyond any government's control. As a result, whether you work for a mayor, a governor, or a president, you need to set ambitious yet realistic goals, figure out your role in meeting them, and then team up with partners outside of government to accomplish them.

The reverse side of goal setting is delegating responsibility and demanding accountability— from both political appointees and career staff. You have to show confidence in the people who work for you—and at the same time have a system for obtaining timely information and measuring results.

Though I believe that I must delegate responsibility and trust my staff, it is important to ac-

knowledge that the secretary must be able to set directions at the top. Delegation is not the same as abdication. When I became secretary, there was a move to delegate all departmental regulations to the individual agencies. There were literally hundreds of these regulations every year. I didn't want to go that far. So I set up four criteria. If a regulation met any one of them—for example, if its impact on the economy was 100 million dollars or more—that regulation would have to be approved by the secretary.

I think about management and leadership as linked processes. Managing in the public sector is quite different from that in the private sector. It is not really possible to think about control in an organization that has very few well-defined goals and technology and has substantial participant involvement in the affairs of the organization.

## Lesson Number Eight: Don't Forget That Politics Is Always Part of Policymaking

There is no way to succeed in the world of government without paying attention to that other world: politics. For HHS, politics means primarily the White House and Congress.

None of us, whether we're a political or career public servant, can operate in a vacuum. A variety of external pressures—from the economy to the press, from the governor's office to regulators in Washington—affect government decisions and raise questions for which there are no simple answers.

I have two rules of thumb in politics. One, be fiercely loyal to the president on policy and appointments. Two, be skillfully bipartisan in the administration of the department. When I go up to Capitol Hill to testify before Congress, I present the Administration's case as vigorously as I can. When I return to the department, it doesn't matter to me if a Medicaid waiver request, or any other request, comes from a Republican or Democratic governor. During the Clinton administration, 80 waivers involving the welfare program were granted by the Department; of those, 49 came from states with Republican governors.[4] Democrats and Republicans get the same professional consideration. When there is a threat to the public health in a particular state, the politics of that state never makes a difference in how HHS responds.

## Lesson Number Nine: Look for Allies Where You Don't Expect to Find Them

To manage a large organization in this age of instantaneous communication, it always helps to look beyond the usual borders and to reach out to non-traditional allies. That's why I believe in being nice to Republicans and spending time speaking to newspapers like *The Washington Times* and *The Wall Street Journal*. Those two papers are not known for supporting Democratic causes.

We work hard to make friends out of adversaries, to cooperate with the leadership of both parties, to disagree without rancor, and to build on areas of agreement. If it helps me communicate better, I will enlist help from people who don't expect me to come knocking on their door.

## Lesson Number Ten: Be Flexible, Be Realistic, and Don't Expect to Win Every Time

Perhaps the biggest mistake that the manager of a large organization can make is to stand in one place for too long. Change comes. And as NASA's Jim Webb once noted, these changes come from both inside and outside the organization (Wilson, 1989, 203). That doesn't mean that there shouldn't be a strategic plan and systems in place for carrying out the operations of a large organization. But it does mean that governing is as much art as it is science.

We must expect the unexpected. We must be nimble enough to change course—even in midsentence—if that's what it takes. In other words, we must keep moving and keep listening to the comments from citizens around the country.

In 1994, we lost on universal health care in part because the other side organized quickly and framed the debate. By 1996 we were flexible enough to find a slower, more incremental, and more successful approach. Last year we passed Kassebaum-Kennedy. This year we passed a budget that will provide up to 5 million uninsured children with coverage. Kassebaum-Kennedy was a great victory. Similarly, the FDA reform was the result of a unique government-industry effort.

The unexpected can also mean having something removed from your plate. In 1993, the Social Security Administration was part of HHS. It no longer is. Downsizing in the federal government—unheard of in 1993—became the norm in 1994 and 1995.

The unexpected can mean a changing economy. Low unemployment is helping to lower the welfare rolls. Listening to people in the country express their concern about waste, fraud, and abuse in Medicare and Medicaid allowed us to focus our activities.

But with unexpected change comes the unexpected opportunity to be creative, to find more efficient and less costly ways to deliver services, to find new partners and break new ground, and to be—in the words of Mark Moore (1995)—an "explorer commissioned by society to search for public value."

I've certainly felt like an explorer since becoming a member of a remarkable president's cabinet. This trip of discovery—although risky, difficult, and once in a while disappointing—has been the trip of a lifetime. I also believe that the disciplines of political science and public administration will be enriched as more students of government have a chance to be practitioners.

## Notes

1. The Department was even larger when I arrived in 1993 since it also included the Social Security Administration.
2. Richard Darman reflected on his experience and advised future managers to reject highly centralized systems that depend on large, central staffs. See Roger Porter (1982).
3. My experience in the Department of Health and Human Services is quite different from that described by Paul C. Light (1995). Light argues that more senior helpers "clutter" the message. I found that these staff have been invaluable to me in running the Department and devising policies and programs.
4. In addition, 20 waivers involving the Medicaid program were approved; ten of those waivers were granted to Republican governors. Similarly, ten waivers were approved for child welfare demonstrations; half of those came from Republican governors.

# References

Blumenthal, Michael (1979). "Candid Reflections of a Businessman in Washington." *Fortune*, 29 January, 36-49.

Dog, James W. and Erwin C. Hargrove (1990). *Leadership and Innovation: Entrepreneurs in Government.* Baltimore: Johns Hopkins University Press.

Hargrove, Erwin C. and John C. Glidewell (1990). *Impossible Jobs in Public Management.* Lawrence, KS: University Press of Kansas.

Heclo, Hugh (1977). *A Government of Strangers: Executive Politics in Washington.* Washington, DC: Brookings Institution.

Levin, Martin A. and Mary Bryna Sanger (1994). *Making Government Work: How Entrepreneurial Executives Turn Bright Ideas into Real Results.* San Francisco: Jossey-Bass.

Light, Paul C. (1995). *Thickening Government: Federal Hierarchy and the Diffusion of Accountability.* Washington, DC: Brookings Institution.

Lynn, Laurence E. Jr. (1987). *Managing Public Policy.* Boston: Little, Brown, 130.

Moore, Mark H. (1995). *Creating Public Value: Strategic Management in Government.* Cambridge, MA: Harvard University Press.

Porter, Roger (1982). *Presidential Decision-Making: The Economic Policy Board.* New York: Cambridge University Press.

Radin, Beryl A. (1992). "Policy Analysis in the Office of the Assistant Secretary for Planning and Evaluation, HHS/HEW." In Carol H. Weiss, ed., *Institutions for Policy Analysis.* Newbury Park, CA: Sage, 144-160.

Taylor, Frederick Winslow (1967). *The Principles of Scientific Management.* New York: W. W. Norton.

Wilson, James Q. (1989). *Bureaucracy: What Government Agencies Do and Why They Do It.* New York: Basic Books, 105.

 **Article Review Form at end of book.**

What relevance do truth, beauty, and unity have to a manager seeking to do a good job?

# Aristotle's Advice for Business Success

Engaging workers' hearts and souls, not just their minds, will be the next catalyst for success in business.

## Jennifer J. Laabs

*Jennifer J. Laabs is the associate managing editor at* Workforce. *E-mail: laabsj@workforcemag.com to comment.*

Tom Morris is a modern-day business philosopher. A former professor of philosophy at Notre Dame for 15 years, Morris is now Chairman of the Morris Institute for Human Values in Wilmington, North Carolina, and author of *If Aristotle Ran General Motors: The New Soul of Business*, which was just published by Henry Holt and Company, New York, last month. Here, in an exclusive interview, Morris discusses such time-tested ideas as truth, beauty, goodness and unity, and why HR professionals, and the workforces they serve, can benefit by tapping the wisdom of the ages.

**Q:** Although the ideas in your book also come from the teachings of other ancient philosophers from Greece, Rome and China, why do you focus on Aristotle?

**A:** Well, I started off surveying all the ancient thinkers and all the great philosophers throughout the centuries looking for the most powerful wisdom I could find to apply to modern-day business. Over and over again, I kept coming back to Aristotle, the person who had the most powerful perspective on any given issue. For example, what really motivates human beings? Many of the great thinkers had a lot of insightful things to say, but it was always Aristotle who seemed to really hit the nail on the head. Then, when I was thinking about what really holds an organization together and how people in an organization should view what they're doing together, it was Aristotle, again, who had the key that unlocked the door to all kinds of powerful insights. Aristotle gives us the way to make the next step forward in our understanding of organizations, of motivation, and those kinds of things.

**Q:** What was the practical advice Aristotle proposed in his day that applies to us now in business?

**A:** Aristotle helps us understand human motivation: that human beings are searching for happiness in everything they do—in their private lives, in their family lives and in their work lives. Aristotle helps us understand, at a deeper level, what that's all about. If business managers can understand what motivates people, they can understand the leverage points in their workers' personalities for helping them attain the highest levels of excellence along with the greatest levels of satisfaction. Too often in modern work, those two things come apart. People are being driven to higher levels of excellence, but it's being attained at the expense of their satisfaction. They feel nothing but stress and pressure. They're disgruntled. Aristotle helps us, as business people, understand human nature so we can see how to build higher levels of excellence on a foundation of happiness and satisfaction, so people feel good about what they're doing in the long run and, thereby, can sustain the kind of excellence businesses hope to achieve.

**Q:** In your book, your first point is truth. How does truth fit into the business picture?

**A:** We're hearing a lot nowadays about businesses being "information societies" and "learning organizations." People appreciate the importance of ideas. But so many organizations are almost desert landscapes when it comes to people telling each other the truth, the whole truth and nothing but the truth. Because of organizational politics, people fear open candor about the problems they're facing and what really needs to be done. But human beings need truth just like they need air, water and food. It's that important. I give lots of examples in the book about how truthfulness, troth-telling in the right way, always strengthens an organization. I show places where it has worked beautifully and try to show how to avoid misusing troth-telling because sometimes it can be a harmful exercise if people are uttering brutal troths in an uncaring and unfeeling way. So I help people understand the importance of truth in organizations and how they can inject more truth into the workplace.

**Q:** Do you think modern businesses have been withholding truth?

**A:** Yes, I do. And it's based on a misunderstanding of a famous insight from philosopher Francis Bacon centuries ago. Bacon said, "Knowledge is power." And a lot of people in modern business concluded from that, "If you want power, hoard knowledge." They think that if you give away knowledge, you give away power. They don't understand there are some things in human life (like love and knowledge) that when they're shared, they're actually multiplied: To share

truth in the right way multiplies truth and strengthens the organization as a result. In the book, I show how that works.

**Q:** How does Aristotle's second point, beauty, fit into the business arena?

**A:** Beauty is seen in the workplace on many different levels: cleaning up a factory, repainting a facility, beautifying a place where people work. Hospitals discovered a long time ago that if you hang beautiful paintings in recovery rooms and if you paint the walls a nicer color, people physically recover from surgery faster. The same thing holds true in the workplace. If people have more pleasant surroundings to work in they're going to feel better about their workplace; they're going to enjoy being there, and they'll work at higher levels. So I talk about that sort of beauty at work. But I also talk about other levels of beauty: performance beauty, for example, delighting a customer, delighting an associate, empowering people to create beautiful solutions to business problems. Nobody wants to feel like a robot. People essentially are creative beings. HR professionals need to turn people loose to be artists, to be creators. There will always be constraints, but if they can help people feel that kind of beauty in their work, they will be helping employees achieve greater satisfaction.

**Q:** How does the third point, goodness, fit in?

**A:** Thoreau once said goodness is the only investment that never fails. Goodness is the power behind business ethics, and I'm talking about the deepest perspective on ethics there is. Ethics isn't about staying out of trouble. Ethics is about creating strength.

A nice side effect typically is staying out of trouble. But goodness is about something positive. That was the perspective of the ancient Greek and Roman philosophers. They believed goodness is a foundation for long-term excellence. So if you have an organization in which people feel they're treated fairly with kindness and respect, that's going to be a stronger organization. We hear so much about how loyalty has been lost in the business world in the last few decades. Goodness brings loyalty back into the equation. Goodness makes a huge difference in both little and big issues.

**Q:** What about the fourth point, unity? How does unity help workers?

**A:** Unity is the target of what I call the spiritual dimension of human experience. Everybody wants to feel part of something greater than themselves. They want to feel like they belong, that they're making their contribution in the world along with other people. So I talk about the different spiritual needs everyone has that have been too neglected in the workplace in the last few decades. And I'm not talking about institutionally religious things. I'm just talking about deep, psychological and spiritual needs that all people have: to feel special, to feel important, to feel like they belong, to feel they're useful, to feel like the deepest parts of themselves are being called into play in their work. People don't just show up at work to make money. They want to make a difference. So the fourth part of the book is all about unity and connectiveness.

This fourth foundation of human excellence helps make the workplace a place of meaningfulness for people. As business managers explore the spiritual dimension of human experience, they're exploring an important and powerful leverage point for excellence in any organization that's been unduly neglected. For such a long time, business leaders have just talked about quantifiable stuff, as if these other issues are the soft issues. But what company managers are working with here are soft beings, human beings. These issues end up being the most important issues for a company's sustainable success, I think.

**Q:** How can human resources professionals begin to influence work processes and people in the workforce with these four points?

**A:** First of all, they've got to expose people to these four points. Then train people on them. These really are the simplest ideas in the world, but they're also the most powerful ideas in the world. But sometimes people miss the simplest things. William of Ockham, a medieval philosopher, always said, "Simplify, simplify. Find the essential core of any situation. Learn to concentrate on that, and all the complications will fall into place." Too often human resources managers try to institute all these different kinds of training programs that focus on how to do this and that. A philosopher is concerned with the whys. If you don't understand the whys, you won't ever get the hows right. For example, if Hewlett-Packard or Toyota do certain things, many managers at other companies think they should do likewise. But, the ancient philosophers always said, "Know thyself." Companies should make alterations that fit their organizations. So first of all, everybody should be exposed to the deep roots of excellence in human nature, the universal human nature that we

## Food for Thought

*By Ann Perle*

*The greatest asset of any nation is the spirit of its people, and the greatest danger that can menace any nation is the breakdown of that spirit.*
—George B. Courtelyou

**Thoughts to Ponder:**

What would our work lives be like if we truly made our employees our most important asset? We may say this is what we do, yet everyone knows that our financial assets and capabilities are the most important thing. Is it possible for us to lead this change? Can we believe it ourselves, that if we practiced the ideas expressed by Tom Morris we could create byproducts of financial assets, satisfied customers and a workplace that hums?

What would our work lives be like if we incorporated ancient truths into the workplace? Employees all wish to utilize their talents, skills and abilities. What if we shifted the orientation of job design and began to structure jobs around the talents we have rather than structuring the job around the tasks of the company? That way, employees would be doing those tasks they do well and enjoy doing. The article begs us to look at the workplace from a different orientation or vantage point. We have valuable employees who want to contribute. Yet, asking them to do jobs that don't produce satisfaction for them doesn't do anything to lead to a stronger company. It only leads to turnover, low morale and mediocre progress. How can that be good? Are we capable and willing to see this in another way?

What would work life be like if we understood that we're more than just our tasks and jobs, defined by job titles? We're human beings with an inner desire for happiness, for using ourselves in a meaningful way, for contributing. Inside each of us is a philosopher, a thinker, a magnificent essence that desires to express. What if we began to see that good business is truly being in touch with people—not calling them "intellectual capital," but seeing them as alive, expressing, interested human beings? What if we helped inspire them to contribute? What would the workplace be like?

Ann Perle is the director of human resources for Leica, GPS, Torrance, California; the founder of Pathways Ministries, Newport Beach, California; and a frequent contributor to this column.

all share. What are those leverage points in human nature for making sure people do their best and feel their best about what they're doing? That's what the great philosophers bring to us. So, HR people could start injecting some of these big-picture perspectives into their training and then talk about how these ideas mesh into people's lives. HR people need to realize that new gimmicks come down the pike every month, but what they've got to do is get their bearings with some of the most fundamental ideas that have never changed.

**Q:** How can American businesses regain the lost hearts and souls of their workers through either Aristotle's plan or your plan?

**A:** Business executives have thought about numbers more than they've thought about people. Of course, they've got to have sustainable, profitable businesses. But they've also got to remember that with all the emphasis on product quality and on process efficiency, if they lose sight of the spirit of the people who do the work, they lose everything. It's the spirit of the people who do the work that's the core of any sustainable enterprise. By losing sight of that, modern American business has drifted so much so that people are instituting all these policy changes, such as process changes, reengineering and downsizing. Yet, managers are saying, "Why isn't it working the way it was supposed to?" So much of modern business thinking is process-oriented rather than people-oriented. But ultimately, it's the people who are the key to success. Relationships rule the world. And if [managers] ignore relationships for the sake of abstract, quantitatively measured process improvement, they're barking up the wrong tree. The science of business has to do with the philosophy of human nature, ultimately. In his famous book *The Republic,* Plato once said, "It's not until philosophers become kings or kings become philosophers that we're going to have a good society." He believed the people in charge better understand human nature. Yet, that's not what business schools train future leaders in.

Per Morris' words, maybe it's time to return to the ABCs of human nature so companies can lead from a humanistic vantage point. Fortunately, Aristotle and Morris give HR professionals a good place to start.

 **Article Review Form at end of book.**

After looking at the history of significant events in the development of modern management, what do you feel will be the next important paradigm?

# Distilled Wisdom:

## Buddy, Can You Paradigm?

### Brian Dumaine

Management must be one of the most unnatural activities in the world. Why else would managers sustain a vast publishing and consulting industry with a huge component of blather whose main function is reassurance rather than the transmission of knowledge? Like diet and golfing books, the hundreds of management guides that come out every year really function as corporate security blankets. Managers, like obese people and duffers, feel so perpetually anxious about themselves that they will tolerate an almost incredible torrent of balderdash in the hope of self-improvement.

Managers can spend an eternity searching for panaceas in the pages of such books, but they won't find them. They may for a few months or even years think that they've found a piece of the true Cross, but eventually the advice, trend, or tool will devolve into just another fad or folly. Yet if you look hard at the history of the Fortune 500 over the past 40 years, there emerges through all the static

a set of golden management rules that have surviving power. They don't have labels—once you stick a name on something, it's fast on its way to becoming a flavor-of-the-month disappointment—but are broad management principles. They are (1) Management is a practice. (2) People are a resource. (3) Marketing and innovation are the key functions of a business. (4) Discover what you do well. (5) Quality pays for itself.

Still, the question nags: Is any of this real? Has it actually generated wealth? As with golf and dieting advice, some fundamentals have proved themselves over time. While no one can measure the precise financial impact of these ideas, the argument that they paid off can be made with confidence. Stanley Gault, who has been to the Fortune 500 over the past decade what Joe Montana is to football, says that basic management principles like empowerment, strategy, and quality contributed greatly to his successes at GE in the 1960s and 1970s, and to his turnarounds at Rubbermaid and Goodyear in the 1980s and 1990s.

The very idea of management as a practice, like medicine or navigation, didn't even exist when *Fortune* published its first 500 list in 1955. Until Peter Drucker published his classic *The Practice of Management* the previous year, management had been seen largely as the expression of rank and power. People managed subordinates; they didn't manage businesses. Says Drucker: "When my book came out, nobody had even thought of managing a business. It led to the whole idea of objective, of what is the mission of a business."

Drucker's insight has had nearly endless ramifications. Once companies like General Electric, Du Pont, and Sears started thinking about management in this way, everything needed to be redefined. What, for instance, was the appropriate role of top management? Rather than trying to control everything, Drucker taught, senior executives should focus on strategy and let the rank and file carry out their objectives. With Drucker's help, General Electric in 1956 opened its now famous Crotonville, New

York, training center and has since taught generations of managers this philosophy.

Odd as it may seem in an age when downsizing has depopulated entire office towers, one of the most important and enduring ideas about management is that managers should treat workers as a resource rather than a cost. Says PepsiCo CEO Wayne Calloway: "It seems to me that over the last 40 years the biggest idea is the notion that management doesn't have the monopoly on brains or judgment. It's this idea of utilizing all the strengths of a corporation."

The shift away from command and control didn't happen fast. It has taken decades to get people—at least some people—to take initiative, to learn, to change constantly. True, in the 1970s, self-realization movements got out of hand. PacBell had to abandon its costly leadership program after employees complained that it was a "dress code for the mind." But more recently companies have put "empowerment" to better use. Hewlett-Packard in the 1980s used it to reduce cycle times, requiring employees to team up and design, develop, and market products and services at record speeds. For instance, in 1988 H-P developed the DeskJet printer in just 22 months—a job like that used to take twice as long.

In the early 1990s books like Peter Senge's *The Fifth Discipline* took empowerment a step further, arguing that people are more than cogs; they are individuals with feelings, thoughts, and insights that need to be aired and understood. What Senge and others articulated was that motivated people are good for business. Says Goodyear's Gault: "The empowerment revolution . . . has allowed our nation to record unprecedented progress in the areas of productivity, creativity, technology, product development, and overall competitiveness in a global market."

This notion has exerted a powerful effect on corporate structure. If people were to have more autonomy, they didn't need as many middle managers looking over their shoulders. Thus, a company could shed organizational layers. Lincoln Electric started experimenting with the flat, or horizontal, organization in the 1950s, but it wasn't until the restructuring movement of the late 1980s that corporate America really began to see the light.

In the management of products, as opposed to people, a similar change has turned out to be a winner. In the Fifties and Sixties, with Japanese and German industry still in ruins, U.S. industry could make virtually whatever its engineers or marketers pleased, the customer be damned. But in the 1970s, especially in the auto industry, global competition began to intensify. American corporations slowly realized they would have to start organizing around the idea of serving the customer. Says Theodore Levitt, Harvard business school professor emeritus and marketing expert: "We call it the marketing concept. It made us run businesses around the principle 'Put the customer first, and then profits will follow.'"

A strong customer focus led companies to adopt disciplines like test marketing, surveys, and focus groups that helped them keep in touch with customers and create new products. Says Andrall Pearson, a partner at the New York LBO firm Clayton Dubilier & Rice: "The idea of a marketing discipline was revolutionary. Before, we had no scientific focus. We were just pissing money away on the market." That attention to marketing detail spread in the 1970s and 1980s and helped build such service giants as L.L. Bean, Nordstrom, and Federal Express. Drucker sums it up best: "You get paid for creating a customer, and you get paid for creating a new dimension of performance, which is innovation. Everything else is a cost center."

Our fourth nominee for a great management idea, strategic planning, took a wrong turn for a decade or so. Although the Pentagon had been doing strategic planning through the 1950s and 1960s, not until the 1970s did the idea gain broad currency in corporate America. Before strategic planning, executives essentially sat around and played what-if: What if our competitors did this or that? Then, starting in 1969, GE began to teach strategy as a discipline. The new idea was to conduct a comprehensive analysis of competitors—their past, present, and anticipated future. GE's strategy course also taught managers to allocate resources based upon how you would categorize your business: Is it a growth business or a harvest business?

The beauty of this kind of planning was that it helped managers focus on what they did best, on competencies (although they didn't use the word at the time) that gave them a competitive advantage. Obvious, perhaps, but the point got lost in the conglomeration-mad Sixties and Seventies. Seeing the inefficiencies that resulted and realizing—with the help of Wall Street raiders—that their best strategy was to focus on what they did well, companies in the Eighties began deconglomerating.

Implicit in the idea of jettisoning the unnecessary was focusing on the essence. Thus it was that corporate strategy came back full circle to one of today's most popular ideas: core competencies. Consultants Gary Hamel and C.K. Prahalad argued that every company has a core strength—be it marketing, manufacturing, or R&D—and that it should focus resources on what it does best. Nike, for instance, concentrates on marketing and design, farming out the manufacture of its athletic shoes.

Sometimes a truly good idea needs an apostle. Before the "quality revolution" of the 1980s and 1990s, managers basically thought that investing in high quality was a cost that couldn't be recouped. More than anyone else, consultant W. Edwards Deming disabused them of that notion. In the 1960s and 1970s, Deming worked in Japan and taught the Japanese that by continually improving the quality of a product or process—kaizen, as it's called—a company could save time and money, reduce waste, and give the customer better products faster. For years Deming couldn't sell his message in the U.S. Then, on June 24, 1980, at 9:30 P.M., he appeared on an NBC show about Japanese quality called "If Japan Can, Why Can't We?" A manager at Ford happened to be watching and brought Deming and his ideas to Ford. The result was Team Taurus, a quality-driven project

## Significant Events in the Development of Modern Management

**1955** Corporations start adopting ideas in Pete Drucker's new book, *The Practice of Management.*

**1956** GE opens Crotonville training center, identifying management as something to be taught.

**1958** Lincoln Electric experiments with flat management, pledging not to lay off workers and obtaining flexible work rules.

**1960** Douglas McGregor publishes *The Human Side of Enterprise*, which outlines Theory X (employees are machines) and Theory Y (employees are extended families).

**1963** Harold Geneen embarks on course of acquisitions that will make ITT one of America's largest conglomerates.

**1969** GE, struggling to cope with a raft of acquisitions, becomes one of the first big companies to adopt a strategic plan.

**1971** Werner Erhard launches Erhard Seminars Training, the taproot of touchy-feely management.

**1980** Rand Araskog becomes ITT chairman; to reduce debt, he begins selling some of the 250 businesses acquired by Geneen.

**1980** W. Edwards Deming appears on NBC TV documentary; Deming is hired as a consultant by Ford.

**1980** Japan overtakes the U.S. as the world's leading producer of automobiles.

**1982** T. Boone Pickens, chairman of Mesa Petroleum, makes his first hostile takeover attempt, for Cities Service Corp. It fails.

**1985** Ford introduces Taurus, one of the first American automobiles to be designed and built using cross-functional teams.

**1987** Manpower becomes largest private employer in the U.S., with over 465,000 temporary workers.

**1988** Hewlett-Packard develops DeskJet printer in just 22 months.

**1990** C.K. Prahalad and Gary Hamel publish "Core Competence of the Corporation" in *Harvard Business Review.*

**1993** Michael Hammer and James Champy publish *Reengineering the Corporation: A Manifesto for Business Revolution.*

that helped Ford turn itself around and eventually led to the development of the company's best-selling car.

After that, quality spread wildly throughout the rest of corporate America. Yes, there were abuses, as some companies like Florida Power & Light got carried away in the 1980s and turned their quality programs into self-sustaining bureaucracies. But overall it works. Stressing high quality makes lots of money for companies. Some 15 years after Deming appeared on NBC, Motorola, one of the great disciples of the quality movement, makes such good pagers that it is now a formidable player in the Japanese market.

 **Article Review Form at end of book.**

# WiseGuide Wrap-Up

- Although managers rely on logic and rationality to accomplish work, the nature of managerial work is full of complexity, ambiguity, and often, chaos. Managers cannot ever fully control organizations or people, and they must learn to appreciate and cope with this reality.

- Management blends knowledge from a wide variety of sources and applies specifically to accomplishing work in organizations. Modern views of management recognize that managers can both enhance or diminish their own lives and/or the lives of those around them by the way they approach their work.

- Although management has been around forever, the field of management has only been studied and developed since the end of World War II. A greater understanding of management shows that good management is both the process of creating organization and "making the trains run on time." However, management also has an inspirational side in that managers must help people to obtain feelings of worth and accomplishment from their work.

- The rapid and sometimes destabilizing pace of change in commerce has changed the nature of management. Technological advances will change the way people communicate and interact, and there are also fundamental differences in people's aspirations and what they seek from membership in organizations. Modern workers no longer simply want work to provide access to goods and services, but seek the fulfillment of higher-order needs.

## R.E.A.L. Sites

This list provides a print preview of typical **Coursewise** R.E.A.L. sites. (There are over 100 such sites at the **Courselinks**™ site.) The danger in printing URLs is that web sites can change overnight. As we went to press, these sites were functional using the URLs provided. If you come across one that isn't, please let us know via email to: webmaster@coursewise.com. Use your Passport to access the most current list of R.E.A.L. sites at the **Courselinks** site.

**Site name:** American Management Association International

**URL:** http://www.amanet.org/start.htm

**Why is it R.E.A.L.?** This is the site of the American Management Association, which modestly describes itself as the world's leading membership-based management development and training organization. On this site, managers and human resources professionals can read daily news reports, learn about upcoming AMA seminars and on-site educational programs, and look through recent surveys published in AMA's research reports.

**Key topics:** nature of management work, research reports, job opportunities

**Try this:** Summarize research available on the site about managers' use of rewards to motivate employees.

**Site name:** Introduction to the Theoretical and Philosophical Basis of Modern Management

**URL:** http://www.city.ac.uk/~sm350/theorymgt.html

**Why is it R.E.A.L.?** At this site are notes covering the basic ideas of Fayol, Taylor, Weber, Mayo, McGregor, Deming, Drucker, Handy, Adair, Mintzberg, Peters, and Kanter.

**Key topics:** nature of management, future management trends

**Try this:** Summarize the contributions of one of the management scholars whose work is summarized at this site.

**Site name:** Business Week Online

**URL:** http://www.businessweek.com/

**Why is it R.E.A.L.?** This is the electronic version of the weekly financial news magazine *Business Week*.

**Key topics:** nature of management , management best practices

**Try this:** Summarize a *Business Week* article regarding excellent management.

# section 2

## Learning Objectives

- List and compare the advantages and disadvantages of small and large organizations.

- Describe the qualities of organizations that support employee satisfaction and productivity.

- Describe means by which managers can effectively manage the tensions between their followers' personal and work lives.

- Explain the nature of organizational culture and cultural change in organizations.

# Where Managers Do Their Work: Organizations and Their Environments

 **WiseGuide Intro**

One way to think about culture is in terms of the organization. The concept of organizational culture borrows theories and principles from the science of anthropology. (In fact, most techniques for understanding management are borrowed from other social science disciplines.) Managers do much of their work in an organizational setting, and their effectiveness is determined to a large extent by how well managerial style and practice match the environment of the organizational culture. Managers also help to create and sustain the culture of an organization.

Have you ever worked at a place where people helped each other, were anxious to do good work, and voluntarily expended extra effort? What about the opposite situation? Have you ever worked in an organization where customers were seen as the enemy, cutting corners was standard practice, and no one made a move unless told to do so? Unfortunately, many organizations are like that—but maybe not for too long if they are affected by competition in an efficient market. No matter which of these two organizations seems more typical to you, many of the unwritten rules that guide people's behavior in an organization are artifacts of what is called the organizational culture.

Your university library probably boasts several linear feet of books primarily concerned with organizational culture. Sometimes, academics have made this concept so complicated, it is difficult for anyone to understand. However, a simple definition of organizational culture is: "the way we do things around here." The readings in this section are about organizational environments and the extent to which they determine and are determined by management.

Reading 5 is by Michelle Cottle, who recounts her move from a small newspaper to the *New York Times* and assesses the relative advantages and disadvantages of small and large companies. She also offers advice to those of you who might be contemplating a move to a larger organization.

Reading 6, from *Fortune Magazine,* describes the 100 best companies to work for in America. What features characterize a really good company to work for? Benefits and working environment are important, of course, but the organizational culture is also significant. One factor that almost all of the 100 best companies have in common is a strong culture, which causes employees to behave in certain ways. For instance, at Southwest Airlines (SWA), a strong premium is placed on being friendly and providing excellent customer service. If you have ever flown on SWA, you know that the flight attendants often make wisecracks, tell jokes over the public address system, or even lead passengers in song. For many, working in a culture with such extroverted interaction and playfulness would be very appealing; however, for some, it would be a nightmare. As you look over the characteristics of the 100 companies featured in this reading, think about how appealing the organizational culture of each would be to you, and look for characteristics these "best" companies share.

James Champy, a management commentator most often associated with the re-engineering movement, describes some unusual management training in Reading 7. Just as all individuals do not view the characteristics of the "best" companies in the same way, the sorts of training experiences Champy describes may appeal to some and be off-putting to others.

Since organizations do not lend themselves well to concrete description, metaphors are frequently used to describe them and their characteristics. One of the most common metaphors refers to "learning" organizations, a view that gained its current popularity following publication of *The Fifth Discipline* by Peter Senge. In Reading 8, Noel Tichy and his University of Michigan colleague Eli Cohen extend the idea to something they call a "teaching" organization and describe their experiences with organizations they feel do a particularly good job of passing along skill and knowledge to others.

Someone asked the psychiatrist and father of psychotherapy Sigmund Freud if, near the end of his own life, he had reached a conclusion about the meaning of life. Freud responded in his native German with the terse comment "lieben und arbeit," which translates to "love and work." By *love*, Freud did not mean just romantic love, but the totality of our relationships with others; and by *work*, he did not mean just the work we do for pay, but all our efforts to accomplish things in our lives. Most of us are constantly trying to find a balance between the amount of attention and energy we devote to our personal relationships and to our work. A tension between these central concerns in our lives seems almost omnipresent. In Reading 9, Stewart Friedman, Perry Christensen, and Jessica DeGroot examine ways in which managers can confront and deal with the competing demands of work and having a personal life—both for themselves and the people they manage.

In general, do you think you would be more satisfied and fulfilled in a small or a large company? Why?

# Seeing the Fruit of One's Labor

## Michelle Cottle

**Q.** I recently switched from a small, hands-on company to a large, hierarchical one. Adjusting has been a bit of a struggle. Before, I had a say in all aspects of the business, and I saw the impact I had. Now, I'm a widget handler and wonder if I am adding any value to the company's products. What should I do: stay put and work my way up to a position where I'll clearly make a difference, or go back to being a big frog in a small pond?

**A.** As far as corporate culture shock goes, nothing is quite as depressing as feeling that you've signed on to be an inconsequential drone in a giant cubicle hive. But before you rush back to your former pasture, make sure you're not just suffering from the grass-is-greener syndrome.

Compile a list of everything you loathed about your old employer and reflect on whether the problems were related to the small, entrepreneurial nature of the place. (To keep you honest, talk with friends who can remind you how you complained while working there.)

Try to assemble as complete a picture as possible of your personality and work style, advised George Zeller, a senior employment specialist with Career Moves, a counseling service in Boston.

You may even want to take one of those personality tests intended to reveal whether you're best equipped to be the chief financial officer of a multinational corporation, a French teacher or a zookeeper. But don't expect any big revelations, Zeller warned. In some ways, these tests just mirror what you already know.

Still, you might be discovering that you have landed in the wrong environment for your personality type. I asked Joseph Frey, a clinical psychologist in Augusta, Ga., for the Highlands Program, a career development firm, about your case, and he said you sounded like a "structural generalist."

The "structural" part of that phrase means that you need a hands-on type of job. You enjoy having a product that you can feel, see, or touch at the end of the day. But as a generalist, Frey said, you also like being part of a team

and want a bit of diversity in your workday.

Smaller companies are ideal environments for structural generalists, Frey said, while large, hierarchical firms often force such folks to choose between their dominant personality traits.

Even if you decide to stay with the larger firm, start planning your rise from dronedom. According to Zeller, a lot of people just want to get lost and be invisible, so you need to make it clear that you are *not* one of them. Volunteer for different assignments.

Acquire as many skills and experiences as you can. Maintain a diary of your accomplishments. After a while, go to the boss and say, "For the past few months I did this. I did that. I went to training and picked up these skills. I helped Sally with that project. Now I want to take on a new project."

Some companies, of course, do not allow such cross-pollination among departments or positions. In that case, your only option may be to seek a less-rigid hive.

 **Article Review Form at end of book.**

Do you think you would love to work at each of these companies?
Why or why not?

# Why Employees Love These Companies

**Ronald B. Lieber**

It isn't complicated: We found that most of the raves workers give their employers are based on just three corporate traits. For many companies they're within reach.

By now, most of us have been schooled to believe we'll spend the rest of our careers jumping from job to job, working ever harder to prove our mettle to cranky bosses, and getting promoted much less often than our predecessors. We've been told over and over that this Darwinian odyssey is the new workplace reality, bleak though it may be. Yet the cheerful employees of our 100 Best companies face a far different, far more benign daily work life. These workers sing their employers' praises and—though it's very un-'90s—even declare pride in their corporate affiliation.

Why? What makes employees not just like but love these companies? We looked hard and found three recurring traits that seem to explain a lot. The great majority of our 100 Best have at least one, and many have all three. The good news is, they're within the reach of just about any employer.

First, many of our 100 Best are run by a powerful, visionary leader. Superstar CEOs like Bill Gates of Microsoft (No. 8), Andy Grove of Intel (No. 32), and Larry Bossidy of AlliedSignal (no. 96) are among the most demanding bosses in business, yet workers seem to feel inspired rather than oppressed by them; non-celebrities running many lesser-known companies have the same effect. Second, many of these companies offer a physical work environment that employees adore. Third, these companies often frame their work as part of a deep, rewarding purpose that employees find fulfilling. Here's a closer look at how a few companies on our list wow their workers.

## Inspiring Leadership

Exhibit A is Herb Kelleher, the Southwest Airlines CEO perched at the pinnacle of our 100 Best list. He spends his business life making sure his employees believe in him and in the operation he has muscled into the top tier of a savagely competitive industry. He smokes, he arm-wrestles, he drinks large quantities of Wild Turkey, he raps in music videos—and it is only slight hyperbole to

say nearly all his employees worship the ground he walks on. But even he can't match the act of devotion displayed for Dave Duffield, the founder and CEO of PeopleSoft (no. 20), the software maker in Pleasanton, Calif. A few years ago employees formed a garage band and decided to call it The Raving Daves.

Remarkably, the well-worn story of Mary Kay Ash also retains its power to inspire. Those who know her well—and almost all who work for Mary Kay Inc. (No. 82) seem to think they do—describe her as a sort of corporate Everywoman: Pushed aside by her male superiors as a saleswoman in the 1950s, she quit her job and built a sales organization intended to empower other women.

Mary Kay's saga of how she grew her business and made a fortune is the chief inspiration for many of the 475,000 women who sell her products. "I was a secretary. I was not voted most likely to succeed in high school," says Lisa Madson, 37, who started selling for the company 11 years ago. "But she reaches so many people by talking about the potential that everyone has inside. And she's the living example."

Though Mary Kay herself is a millionaire many times over, the people who work for her marvel at her ability to remain accessible. Before she suffered a stroke in 1996, she used to invite employees to her home for tea several times a year. "I've sat on her bed and had cookies at her table," says Gloria Mayfield Banks, 41, an executive senior sales director based in Baltimore. "It takes away the mystery when someone totally opens herself up to you like that."

The effective leader inspires employees not just to work hard and succeed but also to become miniversions of the leader. That seems to be happening at Mary Kay. "People understand that for Mary Kay, it was all about fulfilling a mission that was bigger than just her," says Janice Bird, 42, who works at corporate headquarters in Dallas. "They've increased their own self-esteem by being around her, and they want to pass that on to others the same way she did."

## Knockout Facilities

These may be the most persuasive way to tell employees they're valued. Top management at USAA (No. 39), the San Antonio-based insurance and financial services company, demonstrates the value of wooing employees with an impressive corporate compound. "Anywhere you go in town, if you tell someone you work for USAA, they're impressed," says Jeannette Leal, a service adviser in the life/annuity service and claims department. "You become a part of this place, and it becomes everything that you're about."

The amenities begin with an on-site child care center. The facility can handle 300 kids, and there's car-seat storage for families where the mom drops off and the dad picks up. In Tampa, where the company also has a large presence, they've even thought to add industrial-strength fencing around the kiddie playground in case marauding alligators show up in search of snacks. "My wife and I visited ten or 12 day-care facilities all over town," says Raul Nevarez, 30, a USAA security officer. "There was no competition at all."

If you don't want to drive to work, the company sponsors a van pool. If you ruin your hose, you can pick up a pair at the on-site store. There's a dry-cleaning service, a bank, and several ATMs. Even the cafeteria food is tasty enough that, several years ago, employees began demanding dinner to go. At Thanksgiving they purchased 5,620 pies and 188 turkeys to take home to their families.

Then there are the athletic facilities. The three gyms are indistinguishable from those at many upscale health clubs, and one is open all night long. Outside, employees compete in intramural leagues on basketball and tennis courts and softball and soccer fields. If you want to work on your backswing at lunch, there's a driving range too.

USAA employees clearly enjoy these breaks from their desks during the workweek, but they often return to the campus on the weekend with their families. "I enjoy bringing my kids here," says Donna Castillo, 34, a sales manager in consumer finance and auto service. "There are playgrounds where they can run around, and it's nice to take pictures of them here when the bluebonnets come out in the spring."

Amenities like these cost a company a lot, but they buy a lot too. "The facilities say that the company cares about us, that we're a valued asset," says security guard Nevarez. "People are dying to get in here. I have to go direct traffic when the parking lot at the employment center overflows. It makes me feel really good that I work for a company that is sought out like that, but it also means that I have to produce in order to earn the right to stay."

## A Sense of Purpose

What sort of mission turns employees on? Well, it's not shareholder value, that's for sure. "I always try to make this very clear to analysts who cover our company," says Bill George, 55, CEO of Medtronic (No. 47), a medical-products company in Minneapolis. "Shareholder value is a hollow notion as the sole source of employee motivation. If you do business that way, you end up like ITT."

Most of those analysts love Medtronic anyway, largely because its employees turn out so many great new gizmos that a full 50% of revenues come from products introduced in the past 12 months. Shareholder value? The company's total return to shareholders have averaged about 34% annually over the past decade. But that isn't what gets workers out of bed and into a lab coat in the morning. Rather it's the notion of helping sick people get well. Instead of concentrating on shareholders or doctors, workers at Medtronic concentrate on the people who will have the company's products implanted inside them.

This is hardly a new approach for companies in the health and medical industries. Employees at Merck (No. 9), a perennial all-star in surveys of worker satisfaction, have long since memorized the mantra that the medicine is for patients, not profits. Medtronic finds novel ways to teach similar lessons, embodied in the company motto, "Restoring patients to full life." Its symbol is an image of a supine human rising toward upright wellness.

The resurrection imagery comes to life each December at the company's holiday party, where patients, their families, and their doctors are flown in to tell their survival stories. It sounds like the stuff of a made-for-TV tearjerker, but this is not PR gimmickry; journalists are generally not invited. Instead, it's the employees who are moved to tears year after year. "I remember going to my first holiday party, and someone asked me if I had brought my Kleenex," recalls Medtronic President Art Collins, 50, a strapping guy with a firm handshake who is generally not prone to crying fits. "I assumed I'd be fine, but then these parents got up with their daughter who was alive because of our product. Even the surgeons who see this stuff all the time were crying."

Improving human health, though in a much different way, was the deep purpose motivating John Mackey, 44, when he helped start Whole Foods Market (No. 34), a chain of natural-foods grocery stores. That clearly stated mission has helped him draw motivated employees who are more educated than the average grocery worker. Take Lisa Shaw, 30, a Wellesley College graduate who works in Brighton, Mass., for one of the company's Bread & Circus stores. "I remember going to a wedding after I graduated and seeing the looks on people's faces when I told them what I was doing," she recalls. "I just hang on to the fact that my job is good in some larger sense. If people buy the sprouts, they're eating healthier foods, the farmer is doing well, and it's good for the planet because they're grown organically."

Such high-minded talk makes it tempting to dismiss Whole Foods employees as a bunch of hippies running an overgrown cooperative. But Whole Foods is a public company whose margins are roughly 50% higher than the average grocery chain's; its total return to shareholders over the past five years has averaged about 23% annually. And the people who work there make explicit connections between the company's financial success and its larger goals. "We're going to pass a billion dollars in sales this year," says Linda Fontaine, 38, the national tax coordinator at corporate headquarters. "All that means is that we've just made that much more of a difference in the world."

Blissed-out employees working in the best of economic times are fairly easy to please, of course. A better test of worker resolve comes when a company slams up against a serious crunch. TDIndustries (No. 5), a specialty construction and service-repair business in Dallas, fell on hard times when building in that area practically stopped at the end of the 1980s. The company's bank had failed, and private investors wouldn't touch the place. So in 1989 CEO Jack Lowe took the problem to employees, who decided to terminate their overfunded pension plan. They could have put the $4 million thus liberated directly into their IRAs, but instead many of them elected to bet their retirement money on Lowe's bailout plan. All told, TDI employees put about $1.25 million back in the company in return for shares in an ESOP account.

A risky investment? Absolutely— but the value of those shares has more than doubled since then. Besides, it wasn't the money that people were worried about anyway. "Sure, we were fixing to lose a lot of our retirement funds if the company failed," says senior project manager Laura Price. "But the real fear was of having to go work for someone else."

 **Article Review Form at end of book.**

Have you ever considered doing management consulting or organizational development work? How can you balance your need to stay busy with the needs of your client without engaging in "Loony-Tunes" techniques?

# Loony-Tunes Management Training

## James Champy

With the white folds of his kaffiyeh hanging low over his eyes, as if to protect them from the punishing desert sun, the "expedition's" advisor intoned his instructions with a straight face: "The fabled gold of Sheik Yabibi lies high in the mountains to the north. You must organize yourselves carefully in teams to cross the trackless sands. But beware," he added dramatically, "of the winds!" His robed arms fluttered violently. "The haboob!"

Around him stood other corporate executives. They were dressed as camel drivers, desert nomads and Saudi princes. Their faces showed the strain of trying to take the ridiculous seriously. Outside—with a shriek that built to the intensity of a howling sandstorm—a jumbo jet lifted off the runway adjacent to the motel conference room in which we were playing this silly game.

Surveys show that it takes at least five years of persistent effort and outstanding leadership to make cultural change stick. Yet quickie management culture-change courses abound, such as

the one I have just described: treks, walks in the woods, role-playing games, even EST technique and sleep and food deprivation. At that make-believe Arab session, one New York banker got it exactly right. "I think I already know where the gold is," he muttered, fiddling with his desert headgear. "It's in loony-tunes management-training sessions like this."

The only effective short course in radical human transformation I know of takes place at Parris Island. Such heavy indoctrination won't work for businesses. You can't order young executives out of bed at 2 a.m. to shoulder 65-pound packs for a 20-mile forced march.

That New York banker had been sent to the "desert" training because he and his compatriots were treating loan customers badly. The higher-ups deemed this a "culture" problem. Maybe, but the problem wasn't going to be cracked by donning Arab headgear.

A company's culture is no more than a collective set of the beliefs and behaviors of its people. They develop over years and

often start with the founder—like Johnson & Johnson's General Johnson, who imbued J&J with strong beliefs about serving the public good.

More recently, Gary Wendt, the leader of GE Capital, was nearly as relentless as a Marine drill instructor. Over slightly more than five years he developed a new, highly focused culture for this financial services company. His approach: Establish unambiguous business metrics so that everyone understood success.

But let's not kid ourselves about quick fixes. As Peter Drucker said: "Company cultures are like country cultures. Never try to change one. Try, instead, to work with what you've got."

Drucker was right. The quick-culture-change artists are charlatans. Here, from my experience, are some thoughts on what it really takes to effect change:

People on the job change most quickly when they can physically experience the new direction you want. As Wendt did, alter the compensation system. Update the physical environment. If you need bank managers to treat customers better, put them in a new branch where all the customer rules are changed. These changes can be a simple thing, like greeting customers with interest. By changing what people do, you stand a better chance of changing who they are.

Role-playing exercises can be helpful only when people return to find that something really has changed at the company. This could be as aggressive as chang- ing how a company markets and sells, or as simple as how the boss treats people. Otherwise, role-playing happens in an abstraction—and can make people even more cynical and entrenched.

If your business requires a total shift in its culture to suc- ceed, you might do best taking a hint from Peter Drucker and not try. Go out and start a new company—much as General Motors did with Saturn. Or you may need to hire new people. Radical culture shifts require deep personal adjustments, which many people may not want—or be able—to make. After all, the secondary dictionary definition of "change" is "substitution."

 **Article Review Form at end of book.**

Can you identify any organizations, other than the ones named in this reading, that you feel can be characterized as "Teaching Organizations"? What characteristics made you select them?

# The Teaching Organization

In these competitive times, a learning organization isn't enough. Here's how winning companies such as GE and AlliedSignal have become teaching organizations, in which leaders pass along their knowledge every day.

## Noel M. Tichy and Eli Cohen

*Noel M. Tichy is a professor of organizational behavior and HR management at the Graduate School of Business Administration, University of Michigan and director of the university's Global Leadership Program. Eli Cohen is a research director at the University of Michigan Graduate School of Business Administration and a partner in Tichy Cohen Associates.*

Since the early 1990s, a number of companies have invested vast amounts of money trying to become learning organizations. Hopefully, they did a good job because to survive in the future, they have to learn one more big lesson: A learning organization isn't enough. They need to become teaching organizations.

The concepts underlying learning organizations are valuable. But to succeed in a highly competitive global marketplace, companies need to be able to change quickly; their people must be able to acquire and assimilate new knowledge and skills rapidly. Though learning is a necessary competency, it's not sufficient to assure marketplace success.

We have looked at winning companies—those that consistently outperform competitors and reward shareholders—and found that they've moved beyond being learning organizations to become teaching organizations. In fact, we believe that when a learning organization comes up against a teaching organization, the teaching organization will win every time. That's because teaching organizations are more agile, come up with better strategies, and are able to implement them more effectively.

Teaching organizations do share with learning organizations the goal that everyone continually acquire new knowledge and skills. But to that they add the more critical goal that everyone pass their learning on to others.

In teaching organizations, leaders see it as their responsibility to teach. They do that because they understand that it's the best, if not only, way to develop throughout a company people who can come up with and carry out smart ideas about the business. Because people in teaching organizations see teaching as critical to the success of their business, they find ways to do it every day. Teaching every day about critical business issues avoids the fuzzy focus that has plagued some learning organization efforts, which have sometimes become a throwback to 1960s- and 1970s-style self-exploration and human relations training.

A teaching organization's insistence that its leaders teach creates better leaders because teaching requires people to develop a mastery of ideas and concepts. In a teaching organization, leaders benefit just by preparing to teach others. Because the teachers are people with hands-on experience within the organization—rather than outside consultants—the people being taught learn relevant, immediately useful concepts and skills.

Teaching organizations are better able to achieve success and maintain it because their constant focus is on developing people to become leaders. An organization's current leaders are creating the next generation of leaders by teaching people about the critical issues facing their business and by teaching them how to anticipate changes and deal with them. Consequently, teaching organizations have a steady supply of talent to keep the momentum going.

## The Best Leaders Are the Best Teachers

When we set out to write *The Leadership Engine: How Winning Companies Build Leaders at Every Level* (HarperBusiness, 1997), companies around the world were fumbling all over themselves to find the right tools to deal with globalization, technological change, and consumers' rising demands. The many that failed were paying the price. GM, IBM, American Express, Westinghouse, Kodak in the early 1990s, and AT&T and Apple in the latter half of the nineties all said goodbye to their senior leaders and hired new ones. The capital markets were responding to poor corporate results and sending the message to add value or the companies' top leaders would be replaced.

In writing *The Leadership Engine,* we examined some of those failures and compared them with such successes as General Electric, Intel, and Compaq. We concluded that the capital markets were only partly right; leadership was the problem, but the markets were wrong to focus only on top leadership. In the companies we studied, sustained success was a function of leadership throughout. Winning companies win because they have solid leaders not only at the top, but also at all organizational levels.

When we asked why these winning companies had a lot of leaders at all levels, we discovered it was because they deliberately worked at it and had made developing leaders a critical competency. We found that to be true consistently in our research of successful organizations no matter what their size or line of endeavor. Whether they were huge Fortune 500 corporations or not-for-profit social agencies, there was one universal characteristic. It was that everyone, including and especially top leaders, were committed teachers. They had developed leadership engines—systems for creating dynamic leaders at all organizational levels. They made themselves into teaching organizations.

Many executives think that they don't have the time to teach because they're too busy dealing with the immediate issues of running a business. But the best leaders we know are, not coincidentally, the best teachers. Larry Bossidy—who transformed AlliedSignal and led it to become the best performing company on the Dow Jones Industrial Average within five years of his arrival in 1991—accomplished his successes largely by being a dedicated teacher. Bossidy didn't transform Allied by replacing senior managers. He diagnosed the company and decided what had to be done. He taught the senior leaders about strategy and spent hundreds of days teaching other people throughout the company. In his first year on the job, Bossidy reached 15,000 AlliedSignal employees personally.

Now, Bossidy is teaching his people how to create a growth mindset and deliver on it. Many people think that AlliedSignal can't be a growth company any longer because many of its businesses are in mature markets. But Bossidy thinks that defeatist attitude carries the seeds of its own fulfillment. So, he is teaching people at Allied to see that growth is possible anywhere and that if they go looking for it, they'll find it.

Other highly effective leaders known for their teaching include Roger Enrico of PepsiCo, Andy Grove of Intel (see Training & Development, May 1997) and the late Roberto Goizueta of Coca-Cola. By holding classes and workshops regularly, those leader-teachers serve as role models for everyone in their organizations. Their example emphasizes the importance they place on teaching and encourages others to teach. But even more important than the teaching they do in classrooms is the teaching they do in the course of the daily management of their companies. Bossidy, for example, uses the strategy, budget, and employee-review processes to coach the managers who participate in them. After each meeting, he writes each manager a letter that reviews the meeting and states explicitly what he liked and didn't like about the manager's plans. Bossidy also writes what he expects to happen as a result of the meeting. If a manager doesn't understand or disagrees, he or she gets back to Bossidy immediately.

Similarly, Carlos Cantu, CEO of ServiceMaster says, "Every single person has to come away [from a meeting with him] with something positive." His objective is that the people who are responsible to him feel they gain something from the experience.

## No Blueprint

So, how do you create a teaching organization? What does one look like? The answer is that there is no single blueprint. Teaching organizations require the personal input and dedication of the leaders within them. Therefore, each one is unique in that it's based on the knowledge and experience of its leaders and the realities of its business environment. One premier example is General Electric.

Jack Welch has been lauded as one of the great business minds of the century. Many people saw General Electric as an institution that was too successful and too big for it to need change or be changed. But Welch had a very different point of view of GE when he became CEO 17 years ago. Since then, he has creatively destroyed and rebuilt the company. The result is a market value around a quarter of a trillion dollars—the most valuable company on Earth. But, though many people laud Welch's leadership qualities, others miss that he's also a great teacher. He may head a company with annual sales closing in on $100 billion, but he spends 30 percent of his own time teaching and developing others. Equally important, he has made sure that the rest of GE's leaders are also teachers.

The result of Welch's teaching—and the reason GE has achieved marketplace success—is that the company has an abundance of leadership talent. Business Week recently ran a list of the 20 executives "most sought after" by search firms looking for CEOs; five were at GE. That's even after several of GE's brightest stars had been plucked away in the '80s and '90s—including Bossidy; John Trani, now of Stanley Works; Glenn Hiner, now of Owens Corning; Harry Stonecipher, now of Boeing; and Norman Blake, now of USF&G.

Welch was involved personally in transforming GE's Crotonville management development center—directing it less toward packaging information and teaching job skills and more toward testing, coaching, and developing leaders. Twice a month, without fail, he goes to Crotonville to teach and interact with new employees and experienced managers. He also teaches constantly through direct feedback and coaching to leaders throughout the company.

Welch also built a system at GE in which leaders teach other leaders. It has the following basic elements.

## A Leadership Pipeline

Every professional-level employee at GE has a career map that describes where they are in their career relative to positions they've had and may hold in the future. The map includes an assessment of their skills and the specific skills they'll need for the next positions. It also describes primary job assignment, stretch assignments, and formal development and coaching opportunities through which the skills can be acquired and demonstrated. Such tools, to varying degrees, are commonplace in many companies. The difference at GE is how they're used. Managers at every level look at their staffs' maps and use them as the basis for coaching. Everyone at GE understands that the environment will change and that career maps aren't set in stone. But they do provide a context and starting point to develop technical and leadership ability. They also set expectations for what the company wants each employee to achieve at any given point in his or her career.

A main purpose of the maps, along with GE's other HR processes (more on those later), is to keep the leadership pipeline full—a matter GE takes seriously. Dick Stonesifer, who started at GE as a mechanic and became head of GE's $6 billion appliance business by the time he retired in 1996, says, "One of my most important jobs, and one of the things I evaluated people on, was whether there were four people who could [step in suddenly and] fill someone's position."

He explains: "This wasn't about some type of emergency planning, because you don't need four people to fill a job. The point was that you need bench strength; you need people who are that good to run parts of your business and, eventually, they will take bigger jobs in the company. But if you aren't worried about having people who are that good, you'll never improve your business."

That type of thinking is almost a religion at GE. With Stonesifer, a failure to show your faith usually meant career disaster. He says, "If I had a great manager who didn't have strong candidates that could do his job, I'd make a very explicit deal. I'd say, 'You have six months to find people—from outside or inside—who can perform at a higher level or [you can] develop it in your own people. I'll provide any help you need. But if those people aren't here in six months, I'm going to get rid of you because I can't have you making the numbers but not getting people ready to lead.'"

## Coaching Key Leaders

Although GE works hard to develop leaders at every level, the top 500 get special attention. Welch is fanatical that the talents of that distinguished group be upgraded constantly. He demands that whenever one of the 500 positions comes open, several internal and external candidates are examined. That lets him and other senior leaders constantly benchmark GE's talent.

Each of the top 500 leaders regularly receives brutally honest, laser-sharp feedback on their hard-business performance and soft people issues. Welch gives feedback to each of his staff in a two-page, handwritten report on his or her performance and attaches last year's note that's annotated to show what has or hasn't been done. He provides more feedback during annual stock-option awards and salary adjustments, which he accompanies with a face-to-face discussion. The discipline of putting his thoughts in writing forces Welch and his staff to focus on the feedback. It also leaves no room for distortion and misinterpretation. That process cascades so that Welch's staff provide the same level of in-depth, personal coaching to their staff, and so on down.

For example, in the early 1990s, Welch began rating managers on a 2-by-2 grid showing their performance relative to quantifiable targets and the extent to which they "lived" GE values. The tool was effective, and now all of GE's 500 officers use it to evaluate and coach their people.

## Organizational Structure That Encourages Leadership Development

One of Welch's early activities was to dismantle GE's bureaucracy. In place of 240 profit centers, he created 13 global businesses, each of which now reports to the office of the chairman—Welch and two vice chairmen. Together with other senior executives, these people form the 25-person Corporate Executive Council, which meets four times a year to share experiences and plan for the future. At the sessions, these "best leaders" expand their own abilities by learning from each other. Because they're all working on company-wide issues, their thinking about the company and their own businesses is also enhanced. And there's no hierarchy; everyone is expected to contribute.

The CEC structure (think of it as a hub-and-spoke system with the office of the chairman at the center) has been replicated all over the company. GE Appliances has its own business executive council, and GE Capital has set up 27 different businesses—in part to give each unit small-company speed and flexibility and to provide more leadership positions. Though the specific forms may be different, the underlying premise is the same: Bureaucracy stifles people's ability and desire to lead. The CEC-style structure and each business unit encourage people to take the initiative. Several times a year, it lets them stretch their own leadership by thinking more broadly. At these sessions, senior leaders can assess, coach, and teach junior leaders.

## HR Systems and Processes

GE's entire HR system is geared to developing leaders and emphasizes the need for leaders to teach other leaders. Selection for a management job early on in one's career is based on demonstrated leadership talents. Once you manage others at GE, you are evaluated on how well you develop them. Your compensation and career opportunities reflect that.

GE also uses several other HR processes to help leaders teach, such as new-manager assimilation. When a leader is about to take a new job, a professional (usually an HR manager) interviews each of the people who will report directly to the new manager. Next, the HR person discusses the findings with the new manager, who then holds several sessions with his or her new staff to talk about the state of the business and to share his or her personal views on business and leadership.

A good example of that is described by Tom Tiller, who worked in GE Appliances for Stonesifer. The new-manager assimilation interviews for Tiller revealed that people, including the top team, had been demoralized by continued plant closings. So, Tiller used assimilation meetings to discuss that issue and teach people what he knew about turning around bad situations. Basically, he says, he found that people like to be winners and be in organizations where positive things happen. So, in the midst of the cutbacks, GE needed to focus on creating new products and getting people excited about the future. At first, his team members doubted that could be done. But, through the process started in the assimilation meetings, Tiller brought them around to accepting his leadership point of view on how to create positive energy. Nine months later, Appliances had one of the most successful product rollouts in GE's history.

## Becoming a Teacher

In building a teaching organization, leaders must draw on the unique strengths and talents within their organization. There are, however, certain characteristics that we've found mark all teaching organizations. The most important factor is whether individual leaders are prepared to do it. Specifically, they must

- consider developing leaders a core competitive competency

- develop teachable points of view on how to operate and

grow the company, and how to teach others to be leaders

- design and execute methods of teaching on a wide scale, and make sure the teaching goes beyond technical skills to include developing and honing leadership abilities.

Here are those characteristics in more detail.

## Developing Leaders As a Core Competency

Most companies view their competitive strengths in terms of the ability to devise smart strategies and efficiently deliver the goods and services that customers want. Teaching organizations also seek winning strategies and brilliant execution, but they view the cause-and-effect equation differently. They start with the premise that people devise the strategies and implement the execution. Then, they focus equally on developing people.

Leaders with that point of view make decisions differently from people using other metrics. That means not only that the choices they make are sometimes different, but also that the way they arrive at those choices is different. Because decision making is an important leadership skill, leaders in a teaching organization teach others by opening up the decision making process so that everyone can see how and why they reached a particular decision.

Debra Dunn, general manager of Hewlett-Packard's video communications division, is an excellent example. Survival in the hotly competitive markets for video broadcast servers, cable modems, and wireless data communication technologies requires that HP's employees exhibit a lot of what we call, "edge." In other words, they must be willing to

face reality and make clear, definite decisions about which new products HP will invest in. One reason Dunn has been so successful is that she has never had trouble making those types of decisions. She also knows that for her businesses to be successful, she has to help the people who work for her develop that ability as well. Dunn is deliberate in doing that. "First," she says, "I am very open and honest and direct about whether I see people as having the raw material to develop this edge. Second, I use my decisions as a way to coach, showing people how I understand things at a very detailed level. That includes how I think about the market and about communicating things up and down inside our company.

More than a year ago, Dunn and her staff were reviewing the various businesses they were trying to build. In one business in particular, Dunn felt that HP didn't have a sustainable position and would do better to invest resources other places. She thought that there was a teaching opportunity to help people understand the elements of a viable strategy and to get the management team to internalize why that's necessary and important. So, she held a series of meetings. "The objective was to convey the path I was going down," she says. "At the first meeting, I got up and took out the strategy statement from a year ago and began comparing its assumptions to the current reality. I said, 'Let's revisit this. Here's the strategy we're pursuing. Here are the assumptions we're making. Here's what the market size was. What do you think the market size is now?' [Back then], we felt we had to have a major partner to be successful in this business. So I asked, 'Do we have any

reason to think that isn't the case now? Do we have a major partner? Do we see a major partner that we might have?' Next, we walked through every element of the strategy, and I asked, 'What are the options?'"

At the end of the discussion, some people still suggested certain partnerships. But Dunn said, "Guys, I think if we're honest with ourselves, we know enough today to assess, with very high possibility, what is the likelihood of partnerships with [those] people, and none look probable. . . . I know that some of you think the right thing to do is to continue spending time on this. But I am deciding that we are not going to; we don't have time and can't afford to go down every theoretical path. We have to apply some intuitive judgment."

Dunn's teaching regarding her decision didn't stop there. She decided to make dealing with the pain of her decision part of her teaching. She says that she found the decision painful because she had invested a lot of personal energy trying to make the business work. "I didn't like the conclusion. But that didn't cause me to deny it or hide from it or pretend that reality is different. I knew this could be a mind-broadening area for part of my team. I went out to lunch, I went out for drinks, I spent time . . . helping them understand the constraints."

Dunn's decision had both supporters and dissenters. But perhaps more important than the decision was that she gave her team first-class lessons on how to be a good leader. One, she was clear and logical, looked reality squarely in the face, and weighed each option against her ultimate goal to invest resources where they were most likely to pay off. Two, she won people over and energized them to pursue the course she'd chosen. She displayed, up-close and first-hand, the leadership quality called edge. She made a tough decision because she felt it was for the good of the company. In a more traditional organization, Dunn might have made her decision differently. If she hadn't been taught and encouraged to have edge, she might not have made the decision at all or might have made it privately to avoid critical questions from her staff. She could have decreed that the division would get out of the business. But in a teaching organization, that would be unthinkable. If an organization places top priority on developing leaders, then its people look for every opportunity to do just that.

## Teachable Points of View

A commitment to teaching is an important first step to building a teaching organization. But in addition to wanting to teach, leaders must be able to teach, which means that they must have teachable points of view.

Everyone has points of view, and a wealth of knowledge and experience from which we create assumptions about the world and how it operates. We use such points of view every day to orient ourselves in new situations and make decisions about how to proceed. Leaders generally have pretty good points of view. Otherwise, they wouldn't be able to make smart decisions consistently and take the effective actions that made them leaders in the first place. But in order to pass that knowledge on to others, leaders must be able to articulate their points of view in ways that people can understand. In other words, they have to develop their points of view into teachable points of view.

Having a teachable point of view is a sign that person has clear ideas and values. It's also a tool that enables him or her to communicate those ideas and values to others. It isn't enough to have experience; leaders must draw appropriate lessons from their experience and be able to make their tacit knowledge explicit.

We sometimes begin workshops by asking people to think about their own teachable points of view. What are the central ideas driving their business? What are their core values? How do they link them together to direct their own actions and energize other people? Then, we have them stand up and give a three-minute presentation. A few participants are great, but most stumble. Why can't these experienced managers articulate their thoughts? Because the ability to do something, even well, and the ability to articulate how one does it require different skills. For example, a good athlete isn't necessarily a good coach.

Most of us keep our experiences in our hip pockets to use at a later time, but effective leaders keep taking them out and examining them—looking at the lessons they learned and searching for effective ways to express them. Further, they constantly refine their experiences as they accumulate new ones and new information.

Most people have teachable points of view on little things. For example, we frequently hit the save key on our computers, and we can explain why and how that reduces the risk of losing productive work. Effective leaders, however, have teachable points of view on a broad range of less tangible and more complicated topics. They're always coming up with new views because they're always looking to see what can be learned from a situation.

The late Roberto Goizueta of Coca-Cola is a great example of someone who developed teachable points of view and used them—as opposed to using charisma or cheerleading his company to success. When Goizueta became CEO in 1981, he was an underwhelming choice to Coca-Cola veterans and Wall Street. A company built largely on image had just given a 49-year-old, quiet engineer who spoke English with a heavy accent the job of fighting off the threat of a brash and fleet-footed PepsiCo. Goizueta, however, believed that his job was to increase the value of Coca-Cola stock for shareholders, and he was able to teach what was in his head to others. Shortly after becoming CEO, he articulated his point of view on how Coca-Cola would enrich shareholders. He drew on his experience participating in his family's business in Cuba, on the wisdom of his grandfather and Spanish poets, and on his experience leading parts of Coca-Cola's research division. His points of view included how the company would allocate capital and decide on new products—also how to hire, delegate to, and reward talented managers. He taught senior Coca-Cola managers and other employees through speeches, coaching, and actions. Goizueta's teaching allowed him to run the company in a hands-off style. He was notoriously calm because he had groomed talented managers who could run the business day-to-day. When Goizueta died, the final testament to him as a teacher and to the effectiveness of his teachable points of view was the smooth succession of Doug Ivester.

As we outlined in our article in the May 1997 *Training & Development,* leaders need to have teachable points of view in these areas:

- *Ideas.* An enterprise starts with ideas about organizing people, capital, and technology to deliver services or products to customers and value to society.

- *Values.* Many organizations try to launch new strategies without thinking about how the values and behaviors of its workforce need to change— disastrous. Leaders must help people change. That's why when Ameritech, the Chicago-based former Baby Bell, began to enter highly competitive telecommunications markets, it had to abandon its old, plodding corporate values aimed at satisfying regulatory agencies and adopt new ones that prized speed and service.

- *Energy.* In a competitive marketplace, people are constantly buffeted by changes caused by competitors, technology, consumers, and a host of other things. Leaders find ways to turn those changes into positive, energizing events rather than confusing and demoralizing ones.

- *Edge.* Edge is the willingness to make tough decisions. Leaders have clear points of view about how to face reality, incorporate information, and make and communicate decisions.

## Institutionalized Methods of Teaching on a Wide Scale

When a company recognizes that developing a lot of leaders is a strategic imperative, then its teaching isn't haphazard or targeted to just a few high-potential players. A company that has chosen to be-come a teaching organization has formal processes and channels for making sure that teaching takes place throughout.

Because circumstances change quickly in business these days, the company with the fastest and best response is the one that wins. In order to meet the challenges, a company needs all of its people aligned and pulling in the same direction. Everyone must understand and internalize the company's business purpose, operating ideas, and values. Command-and-compliance hierarchies are too slow, and they don't work as well. Welch was able to pull off GE's major culture shift only when he put in place a systematic program to teach new values and operating norms. The original vehicle, Work Out, reached 200,000 people in the first few years. Welch has repeated the pattern of wide-scale programs again and again to advantage, each time learning from the last experience.

The latest incarnation is GE's Six Sigma quality effort. Like Work Out and the Change Acceleration Program that grew out of that, Six Sigma involves teaching GE's ideas and values, such as the importance of having Six Sigma quality (no more than 3.4 defects per million) in all processes. The concept is simple: In the world's current deflationary environment, the cost efficiencies of Six Sigma are a competitive advantage. Further, Six Sigma will aid GE's transition from a product company to a service company by assuring customers about the value of a long-term agreement with GE. Six Sigma training shows how the GE values of boundarylessness, speed, self-confidence, stretch, and simplicity are important. The tight deadlines and high performance expectations of Six Sigma projects encourage people to operate within those norms.

Welch is running Six Sigma with incredible speed and making it the responsibility of tens of thousands of GE leaders to teach others. He has created a stable of black-belt Six Sigma teachers and decreed that anyone wanting to be a senior leader at GE has to be a Six Sigma expert with a proven record of developing Six Sigma knowledge and capabilities in others. The black-belt leaders teach the fundamental Six Sigma goals, rules, and values to hundreds of people, who then design quality projects that engage thousands more. Project teams implement Six Sigma projects, while the black-belt teachers offer coaching and assistance. Though quality-improvement programs have had mixed results at many companies, GE's is going gang-busters. Prudential Securities analysts are projecting a $10 to $12 billion increase in net earnings due to the program over the next five years.

Another leadership example is Bob Knowling, who went from Ameritech to US West in February 1996, as vice president of network operations—which meant he would lead more than 20,000 employees in a company that was up to its eyeballs in trouble.

Knowling describes what he saw when he walked in the door: "The company was experiencing service performance problems. Many customers had to wait more than 24 hours for a repair. New service orders and activation took an unacceptably long time to deliver. . . . My first week on the job, it was apparent that nobody had been accountable for a reengineering effort . . . [and] it was acceptable to miss budgets. Service was in the tank; we were overspending our budgets by $100 million. Yet, people weren't losing their jobs and still got all or some of their bonuses."

Knowling came in with a simple point of view: Hold employees accountable for meeting customers' expectations and for their own commitment to the company. He began teaching people what he meant by "walking the talk." Rather than spend time at Denver headquarters, Knowling told his boss that he was going "to put on fatigues and get out with the troops." After removing some senior people on his team, Knowling spent several hours with the people who worked for them, explaining the firing decision and discussing how they could improve the situation. He brought in people from the outside to help create a new leadership cadre. To get people's attention, he did things in an unorthodox fashion—such as holding phone-call meetings at 6 a.m. to review service performance. His message to the troops: "You're going to serve customers between 8 a.m. and 5 p.m., so the call happens at 6 a.m." When it proved difficult to have the right data at 6 a.m., Knowling relented and moved his conference calls to the lunch hour.

Having literally awakened his top team, Knowling turned his attention to spreading the word throughout the company and doing it quickly. Working with his senior group, he mapped out a program called Focus Customer, which was designed with the twofold purpose to deal with the technical issues of fixing problems and to deal with the emotional issues of fear, distrust, and feelings of chaos.

Like most successful wide-scale teaching efforts, Focus Customer was action-based. Knowling and the top team brought together more than 100 of the company's leaders to analyze and understand the most pressing problems. Then, they went back to their departments with a 10-week deadline for taking on a significant project that would engage their people and help solve the identified problems.

The results of Focus Customer include such projects as

- mapping the root causes of repeat customer complaints, and helping people in the field diagnose and deal with the causes

- changing the scheduling process of service operators to reduce overtime and the amount of time a customer is put on hold

- improving the scheduling of repair trucks to reduce dispatches.

Overall, the projects have produced tens of millions of dollars in benefits for the first year of the program, with more projected for next year. Moreover, 100 people felt that they'd reclaimed leadership ground, and acquired a new appreciation of (and practice with) the skills they'd need to keep exercising that leadership. Knowling is now expanding the effort to include more people. His next target is the more than 2,000 supervisors on the front lines. He's starting a program in which they will develop their own points of view on how to manage change and on the most important priorities for their part of the business. Then, they'll teach that to others while launching important projects to get the changes rolling.

We've seen similar processes in other settings. At Royal Dutch/ Shell, for example, the committee of managing directors is a small group of people who lead more than 100,000 people spread across 100+ countries. In 1995 and 1996, the committee took the top 50 people in the company through a series of meetings and workshops, in which they challenged the company's direction and developed a new point of view on where it was going. Over the course of the next year, they used that to transform some of Shell's key businesses. Now, in an effort called Focused Results Delivery, Shell is engaging close to 25 percent of its vast workforce by pulling together various business or geographic units to work on what leaders want to teach the employees. They, in turn, put what they learn to use in a real project. The approach gives thousands of Shell employees common goals and ways to achieve them—plus the projects will net hundreds of millions of dollars in such countries as Argentina, Australia, and Brunei.

## It Takes a Teaching Organization

The learning organization may be a popular model in business circles these days, but becoming a teaching organization is what truly makes a company a winner. Building one requires commitment and determination on the part of a company's leaders. They must be willing to invest not only the resources of the company, but also themselves. They must put in place serious career development mechanisms for people at all levels of the organization, not just at the top. They must build operating structures, create incentives, and instill cultures that encourage teaching. They must also develop broad-scale programs to quickly teach ideas and disseminate new ways of thinking and working.

Most importantly, leaders must be dedicated teachers. They must be willing to open up and share their experiences. They must make the effort to distill from those experiences their own teachable points of view—not only about how to make money in the marketplace, but also about leadership. Last, they must teach.

They must use every opportunity to impart their knowledge and understanding, and act as role models for other teachers.

That may sound like a tall order. But for leaders who are dedicated to winning—and who understand that success is the product of having a lot of leaders throughout an organization—it's the smartest way to operate. Building a learning organization may make your company more successful than it is now, but it won't be able to match the num-

ber and talent of leaders in a teaching organization.

Warren Bennis notes that the basis of leadership is the ability to change the mind-set, the framework, of others. To paraphrase Larry Bossidy: When you want to know how you are doing as a leader, consider how you are doing as a teacher.

 **Article Review Form at end of book.**

Many of America's most successful companies are legendary for the demands they put on the personal lives of their employees, particularly their managers and technical staffs. How effective would the recommendations of these authors be in helping you to reduce the tension between your work and personal life?

# Work and Life:
## The End of the Zero-Sum Game

Managers on the front lines are using three principles to benefit their organizations and individual employees alike.

## Stewart D. Friedman, Perry Christensen, and Jessica DeGroot

*Stewart D. Friedman is the director of the Leadership Program and the Work/Life Integration Project at the University of Pennsylvania's Wharton School in Philadelphia. Perry Christensen, the former director of human resource strategy and planning at Merck & Company, is now with WED Consulting in Boston, Massachusetts. Jessica DeGroot is founder and executive director of the Third Path, a nonprofit agency based in Philadelphia focused on the integration of work and personal life. The three are coorganizers of the Wharton Work/Life Roundtable, an applied research group drawn from academic and industry experts.*

The conflicting demands of work and personal life have always been with us. People have always had children and elderly parents to care for; they have always pursued hobbies and devoted time to community activities. In the past, many managers dealt with such personal needs summarily: "What you do in the office is our

business. What you do outside is your own." It was assumed, too, that employees would put the company's interests first. Work versus personal life, after all, was a zero-sum game.

Have times changed? Yes and no. On one hand, striking demographic shifts, such as the increasing number of women in the workforce, have put more mothers on the job, heightening awareness of work-life issues. New economic forces, such as global competition, have also changed the landscape, creating an unprecedented need for committed employees at a time when loyalty is low in the wake of corporate downsizings. On the other hand, most executives still believe that every time an employee's personal interests "win," the organization pays the price at its bottom line. They consign work-life issues to the human resources department, where the problems are often dealt with piecemeal, through programs such as flextime and paternity leave. Such pro-

grams, however, rarely help more than a few employees strike a meaningful, sustainable balance between work and personal life because they do not permeate a company's culture or fundamentally change managers' behavior.

## Under the Radar

In recent years, however, we have observed that a small but growing number of managers—many of them flying under the radar of officially sanctioned programs—approach the work-life question differently. They operate under the assumption that work and personal life are not competing priorities but complementary ones. In essence, they've adopted a win-win philosophy. And it appears they are right: in the cases we have studied, the new approach has yielded tangible payoffs both for organizations and for individual employees.

These managers are guided by three mutually reinforcing

principles. First, they clarify what is important. That is, they clearly inform their employees about business priorities. And they encourage their employees to be just as clear about personal interests and concerns—to identify where work falls in the spectrum of their overall priorities in life. The objective is to hold an honest dialogue about both the business's and the individual's goals and then to construct a plan for fulfilling all of them.

Second, these managers recognize and support their employees as "whole people," open-mindedly acknowledging and even celebrating the fact that they have roles outside the office. These managers understand that skills and knowledge can be transferred from one role to another and also that boundaries—where these roles overlap and where they must be kept separate—need to be established.

Third, these managers continually experiment with the way work is done, seeking approaches that enhance the organization's performance while creating time and energy for employees' personal pursuits.

The three principles lead to a virtuous cycle. When a manager helps employees balance their work lives with the rest of their lives, they feel a stronger commitment to the organization. Their trust redoubles, and so do their loyalty and the energy they invest in work. Not surprisingly, their performance improves, and the organization benefits. Strong results allow the manager to continue practicing the principles that help employees strike this work-life balance.

In the following pages, we will explore the three principles in more detail and illustrate how managers apply them. The cases are drawn from our research into several dozen U.S.-based companies of varying sizes in a variety of industries, supplemented by over 100 interviews conducted and analyzed by our colleagues at the Wharton Work/Life Roundtable. Each case shows that striking a balance between work and personal life is not the task of the manager alone; rather, it is a process that requires a partnership between the manager and individual employees. Ultimately, all the strategies call for an honest two-sided exchange, as well as a mutual commitment to continual change.

## Clarify What's Important

In most organizations, employees rarely feel comfortable discussing their personal priorities. They worry that admitting a passion for singing with the local opera company, for instance, will be seen as a lack of passion for work. Such fear is not misguided. Most managers believe—or at least hope—that work is at the top of an employee's list of life priorities. For some, it is. For others, of course, work is just a means to the end of achieving other priorities. These people are often put in the uncomfortable position of having to pretend they care primarily about work-related issues that are actually of secondary importance to them.

The managers who strike a work-life balance with their people cut through the charade about priorities. They make business objectives crystal clear, and they define them in terms of outputs—in terms of results. Simultaneously, they ask employees to identify the important goals, concerns, and demands outside the office that require time and energy. One person might be responsible for his elderly mother's health care, which involves three trips to the hospital every month. Another might be in the process of qualifying for a Gold Star in figure skating. Still another may feel strongly that, at this point in her career, none of her priorities is more important than success at work.

Such a discussion of priorities can take place only in an environment of trust, and the managers who are striking a balance between work and personal life with their employees know that. They do not penalize people for putting personal concerns first or for putting them right alongside work. They do not try to persuade people to give up their extracurricular interests. Rather, they use the information about personal priorities to draw a road map toward a singular destination: business success achieved hand in hand with individual fulfillment.

The fact that these managers define business success in terms of results is key. To them, outcomes matter more than process. To that end, they give their employees specific goals but also great autonomy over how to achieve those goals. That way, the woman who is trying to receive a Gold Star in figure skating can practice in the morning when the rink is empty and rates are lower. She can arrive at work at noon, stay until 5 P.M., and then take unfinished tasks home with her to complete in the evening. To her manager, such a schedule is acceptable as long as she is producing the work her job requires.

Steve, a senior operations executive at a global bank, demonstrates the benefits of putting both business and personal priorities on the table. For many years, Steve was a classic hard-driving boss, given to starting the day with 7 A.M. breakfasts with his staff. He also expected his top people to work as late as he did—sometimes close to 10 P.M.

One of those people was a vice president named Jim. At first, Jim played by Steve's rules, "living at work," as he describes it. Then one weekend, Jim's young son fell and cut his knee. To Jim's shock and dismay, the child refused to let Jim comfort him. Indeed, he treated Jim like a stranger. The event was a turning point. Although fearful for his job, Jim approached Steve and said that he had let slip the single most important priority in his life—a close relationship with his son. He made an offer: "Judge me by the quality of my work, not by the amount of time I spend at the office."

The request clearly disconcerted Steve, but because he valued Jim enormously, he agreed to evaluate Jim's performance based solely on his contributions to the bank's success. Both men then had to change how they got things done. They began to plan their time together more carefully. Their meetings became more focused; they cut down on the length and number of reports and memos they sent to each other and got right to the essentials in their communications. Until that point, Jim had helped Steve prepare for the 7 A.M. staff meetings in the half hour prior to them. Under the new arrangement, Jim briefed Steve the day before; soon, in fact, Jim was routinely skipping the 7 A.M. meetings, and his absence had little or no adverse impact. What's more, Jim was able to leave the office regularly at 5 P.M.

For his part, Steve found that Jim's energy and concentra-

tion at work soared. Indeed, having made his business and personal priorities explicit, Jim was able to pay unrelenting attention to key business issues while at work. As a result, his performance improved dramatically. He was rewarded with several promotions, rising quickly through the company's ranks.

In time, Jim went on to run a large credit-card business, and he is currently the chief operating officer of a major manufacturing company. Along the way, clarifying what's important has become a fundamental part of his managerial style. In fact, he is well known throughout his current organization for taking family and personal considerations into account in scheduling both his own time and his employees' time.

Steve recently retired. In his farewell address to the organization after a long and successful career, he noted that his experience with Jim was a milestone in his development as a leader. He learned, he said, the business value of allowing employees to meet personal commitments as they pursue organizational goals. An essential role of a leader is to make sure all priorities are part of the discussion of how to achieve success.

## Recognize and Support the Whole Person

Most managers know about their employees' personal lives to some extent. They know, for instance, that one person has three children or that another is about to be married. Occasionally, they are aware of people's hobbies or community activities. This kind of incidental knowledge, however, bears little resemblance to the second principle as managers who balance issues of work and personal life

practice it. Their understanding of employees is deeper and more detailed. Instead of knowing casual facts about people, and beyond learning about priorities, these managers recognize and support the full range of their people's life roles: not just mother or caretaker, but also volunteer with autistic children, aspiring concert pianist, or passionate golfer.

Why do these managers tune into their employees' roles outside the office? First, being sincerely interested in an employee's personal life creates a bond and, with it, trust—which brings organizational benefits familiar to any manager. Second, identifying the various roles helps these managers tap into the full range of their employees' talents. Third, it is necessary for individuals to understand how their roles relate to one another—where they mesh and where they need to be kept separate—to establish effective boundaries. Establishing the boundaries helps remove distractions, allowing people to be more fully focused on the task at hand. Finally, knowing about an employee's personal life is critical if a manager wants to put the first work-life principle to work, crafting a strategy to meet both business and personal goals.

Just as employees don't usually volunteer details of their personal priorities, neither do they openly offer information about their life roles. Indeed, such revelations are countercultural in most big companies today. That is why managers who adopt this principle demonstrate their commitment to it by acting as role models. They openly discuss the benefits and demands of their own roles outside work. The manager of a 15-person work group at a manufacturing company, for instance, freely discusses the challenges of her role as the head of a blended family. At home, she cares for six preteen children from her previous marriage and her husband's two previous marriages all living under one roof. Not only does she apply her experience resolving conflicts in her own family to settling differences within the work group, but she also openly admits, "Everything I know about negotiation I learned at the dinner table." The manager's honesty about her roles as a mother and stepmother invites her employees to be similarly candid about their personal roles.

Another way managers recognize and support the whole person is by valuing the knowledge and skills employees bring to the business from their lives outside work. In one company we studied, for example, a manager named Jose found out that one of his key sales representatives, Sally, was intensely dedicated to her alma mater, a Big Ten university. She was an active fund-raiser for the school and often used her free time to recruit local high-school students.

After receiving Sally's permission, Jose called the company's recruiting director. He described Sally's knowledge of and commitment to her alma mater and asked if it would be possible to get her assigned as the company's liaison in its recruiting efforts at the school. As it happened, the company had been having limited success at the school, and the recruiting director was looking for ways to both improve the company's reputation on campus and increase the number of students it was able to recruit, particularly for the sales force. The recruiting director welcomed the chance to talk with Sally, and they met soon thereafter.

The recruiting director was impressed with Sally's energy, ideas, and the relationships she had already forged with the university. He offered her the position of liaison, a task that would likely take up to 20% of her time for half the year. She would replace another sales rep—an individual without personal ties to the school—who was currently doing the job. Sally brought the liaison proposal to Jose who, despite the fact that it would mean that Sally would spend less time with her customers, recognized the business value of increasing the organization's ability to hire more sales reps from the university.

Why did he agree? First, he correctly anticipated that because of her feelings about the school, Sally would do a great job, and her relationship would bear fruit in the company's recruiting effort. Second, he accurately predicted that the loss of Sally's time with customers in the short term would be minimal since she was already spending some of her discretionary time on school events. Finally, Jose expected that Sally would be grateful for this opportunity to combine her interest in the school with her work. And she was. Sally told us that after she received the liaison position, her commitment to the company skyrocketed. As often is the case, exercising the principle of recognizing and supporting the whole person benefited not just the individual but the company as well.

These managers encourage employees to question basic assumptions, such as the common sales mantra: "Real commitment means total availability." "Does it really?" they ask. "Can we find creative ways to demonstrate total commitment to our customers without being available every waking moment?" They

also encourage employees to learn, through trial and error, about new ways to organize work that might well challenge the legitimacy of existing practices.

## Continually Experiment with the Way Work Is Done

Most managers in today's rapidly changing business environment know how important it is to find ways to increase efficiency and productivity. Still, new methods and different ways of thinking about work can be daunting, if not threatening. Managers who embrace the third work-life principle, however, see experimenting with work processes as an exciting opportunity to improve the organization's performance and the lives of its people at the same time. They have discovered that conflicts between work and personal priorities can actually be catalysts for identifying work inefficiencies that might otherwise have remained hidden or intractable. That's because taking a new set of parameters into account can allow people to question ways of doing business so ingrained that no one would think to consider changing them otherwise.

Many work practices are legacies of outdated industrial models in which employees had to be physically present during "normal" business hours. The managers who strike a work-life balance with their employees, however, recognize that newer telecommunication tools—such as e-mail, voice mail, teleconferencing, and computer networks—can create greater flexibility in how, when, where, and with whom work is accomplished. In addition, they are willing to explore alternative arrangements like job sharing to see if they can improve organizational efficiency while freeing up employees' time.

Hallie is a manager who—by meeting both business demands and her employees' personal needs—was able to reinvent the way work was done in her organization. As the new department director at a food services company, Hallie learned that she had inherited an older employee named Sarah, an administrative assistant who was perceived to be unmotivated and cynical. Her attitude, Hallie was told by other employees, badly hurt morale. They recommended, in fact, that she fire Sarah if she could.

At Hallie's first meeting with Sarah, she learned that Sarah enjoyed working with numbers but was not permitted to do finance work because of her inexperience with computers. Hallie also learned that Sarah was caring for her mother, who was in the late stages of a terminal illness. As her mother's condition deteriorated, Sarah found she had to go to her home in the morning and again at lunch to tend to her mother's physical and household needs. In addition, Sarah also managed her own home—chores, yard work, and paying the bills.

Hallie could have heard Sarah's story and asked, "How can I rid myself of this burden?" Instead she asked, "How can we work differently, in a way that will improve the department's performance and preserve the dignity of the employee?"

Together, Hallie and Sarah explored possible answers. They were able to identify inefficiencies in the department's work processes, including those in Sarah's job. The department had been formed recently as a result of the consolidation of several different groups. Yet Sarah was maintaining separate budgeting and inventory control systems. Combining them would streamline data collection and analysis.

Knowing of Sarah's interest in finance, Hallie arranged for her to be trained on Excel, on a new Excel-based budgetary system, and in basic analytical processes, which gave her greater control over the department's finances. The change had immediate effects. Sarah now gathered more relevant data in a streamlined and logical manner, allowing managers to interpret the information faster and more intelligently. At the same time, working with numbers greatly increased Sarah's interest in her job. Her morale and performance improved markedly. And working on a computer made it easier for her to care for her mother; she could even work from home when her mother needed more attention. As a result of the change in the content and flexibility of her job, Sarah had an easier time coping with her mother's final days.

## A Mutually Reinforcing System

Each of the three work-life principles might be practiced by itself, but more often they are practiced together. That's because the principles reinforce one another and, in fact, overlap to some degree. Encouraging employees to be explicit about their personal priorities, for instance, is a necessary element in recognizing and supporting an employee as a whole person. Valuing productivity over face time is a necessary element in experimenting with work processes. Both involve a manager caring more about the ends than the means. Let's look more, then, at all three principles working together.

Consider first the case of Sam, the director of a 24-hour command center at a pharmaceutical company's largest site, a plant with 8,000 employees. The 30-person center monitors more than 10,000 "hot spots" at the site, such as fire alarms; sewage lift stations; and, in particular, a hazardous manufacturing process. For example, the command center oversees several vaults that house chemicals being stored at minus 70 degrees Fahrenheit. Employees working in the vaults must wear special protective suits and are allowed to stay for only ten minutes at a time; if they stay longer, the center considers it an emergency and responds in kind. Such incidents are not uncommon and, as you might expect, work in the command center can be stressful.

Because the command center needed to be staffed around the clock, its schedule was always a challenge. Sam frequently had trouble filling the midnight to 8 A.M. slots in particular. Shifts changed 21 times each week, and exchanging information between members of incoming and outgoing shifts was cumbersome. To make matters worse, the command center was about to be handed more work. The number of hot spots under its supervision was set to increase by 50% to 15,000 within the next year and perhaps even to double to 20,000 within two years.

Sam could have seen the burgeoning workload at the command center purely as a business problem and sought an exclusively business solution. How could he fill the center's schedule, keep overtime down, and make sure information was exchanged efficiently? But Sam also realized that a heavier workload was bound to have an impact on his staff's personal lives. Financial constraints made hiring more people out of the question. The existing staff would need to work longer hours under more stressful conditions. If he ignored those facts, Sam believed, any solution he arrived at would not be sustainable. The members of his staff were not robots but whole people with rich and varied lives. Just as the business imperatives had to be accounted for, so did his people's personal needs and concerns.

Sam's first step was to call his staff together and explicitly define the command center's business goals. He talked about how the group's work was essential for the safe operation of the entire site, including the critical research and manufacturing processes. He was open about how the center's workload was sure to increase and about the fact that they could not just throw more people at the problem.

Sam had a vision of the command center as more customer focused, proactively anticipating the needs of the site. He described to the group, for example, the need to improve the way manufacturing lines were shut down for maintenance and repair. He stressed the importance of forecasting needs as far in advance as possible, rather than waiting for an emergency to galvanize everyone to action. Sam knew that to achieve his vision, everyone would have to pay more attention to feedback from the center's customers, that the staff would need more training, and that there would simply be more plain, hard work—and he told them so. At the same time, he explicitly acknowledged that the demanding workload might have a negative impact on his employ-

ees' personal lives, and he invited them to describe to him and to one another how the schedule could adversely affect them.

After that discussion, Sam opened the door for radical experimentation with the way the command center was run. He asked the staff itself to design a solution to the scheduling problem that met not only the business needs he had outlined but also their own personal requirements. As many executives who operate according to the three principles do, Sam told the employees that no solution was out of bounds as long as it produced the results they were looking for. He also told them that they did not have to solve all the center's problems at once. They could test possible plans of action, gradually learning from those experiences what would work and what would not.

Within several weeks, Sam's people had developed a comprehensive new approach to staffing the center. They would work 12-hour shifts, three days on and four days off one week, four days on and three days off the next week. Over the course of two weeks, they would work 84 hours, which worked out to four more than they had in the past. But at the same time, work schedules would be steady and predictable, and their time off more concentrated. It added up to an acceptable trade-off.

The system has now been in place for more than two years, and it has far exceeded expectations. At work, the new schedule has eliminated seven shifts, which means that information is now exchanged seven fewer times, reducing errors and oversights during shift transfers. The predictability of the schedule has reduced overtime considerably, as

well as the number of personal days the employees take. In addition, the new schedule has led to a better way to train supervisors. In the past, they had been stuck in the command center whenever there was an unexpected hole in the schedule. Often they were alone on the night shift, during which they learned little and potentially compromised safety. But now they are rotated systematically into the command center in all shifts to learn the processes, systems, and safety procedures.

Much to Sam's delight, the new system has allowed the center to become the proactive, customer-focused group he had envisioned. Now that staff members work on a set schedule and aren't scrambling to fill empty spots, they can spend more time on coordination and process improvements. For example, there was a time when sales of a new drug boomed, exceeding forecasts by 300%. Unfortunately, the drug's manufacturing line was scheduled to be closed for six days of maintenance. Working with production and maintenance supervisors, the command center was able to reduce shutdown time to two days.

Finally, because the schedule has become predictable and acceptable to all, there's less strife among employees and less strife between employees and management. In short, morale is up and stress is down. Not surprisingly, productivity has improved.

At home, the new schedule has allowed employees to meet their personal needs in ways that were not possible under the old system. One person was able finally to go to school during the day to earn a master's degree. Another earned a certificate degree on her days off. Many employees have told Sam that simply feeling that their lives are predictable has allowed them to relax when they are home and plan more personal projects and events. The new schedule has been so successful from a lifestyle point of view that, somewhat ironically, it has created a high demand to work in the command center. "We are a magnet now for transfers and new hires," Sam recently observed.

We found another example of the three principles working in tandem at a global, 80,000-employee manufacturing company where senior executives were anxious to determine the best way to transfer knowledge from region to region. They decided to test a radical new approach that had two parts: a computer-based data warehouse that would allow sales representatives to collect and share sales and marketing information in real time and a territory management system that would allow each sales rep to run a fully functioning, independent operation. The success or failure of the two pilot projects would determine the company's direction for global marketing and sales.

A task force consisting of three men and three women was created to oversee and coordinate the pilot projects. It was headed by one of the women, Terry. From the outset, pressure on the group was intense; the company's leaders believed that the way the organization managed the process of learning and of transferring information was critical to its competitive success. Despite the pressure for results, Terry strongly believed that if she let business objectives nullify personal ones, the task force would fail on all counts. "To ignore people's personal issues was unrealistic," she noted. At the time, all the team members had significant personal issues: two pregnancies, three recent births, one person on a part-time schedule, another in a demanding M.B.A. program at night, and still another in the midst of a family separation.

Before the task force's first meeting, Terry met individually with each member to discuss the demands he or she faced in the coming year and to help identify each person's spectrum of priorities. Then, at the first group meeting, Terry led a discussion of business objectives. She explicitly defined what the company's leaders expected of the team, as well as the timetables and specific tasks involved. She identified how the team's performance would be measured and what kind of results would constitute success.

Next, Terry opened up the dialogue on personal priorities and brought in the discussion of roles. She asked a couple of questions to get it going: "Despite the amount of work we will all have to do, what personal priorities do you want to make sure are not compromised? In other words, what is most important for you from a personal perspective as we embark on this work?" Team members voluntarily disclosed challenges in their personal lives, which they felt comfortable doing because of their prior separate conversations with Terry. The meeting concluded with the team brainstorming about how business and personal objectives could be reached at the same time. Members decided, for instance, that they needed to know how to do one another's jobs so that they could cover if anyone had to miss work. They also decided that they needed to constantly keep abreast of everyone's schedules and personal demands so that no one could be taken by surprise, and the flow of work would not be disrupted, if a member was absent.

As the pilots progressed, weekly planning meetings continued to focus on both business and personal priorities. Members did learn one another's jobs inside and out, and constantly updated everyone on the demands of their personal lives. As one team member said, "We knew each other's home routines, school holidays, and soccer practice schedules. It was easy to do this because we talked about everything up front." The lengthy stretch needed for a christening in Paris or for a six-week vacation that had been booked a year in advance—and other personal time constraints—were known and accounted for as legitimate business issues.

As the pilots concluded, there could be no doubt that the team's results were impressive. All of their ambitious deadlines were met or beaten. Moreover, the fact that everyone knew everyone else's job added to the creativity and value of the team's output. Most important, the team achieved its goal of developing systems for knowledge transfer that could be used throughout the company worldwide. They were evaluated in a 360-degree process by their customers, team members, and their senior management sponsors. The project was successful from every business measure they had established.

Not surprisingly, the team members' lives and careers were enhanced by their experience on the task force. No one had to compromise personal priorities because of work. And, as one team member said, because of the openness and trust created within the team, "the project was the most satisfying work environment I have ever been in." Professionally, members of the team flourished after the project was completed. Terry, for instance, received a major promotion and now heads up the strategic-support function for one of the company's largest regions.

## Getting beyond the Status Quo

As we've said, the three principles are typically put into practice by managers "flying under the radar." Our next case, however, involves the manager of an HR department at a prominent accounting firm who actually used the principles to put the issues on the radar screen, thereby enhancing the performance of his organization's business-assurance department and the life of one of its senior associates, an aspiring novelist we'll call Jane.

Jane had joined the firm after graduating from college with a double major in accounting and English. She enjoyed her work—and was considered a strong performer by her superiors—but she also yearned to find time for her real passion, creative writing. After rummaging through the materials that were handed out back at her orientation, Jane came across a pamphlet that discussed the company's policy on alternative work schedules. She had hoped there would be a way to develop a schedule that would take advantage of the seasonal nature of the accounting business and allow her to carve out significant blocks of time for writing. But none of the examples of alternative schedules in the pamphlet came close to meeting her needs. Even though it felt risky to ask for something radically different, Jane approached Harry, the HR manager responsible for her department. In a way, there was no one else to turn to. Because of the project-based nature of Jane's work, the managers supervising her job were always changing. Much to her surprise, Harry was receptive and said he would be glad to work with Jane to craft a solution to her work-life dilemma.

Jane began by suggesting she reduce her workload from 12 to 8 clients. The change would mean that in the off-season she'd have sufficient chunks of time to focus on writing. Client by client, Harry and Jane decided which ones to keep and which to pass on to other associates. They then charted out the expected work for the upcoming year, making sure there would be enough time both for fulfilling her clients' needs and for writing.

At first, the plan seemed like a good one. Unfortunately, Jane quickly began to doubt how realistic it was. Often during her writing time, she would get a call from the central assignments department, putting her on another job. Although Jane knew she could legitimately decline those assignments because she had already completed the work she had contracted for, she was concerned that refusing work might have ramifications for her career later on. Hesitantly, she approached Harry a second time.

Harry was again receptive, inviting Gabriel, a member of the central assignments department, to join the discussions. The three of them then developed a method by which Jane's hours were logged so that there no longer would be any confusion about when she had extra time available for work and when the extra time was reserved for writing. Jane also suggested that she change the way she did her work. Could she try e-mailing and faxing her clients, she asked, instead of assuming that a face-to-face meeting was always necessary? Harry agreed to let her experiment.

The benefits of the new arrangement became apparent within the year, particularly with regard to Jane's capacity to contribute to the firm. With fewer clients, Jane felt more focused at work and thus more committed and effective. Previously, she had been moved from project to project and sometimes from crisis to crisis. Now she could plan her time in advance and concentrate on end results more creatively. In fact, she found that for the first time she had enough energy and time to reflect on better ways to get her projects done. Her clients responded positively; Jane's efficiency allowed her to work more quickly, which in some cases reduced their fees. And meanwhile, Jane was able to write two novels.

Three years later, still following this alternative work schedule, Jane was promoted to manager at the same time as others in her cohort. As a manager herself, Jane now practices the three principles. She believes they help her keep and motivate quality employees. Not only is it costly to replace a good employee, but, she notes, "people who are constantly under pressure will take the path of least resistance, doing things the way it was done last year instead of looking for ways to improve on the product." Furthermore, Jane points out that, unlike in other work groups at the company, "my group doesn't have to work weekends. Instead, we've found out everyone's parameters, discussed what work needs to get done, and focused on the end results."

Recently, Harry and Jane served together on a task force that's looking for ways to apply more broadly what they learned from practicing the three principles. They are exploring the development of a project database that would make it easier to anticipate the workload in advance and even out the assignments among the associates. They are looking into the possibility of defining expected work hours more explicitly. They believe that this will encourage a new attitude whereby excessive work hours will be seen not as a measure of commitment but as an indication of the need for better planning.

Although Jane and Harry are plainly aware of the benefits to the business of the approach they've developed, Jane is also absolutely clear about the personal benefits. "Neither activity, work nor writing, was appealing in isolation. I didn't want to be a starving writer, forced to write to earn a living. But I also felt that if I stopped practicing my writing, my creative side would die, and then the job would just become a job. Until we worked out this solution, I felt like it had to be an either-or choice, but now I see it doesn't have to be that way. Both sides can win."

## A New Breed of Managers

If the three principles are so effective, why aren't they more widespread? There is no single answer. Some managers block the new approach to balancing work and life because they are bound by tradition and continue to value face time for its own sake. They believe that productivity is a function of time spent in the office—not energy invested in the work. Other managers are simply unaware that their employees might be able to bring skills and knowledge to their jobs from their lives beyond work. And still other managers consider the whole topic of striking a balance between work and personal life as a women's issue—in other words, not their problem.

We have also found that managers resist the three principles because they fear that taking an employee's personal priorities into account will create either a sense of entitlement or feelings of resentment. Take the case of Sarah and Hallie again. Once Hallie allowed Sarah to work at home to care for her ailing mother, these managers might reason, what's to stop everyone in the office from asking for some sort of special treatment to make his or her life more convenient or enjoyable? If we oblige, these managers might argue, we risk creating a slippery-slope situation in which the organization is expected to strike a work-life balance for every employee. If we don't, we are certain to anger people who feel slighted. Why should Sarah be allowed to work at home, another employee may ask, if I still have to come into the office when my child or husband is sick? What makes her more deserving than me?

It's understandable that managers worry about setting off waves of entitlement and/or resentment. But interestingly, the managers in our research who use the three principles rarely run into that. Because these managers deal with all of their people individually, every one of their employees does, in fact, receive "special" treatment in terms of a work plan that takes personal priorities into account. Therefore, there is less chance for resentment to fester. As for entitlement, the enormous loyalty these employees feel toward their managers usually outweighs it. Indeed, when a manager helps his or her employees strike a work-life balance, they feel grateful more than anything else.

Even when managers are inclined to operate with the three principles, many tell us that they don't because they believe it would be impractical and complicated. How time consuming it must be to delve into the varied priorities and life roles of every employee, they argue. And imagine how much energy it would take to create a series of individual action plans that fulfill both professional and personal goals.

But we have found that, in reality, following the three principles does not involve that much more time or energy than managing in more traditional ways. Virtually all managers today are held accountable for developing their employees professionally— that is, they already engage in discussions about what their people want and need from work and what they are expected to contribute. To bring personal-life priorities and goals into the conversation really only involves asking two or three more questions. And often the answers to those questions are so illuminating, they make the development process more honest—and more efficient.

Sometimes the "work" of the three principles can be delegated to the employees themselves, who can apply them personally and to their dealings with one another. In fact, we have seen that people become quickly engaged in this process as they come to realize that the solutions they develop will benefit both the business and their own lives. Consequently, the principles need not sap any more time or energy than conducting management as usual.

## Out from under the Radar

No two companies—indeed, no two managers—approach the relationship between work and personal life exactly the same way. But it is fair to say that all organizational practices fall along a continuum. On one end is the trade-off approach, whereby either the business wins or personal life wins, but not both. Further along is the integrated approach, in which employee and manager work together to find ways to meet both the company's and the employee's needs. That approach is indeed becoming more common, as an increasing number of companies use "life friendly" policies to attract and retain talented people.

Taken together, the three principles fall at the far end of the continuum—the leveraged approach, in which the practices used to strike a work-life balance actually add value to the business. Not only do the three principles seem to help people live more satisfying personal lives, but they also help identify inefficiencies in work processes and illuminate better ways to get work done. Think of the pharmaceutical company's command center, for example. Using the three principles, its staff created a new and successful solution to its managerial problems that neither the trade-off nor the integrated approach could have achieved.

The growing cadre of managers who use the three principles to help their employees strike a work-life balance typically do so without official sanction. But perhaps as the business impact of their approach becomes better known and understood, a shift will occur. Managers who once flew below the radar will themselves become beacons of change.

## Where to Begin

Putting the three principles into practice does not happen overnight. It can't—the changes required by this new approach are too substantial to be instituted without stops and starts, and periods of evaluation. Therefore, when managers ask us how to get started, we often suggest that they begin by applying the principles to one employee. Think of Steve, the senior executive who once expected his staff to work from 7 A.M. to 10 P.M. He used the three principles to help one person—Jim—strike a meaningful balance between work and personal life. The arrangement—and its successful impact on both Jim and the business—gave Steve the experience and the confidence he needed to apply the three principles more broadly. Eventually, the principles became the foundation of his management style.

A second way to get started with the principles is to initiate an organizational dialogue about integrating work and personal life goals. In small-team settings, a manager might even lead the process of creating a work-life philosophy statement. We have seen such dialogues facilitate the implementation of the principles by bringing to light thorny issues such as the organization's level of commitment to striking a work-life balance or employees' fears about sharing private information about their personal priorities and life roles.

As a third starting point, we suggest that managers try applying the three principles to themselves to find out how well they personally have leveraged work and personal life. First, a manager might ask, "How well do I clarify my own life goals? Do I know where work falls in my list of priorities? What trade-offs am I willing to make to achieve my goals?"

Second, a manager might consider, "Do I understand my varied life roles—such as parent, child, cub scout master—in terms of how they overlap and when they must be kept separate? That is, have I considered what skills and knowledge can be transferred from one role to another, and have I explicitly formulated the boundaries of each role?" Some executives, for instance, will not check voice mail on weekends; others let their work and personal lives blend.

And finally, a manager can explore his or her comfort level with the third principle of continual experimentation by asking, "Do I regularly challenge the way I myself approach tasks, both at work and at home? How do I react when other people suggest new ways to get things done? Am I defensive or intrigued?"

A self-assessment is useful because it shows managers who want to embark on the journey of striking a balance between work and personal life how sensitive they may or may not be to the struggles of employees trying to do the same. Does that mean people who don't have their own house in order should avoid managing with the principles? Not necessarily, but they should be aware that striking a work-life balance, like many other aspects of effective management, can take time, energy, and commitment. Given its added value, however, the process appears to be well worth the investment.

 **Article Review Form at end of book.**

# WiseGuide Wrap-Up

- All organizations have cultures that are created, sustained, and passed along to new employees through informal means. The culture has a powerful influence on the behavior of the members of the organization and is sometimes described as "the way we do things around here."

- Managers can influence the nature of the organizational culture so as to either facilitate or hinder the accomplishment of work. Effective organizations have formal work rules and an organizational culture that shares the same goals and objectives.

- Some organizations are able to create the capacity to "learn" from their experiences. In business organizations, the rapid rate of change and the hypercompetitive nature of markets make this capacity a key success factor.

## R.E.A.L. Sites

This list provides a print preview of typical **Coursewise** R.E.A.L. sites. (There are over 100 such sites at the **Courselinks**™ site.) The danger in printing URLs is that web sites can change overnight. As we went to press, these sites were functional using the URLs provided. If you come across one that isn't, please let us know via email to: webmaster@coursewise.com. Use your Passport to access the most current list of R.E.A.L. sites at the **Courselinks** site.

**Site name:** The Fifth Discipline FieldBook Project

**URL:** http://www.fieldbook.com/

**Why is it R.E.A.L.?** This site provides strategies, tools, and connections for building a learning organization based on Peter Senge's influential book *The Fifth Discipline*. This is a good site for someone considering doing some small group or consulting work.

**Key topics:** change management, management consulting, research reports, learning organizations

**Try this:** What does Senge describe as the ten challenges to the implementation of change?

**Site name:** Learning, Change and Organizations

**URL:** http://www.euro.net/innovation/Management_Base/Man_Guide_Rel_1.0B1/LCOrg.html

**Why is it R.E.A.L.?** This is an interesting hypertext version of a book on the subject of learning organizations.

**Key topics:** learning organizations, technology and management

**Try this:** Find and summarize a model of organizational change that you think is useful to managers.

**Site name:** Six Management Concepts

**URL:** http://www.timesystem.com/timesystem/methods/book/default.htm

**Why is it R.E.A.L.?** An online book that examines the contemporary concepts of benchmarking, networking, business process reengineering, organizational learning, core competence and empowerment.

**Key topics:** organizational control, organizational development

**Try this:** Compare and contrast benchmarking and reengineering as methods for organizational improvement.

# section

3

- Articulate the ethical and moral dimensions of the performance of managers.

- Explain the nature of the ethical-moral dilemmas that confront managers.

- Describe effective managerial approaches to ethical-moral challenges.

# Ethics, Diversity, and the Social Responsibility of Managers

**WiseGuide Intro**

As the economy burgeons and becomes increasingly global, the interest, attention, and roles of managers go well beyond maximizing the economic value of their enterprises. In the United States, much social legislation regarding business employment practices has been passed. Whether for reasons of personal preference or a desire to avoid regulatory intervention, contemporary managers are responsible for advancing a social agenda. The management orthodoxy tends to be that you can embrace diversity and social responsibility for one of two reasons: because you have to, or because it makes good bottom-line business sense.

All too frequently, we are saddened and outraged to learn of the misdeeds of a prominent business manager, largely because the way an individual manages is inevitably and inextricably intertwined with personal values. Often, the press of circumstances leaves little time to carefully consider all the implications of a decision; however, preparation for management work must include a consideration of the personal values that underpin decisions. Perhaps, the lessons of the perspectives, missteps, and dilemmas of those who have gone before will help in making that preparation.

This section begins with three readings about one of the more controversial figures in contemporary management, Al Dunlap—or, as he is more widely known, "Chainsaw Al." Dunlap has gained a reputation as an expert at reviving failing companies and returning them to profitability. Having taken charge of seven companies in the last 15 years, his most notable achievement was the turnaround of Scott Paper, a formerly successful company that had fallen on hard times and was struggling under a crushing debt load.

Dunlap's methods are anything but subtle. He is famous for Draconian cost cutting and massive employee layoffs to restructure companies and rescue them from their current circumstances. Although the focus of considerable resentment and hostility among laid-off workers, Dunlap enjoys the respect and admiration of many boards of directors and shareholders who have seen values restored and added as a result of his management.

The three readings offer different perspectives on Al Dunlap as he began, then ended, a short stint as the CEO of Sunbeam, his most recent turnaround effort. Although Dunlap's personal style tends to attract considerable attention, the underlying issue is the tension that arises between the need to make a profit and the company's responsibility to its employees and community.

**Readings 10, 11, 12.** Managers, like everyone else, are combinations of strengths and weaknesses, things that are personally commendable and things that represent failings. Following his departure from Sunbeam, even more people than usual have been critical of Al Dunlap and his managerial practices. After reading the three articles on Al Dunlap, what conclusions do you reach about his positive and negative managerial attributes? What lessons do you think you could or should learn from his career?

**Reading 13.** If you were a human resources manager and were asked to make a recommendation to top management as to the three most important aspects of an organization-wide ethical program, what would you suggest?

**Reading 14.** Are there any elements of health-care delivery that are potentially at odds with business values? To what extent might these tensions create ethical problems for a company?

**Reading 15.** What is the dilemma of "right vs. right"? Give some examples of this problem other than those mentioned in the reading.

A basic tenet of free market capitalism is that profits flow to the most efficient producers and away from inefficient producers. Much of the prolonged period of economic growth enjoyed in the U.S. economy in the 1990s is attributed to managers' willingness to reduce costs and create lean, profitable organizations. As Readings 10, 11, and 12 clearly demonstrate, Dunlap makes no apology for his approach to business management. Is he the managerial prince of darkness, or simply a manager making necessary adjustments to match market conditions and realities?

In Reading 13, Louis Larimer, one of the most significant commentators on business ethics, points out some of the steps that managers and companies can take to engender and promote ethical behavior. In particular, Larimer directs his suggestions toward those responsible for the human resources of their organizations.

Reading 14, profiling Columba/HCA's CEO Rick Scott, is reminiscent of Readings 10–12 in that it concerns another eminently successful manager who encountered much criticism and eventually lost his job. Scott gained a reputation for incredibly tough management in the hyper-competitive world of health care. Like Al Dunlap, he became known as a fierce cost cutter and profit maker. Again, this reading draws attention to the distinction between tough business practices and social responsibility.

In the classroom, we often study cases of blatantly unethical or illegal managerial actions. Students frequently criticize these actions and condemn both the practice and the perpetrator. Although such criticism is appropriate and commendable, this is not the real problem in business ethics. If someone brings you an obviously incorrect statement of assets to sign, you know if you choose to sign it that you have committed an unethical and possibly illegal act. The much more common ethical/moral dilemma, however, is when someone brings you a choice between two acts, neither of which is wrong, but either of which may inevitably cause some harm or damage to innocent parties.

Recalling the cost-cutting fervor of Al Dunlap, is it better to close one inefficient plant immediately and try to save the entire company, even if it means that hundreds of workers will lose their jobs, or is it better to delay that decision until a later date, hoping for improved efficiencies while running the risk that everyone in the company will lose their jobs? In Reading 15, the final article in this section, Perry Pascarella more fully explores the dilemma that managers face most often—not the decision to avoid an illegal or unethical practice, but the need to choose between two alternatives, both of which have attractions and drawbacks.

Managers, like everyone else, are combinations of strengths and weaknesses, things that are personally commendable and things that represent failings. Following his departure from Sunbeam, even more people than usual have been critical of Al Dunlap and his managerial practices. After reading the three articles on Al Dunlap, what conclusions do you reach about his positive and negative managerial attributes? What lessons do you think you could or should learn from his career?

# Ready, Fire, Aim

Al Dunlap, the boss of Sunbeam Corporation, has saved several big companies by acting rather than thinking. Can others learn from his approach?

One of his favourite words is "Bam!" When his blood is up, he is capable of rattling off four "verys" in half a second. And although he credits the British for teaching him to say "rubbish" instead of "bullshit", he often regresses. In short, Al Dunlap is not fond of management jargon.

Nor, for that matter, is he particularly impressed with management theory. Mr. Dunlap believes that his time at West Point military academy was all the formal training he needed for a life in business. And having spoken at several business schools, he remains convinced that the students would be better off without most of their teachers. In fact, the 60-year-old Mr. Dunlap holds a dim view not only of the management profession's trappings, but also of managers themselves. Most of them, he believes, along with the directors they report to and the journalists they talk to, are "fundamentally lazy".

These are strong words from a strong manager. Fortunately for Mr. Dunlap, he backs them up with strong performance. In the past 15 years he has taken charge of no fewer than seven companies in three continents—most of them in the pulp and paper industry, and all badly wounded. Each time he has proceeded to transform the company: quickly, forcefully and unforgettably. When Mr. Dunlap arrives on the scene, "Bam!" is precisely the word for the occasion.

## An Unconventional Weapon

Mr. Dunlap's self-image is linked to his roots. The son of a shipyard worker in Hoboken, New Jersey, he says that he has spent his career "trying to prove he was worth something". Worryingly for anyone who has spent more than an hour with the man, Mr. Dunlap was once an executive officer at a nuclear-missile installation in eastern Maryland. After finishing active duty, he began his business career as a junior executive at Kimberly-Clark, an American pulp and paper com-

pany. His very next career move, at the age of 29, made him the head of Sterling Pulp & Paper, another American firm. After a stint as a subordinate at American Can, Mr. Dunlap has been running the show ever since.

His most publicised turnaround took place at Scott Paper. Before he arrived in April 1994, the firm was saddled with a bloated cost structure, an incorrigible labour union and an unfocused, undisciplined management team. Small wonder that its share price was going nowhere.

Over the next 20 months Mr. Dunlap laid off more than 11,000 people—35% of Scott's workforce—and sold $2.4 billion of assets. When he failed to overcome the firm's entrenched culture, he moved its head offices from Philadelphia to Boca Raton, Florida. It was not long before his two fearsome nicknames— "Chainsaw Al" and "Rambo in pinstripes"—both of which had been doled out by admiring colleagues at previous companies, were picked up by an unflattering business press. Happy shareholders, Mr. Dunlap seems to have concluded, provide more compelling proof of his worth than popularity.

His efforts may not have made him popular, but the changes Mr. Dunlap made were probably inevitable if Scott was not to go bankrupt. The difference between Mr. Dunlap and previous managers was that he accepted—indeed, relished—what needed to be done. By the time Scott merged with Kimberly-Clark in December 1995, he had tripled its value (see chart)*.

Seven months later Mr. Dunlap took over at Sunbeam, an American firm that makes small appliances and other household products, and began to apply the same approach. He handpicked new managers, tied their pay to the share price, cut costs ruthlessly, sold non-core assets and forced the marketing team to stick to a focused strategy—which, in Sunbeam's case, means selling more aggressively over-

*Not included in this publication.

seas. The results, once again, have been impressive.

But if Mr. Dunlap's formulaic method is so successful, why doesn't everybody apply it? Unsurprisingly, Mr. Dunlap has a simple answer: they are, of course, too lazy. Yet this is where his glibness becomes unconvincing.

Mr. Dunlap is surely right that some firms need shock therapy. Many run into temporary trouble because of bad luck, but those that stay bedridden tend to have several nasty symptoms in common. Typically their strategy is flawed, most of their managers fail to see that it is, and those who do spot the problem cannot overcome cultural resistance to change. Only after a few feeble restructurings is such a firm sick enough to seek outside help. By that point, it badly needs the Dunlap treatment.

But how many firms are really like this? Mr. Dunlap himself admits that his approach will not work for many high-tech or knowledge-intensive firms. Nor does he think he could tackle continental Europe, where unions

and other opponents of change are more powerful than in America. And even in low-growth industries, many firms are healthy to begin with. Usually these companies face problems that are varied and complicated. Solving them requires thought, tact and an ability to weigh up the circumstances.

Yet Mr. Dunlap, a man who has the answer to every question off pat before it is even asked, is more prone to blustering assertions than to analysis. Watching him launch into a well-rehearsed tirade, it is hard to imagine him listening carefully to dissenting views, or pausing to adapt his ideas to the facts at hand. Why would a busy executive learn what is best in a company, when he arrives already knowing what needs to be done? The same lack of self-doubt that makes Mr. Dunlap so successful in the sickest firms would make such a man disastrous in most of the rest.

 **Article Review Form at end of book.**

Managers, like everyone else, are combinations of strengths and weaknesses, things that are personally commendable and things that represent failings. Following his departure from Sunbeam, even more people than usual have been critical of Al Dunlap and his managerial practices. After reading the three articles on Al Dunlap, what conclusions do you reach about his positive and negative managerial attributes? What lessons do you think you could or should learn from his career?

# Is That You, Al?

## A Famous Cost Cutter Decides to Build, Not Sell

Sunbeam CEO Al Dunlap buys three appliance makers.

### Daniel Kadlec

*Daniel Kadlec is* Time's Wall Street *columnist.*

The man known as Chainsaw Al pulled a fast one last week, buying three companies when everyone assumed he would be selling his own. In the process, the CEO of Sunbeam Corp., the small-appliance maker, carved a kindlier image for himself: Al Dunlap, builder. No, the Chainsaw did not have an attack of conscience. Dunlap, who seemed primed for an exit, decided to try something different. And in keeping with his flair for drama, he spent $1.8 billion in a single day for three companies—all with striking possibilities to complement one another: Coleman Co., which makes leisure equipment; Signature Brands, which produces Mr. Coffee coffeemakers;

and First Alert, which manufactures smoke detectors. "We have a potential Procter & Gamble of world-class, branded durable goods," Dunlap crows.

This is no ordinary builder. Dunlap adds by subtraction—and he will run these appliance makers through his corporate Cuisinart. Jobs will go; tears will flow. But that doesn't mean Dunlap's makeover is a farce. He has an ambitious growth strategy, which he appears determined to stick around to oversee. That's new stuff for Dunlap, 60, a churn-around pro who in the past has followed swift cost cuts with the well-timed sale of his company. The formula worked wonders for shareholders in 1994–95 at Scott Paper, where he cut the head count 35%. The stock tripled. The script was being rewritten at Sunbeam, where the stock has quadrupled.

His new lineup gives him a leading global position in camping gear, gas grills, coffeemakers, smoke detectors and more. But for all the synergies, it is the potential for tried-and-true Dunlapian cost cutting that excites Wall Street. The biggest of his buys, Coleman, with '97 revenues of $1.2 billion, is roughly the same size as Sunbeam and has problems similar to those Dunlap faced at Sunbeam when he arrived in July 1996. Coleman essentially becomes Dunlap's next turnaround gig. Only he bought it instead of being hired. (Job hunting is such a drag.) If he can work his formula at Coleman, Sunbeam's stock will shoot much higher. With that in mind, Wall Street rolled out the red carpet, pushing Sunbeam shares up 24% in a week. Remember, an acquirer's stock generally goes down at first.

That is especially sweet music to Dunlap, who before signing those deals inked a more personal one that has already added a small fortune to the $100 million he made at Scott. Sunbeam gave Dunlap a new three-year contract granting him 300,000 shares and a staggering 3.75 million stock options—one of the 10 largest option grants ever, according to compensation experts SCA Consulting. That is on top of one he got in '96, a package now worth $130 million on paper. The new package, barely a month old, has already yielded Dunlap paper profits of $73 million. Never shy, Dunlap is quick to say he is well worth it.

And I'm not so sure he's wrong. He may be Chainsaw Al to the tens of thousands he has fired. But that name doesn't fit for the even greater numbers who have prospered with him. I hereby dub thee Equity Al, money in the bank. Maybe that moniker, like Dunlap at Sunbeam, will stick around awhile.

 **Article Review Form at end of book.**

Managers, like everyone else, are combinations of strengths and weaknesses, things that are personally commendable and things that represent failings. Following his departure from Sunbeam, even more people than usual have been critical of Al Dunlap and his managerial practices. After reading the three articles on Al Dunlap, what conclusions do you reach about his positive and negative managerial attributes? What lessons do you think you could or should learn from his career?

# Yep, He's Gone

## Patricia Sellers

## Abstract

Fortune *was the only publication to predict that CEO of Sunbeam, Al Dunlap, would get the ax. It was an inevitable end to 3 disastrous months in which the CEO's turnaround attempt stalled badly and Sunbeam stock lost two-thirds of its value. The new CEO, Jerry Levin, is just the boss the fading Sunbeam needs.*

My ears are still ringing from the shrill sound of Al Dunlap fighting to hold on to his job. There he was, the embattled Sunbeam CEO, yelling at me through his speakerphone as he read laudatory blurbs about himself from the back cover of his autobiography, *Mean Business.* "Ron Perelman gave me a testimonial," he screamed. "And [Bear Stearns Chairman] Ace Greenberg—he says, 'Dunlap is corporate America's ultimate change agent.' These guys are giants of industry!" "Chainsaw" Al was a mite apoplectic that mid-May day because I'd just told him that *Fortune* planned to report that some big Sunbeam investors

wanted him out. "Geez, this idea that Dunlap's in jeopardy. That's bullshit!" he raved. "Am I afraid of losing my job? Get goddamn serious!"

Of course, we were serious. And correct. As it turns out, we were the only publication to predict Dunlap's ouster. It was an inevitable end to three disastrous months in which the CEO's turnaround attempt stalled badly and Sunbeam stock lost two-thirds of its value.

The story in our June 8 issue played an interesting role in the drama. When Dunlap read the piece, he flipped out over a quote from Michael Price, who, through his Franklin Mutual Series funds, is Sunbeam's largest shareholder. ("We're not going to sit around and let Al wreck the company," Price had said.) Dunlap threatened to quit that day, but Price wasn't ready to give up on the boss he'd brought in two years earlier to save Sunbeam. To mollify Chainsaw, Price issued a statement saying he remained "completely supportive of Dunlap." Of course, "support" is relative on Wall Street. During the

next few weeks, Sunbeam's shares fell further on news of Dunlap's accounting gimmickry. Price and Ronald Perelman (the second biggest shareholder) talked several times, sharing their concerns. In his final meeting with the directors who fired him, Dunlap was still griping about Price's wavering support—and what he saw as Price's tepid response to the *Fortune* article.

The new CEO, Jerry Levin, is just the boss the fading Sunbeam needs. Levin, one of Perelman's top lieutenants, is a turnaround expert (he resuscitated Revlon for Perelman) and a realist. As for Chainsaw, he's going down fighting—for his severance pay, which the board wants to deny him. Dunlap hasn't returned my calls, but I bet he's rooting for Levin. If he isn't, he should be: Dunlap told me his Sunbeam shares, once worth $275 million and now worth about $60 million, represent virtually his entire investment in the stock market.

**Article Review Form at end of book.**

If you were a human resources manager and were asked to make a recommendation to top management as to the three most important aspects of an organization-wide ethical program, what would you suggest?

# Reflections on Ethics and Integrity

Corporate America does little to inspire, demand and reward ethical behavior.

## Louis V. Larimer

*Louis V. Larimer is president of The Larimer Center for Ethical Leadership Inc., a management training and consulting firm specializing in ethics and compliance issues.*

The business environment is hostile. Employee misconduct is reported in the press with increasing frequency. Litigation is at an all-time high. Not a week goes by without some corporate fraud or scandal appearing in the national press. Last year alone, we endured the public flogging of Mitsubishi (for alleged claims of sexual harassment), Texaco (for alleged claims of racial discrimination), State Farm Insurance (for alleged claims of failing to properly investigate and settle policyholders' claims), Prudential Insurance (for alleged claims of fraud, deceit and improper sales practices) and Archer Daniels Midland (for price-fixing and antitrust claims).

## Steps to Take

Clearly, corporate America does not do enough to inspire, demand and reward ethical behavior. Few top executives promote and model the highest ethical standards, and even fewer corporations offer training in ethical conduct. Ask yourself: Does my organization have a high-level ethics officer or committee to investigate charges of impropriety? Has it communicated its core ethical values? Does it respond in a meaningful way to allegations of impropriety?

If not, your company has work to do. Here are some steps it can take to promote ethical behavior and thereby prevent misconduct and litigation:

- Make a formal commitment. The leaders of an organization must make a genuine formal commitment to advance ethics, integrity and honor throughout the organization. The commitment needs to be formalized in writing and communicated to employees.

- Develop an ethical vision. The organization's leaders must develop and communicate a vision of responsible business conduct. This means creating a strong corporate mission statement, a viable code of business conduct and a statement of corporate values to shape employee behavior.

- Demonstrate ethical conduct. Corporate executives must lead by example. They must carefully examine their personal conduct and eliminate questionable business practices. They must act in a manner that is above reproach.

- Establish appropriate performance criteria. There is a basic management doctrine that is often overlooked, namely: You get what you measure. Corporate leaders must establish clearly defined, realistic performance goals for employees that include ethical criteria such as the extent to which the employee acts ethically, reflects honesty and demonstrates integrity.

- Reward ethical achievement. When an instance of ethical achievement occurs—for instance, when someone acts with integrity and honor—the organization's leaders must find creative ways to reward it.

- Respond to allegations of misconduct. When allegations of misconduct arise, they must be investigated in a timely and thorough fashion. If the allegations are found to be true, the organization's leaders must respond with appropriate discipline and remedial action.

- Demonstrate ethical courage. Doing the right thing requires inner strength and courage. During an ethical crisis the stakes are incredibly high. Careers, reputations, relationships, lives, opportunities and money are on the line. The temptations sometimes appear irresistible. It is during such times that corporate leaders must have the personal courage to stand tall and face whatever consequences may follow from making an ethical decision.

- Err on the side of goodness. In making a difficult decision, corporate executives must seek to move the organization toward goodness. They must be prepared to explain why and how their decision advances ethics, integrity and honor.

- Conduct ethical training. Highly effective organizations have implemented ethics training as a means of providing employees with a set of fundamental skills to help them deal with ethical issues and dilemmas in the workplace.

## HR's Role

As an HR professional, you must take responsibility for the design and implementation of your organization's ethics program. Your first and foremost challenge is to educate and influence the organization's CEO to make ethics a priority. You must be the constant voice that calls for ethical commitment, vision, behavior, achievement and courage. Someone must be the keeper of the corporate conscience. Someone must remind the organization of the need to err on the side of goodness. As a human resources professional, you possess the unique blend of personality traits, skills and knowledge that makes you worthy of fulfilling this vital organizational role.

Are you willing to step up and accept this challenge? If you do, you will find the rewards to be personally and professionally satisfying.

 **Article Review Form at end of book.**

Are there any elements of health-care delivery that are potentially at odds with business values? To what extent might these tensions create ethical problems for a company?

# Code Blue at Columbia/HCA:

## Why the For-Profit Hospital Chain Needs to Clean Up after Former CEO Rick Scott

**Susan Headden**

It is the seventh-largest employer in America. Its annual sales are higher than Xerox's. It is the largest buyer of medical supplies in the world. To these superlatives and others it has earned as the leader among for-profit hospitals, Columbia/HCA Healthcare Corp. can now add that it is the target of the most sweeping single-company fraud investigation in Medicare history. As a result, it faces the future under an ethical cloud—and without the man who built Columbia from two little hospitals in El Paso, Texas, into a 68,000-bed medical empire.

The resignation on July 25 of Richard Scott, Columbia's visionary founder and chief executive officer, is part of an extraordinary series of events that have shaken the health care behemoth with a reputation for hyperaggressive business tactics. In an indict-

ment unsealed last week, three Columbia executives were charged with overbilling Medicare at a Florida hospital. Just days before, federal agents served at least 35 search warrants on Columbia facilities in seven states. More indictments appear likely.

Although his culpability, if any, remains unknown, Rick Scott was to many a symbol of Columbia—and to critics of corporate medicine he epitomized what they deplored. Over the course of a decade, the 44-year-old mergers and acquisitions lawyer built the Nashville-based corporation into a $20 billion hospital chain by aggressively pursuing mergers, cutting staff, driving tough bargains with suppliers, and buying nonprofit hospitals—often over loud opposition from their communities. He also challenged traditional concepts of medical ethics by encouraging doctors to invest in Columbia hospitals.

Scott's boast that he has done more to reform the nation's health care system than Bill Clinton is partly true. He was by all accounts one of the most energetic figures in the business—his Monday staff meetings began at 6 A.M.—and a skillful dealmaker who drove down prices by buying in bulk and rescued some local hospitals close to extinction. His difficulties arose from the sweep of this process—and from what industry analyst Jeff Goldsmith calls his "towering arrogance."

Last week, Columbia attempted to repair its scarred image by replacing Scott with Thomas Frist Jr., a respected Nashville cardiologist and philanthropist who had been serving as the company's president. He appears to be his predecessor's temperamental opposite. Frist—the brother of Tennessee Sen. Bill Frist—immediately commissioned an independent corporate audit, demanded an end to physician investment, and stated that Columbia would no longer buy nonprofits in communities where it was not welcome. "I felt that the style that was in place was not appropriate for this company long-term," Frist told *U.S. News.*

While the actions announced by the courtly Frist may appease anxious stockholders and limit criminal penalties down the road, they do not resolve questions about the place of for-profits in a traditionally nonprofit field. Some health care experts suggest that because of its high profile, Columbia is being singled out for offenses that may be common throughout the industry. Others wonder whether for-profits can increase their margins further without bilking Medicare. "For not-for-profits and for-profits, all the [operating] costs are about the same," says Gerard Anderson, a health care finance expert with Johns Hopkins University in Baltimore. "After you've cut costs, one way you boost revenue is by taking liberties."

Scott founded Columbia Hospital Corp. in 1988 with $125,000 and crucial help from billionaire investor Richard Rainwater. He acted at a time when the government had drastically reduced the amount it was reimbursing hospitals for Medicare services, forcing many for-profits out of business. But where others saw danger, Scott—a truck driver's son whose previous holdings consisted of two doughnut shops—saw opportunity. There were still too many hospitals in America, he reasoned, and thus there was money to be saved through consolidation.

But Columbia's strategy for building the highest-volume, lowest-cost health care chain allegedly didn't end with simple efficiencies like bulk purchasing. It included other tactics that have proven far more controversial:

*Alleged fraud.* According to the federal indictment, three Columbia executives overcharged Medicare, as well as a Defense Department health insurance program, by claiming improper reimbursement for capital expenses. Future inquiries are expected to focus on Columbia's home health care business and on suspicions that it may have engaged in a practice called "upcoding"— inflating the seriousness of diseases to get reimbursed at a higher rate.

*Doctor-investors.* Central to Columbia's remarkable growth was Scott's practice of inviting doctors to become investors in the hospitals where they worked. Scott figured that ownership gave the doctors an incentive to fill beds and improve quality. These unorthodox arrangements drew fire from officials of the American Medical Association, who claimed they undermined doctor-patient trust, and from Frist himself, who says: "A doctor is a psychological partner with a hospital; he doesn't need to be a financial partner." When doctors have a monetary stake, critics say, they are more apt to keep well-insured patients at their own hospitals and send charity cases elsewhere. Indeed, a study by the Florida Agency for Health Care Administration found that at two hospitals, Columbia's doctor-investors appeared to skim off the patients most likely to pay.

Scott realized that attracting high-quality doctors was an important ingredient of success. But Columbia took this concept to extraordinary lengths, physicians say. In a lawsuit, Dr. James Thompson, a family practitioner from Corpus Christi, Texas, says Columbia wooed him with a Venezuelan fishing trip, a vacation at an Arizona dude ranch, half-price office rent, and what became a 1,000 percent return on a $19,000 investment.

*Secret buyouts.* Columbia is notorious for its aggressive efforts to buy out nonprofit hospitals. Scott made few friends when he commissioned a study that found that not-for-profits were "net community burdens" because the value of their tax exemptions exceeded the value of their charity care. His insistence on keeping the terms of deals secret only fed suspicions that officials of the purchased hospitals were benefiting from the transactions at the community's expense.

*Driving out competitors.* The health care group has not been shy about using its clout to punish competitors and perceived enemies. According to the *New England Journal of Medicine,* a memo from a Columbia administrator in Fort Pierce, Fla., promised to "utilize all appropriate resources to ensure the failure of any competing surgery center in our community." Outside Wellington Regional Medical Center in West Palm Beach, Fla., Columbia erected a billboard inviting motorists to bypass Wellington in favor of

Columbia. And when the *St. Petersburg Times* wrote an editorial critical of Columbia's efforts to buy Tampa General Hospital, Columbia pulled its ads from the newspaper and banished the publication from its hospital gift shops.

*Maximizing profit.* It is impossible to say whether Columbia's practices have diminished patient care. Cost-cutting is prompting complaints throughout medicine. But Columbia doctors and employees say that Scott set such ambitious profit goals—seeking margins of 20 percent, compared to a for-profit industry average of just over 4—that sacrifices in quality were inevitable. Dr. Jamal Modir, a surgeon at Columbia's Good Samaritan Hospital in San Jose, Calif., says he depends increasingly on inexperienced nurses. At Columbia's Suburban Hospital in Louisville, Ky., a bath now consists of a wipe-down with a premoistened, disposable towel. None of Columbia/ HCA's hospitals was among the 136 institutions listed in the 1997 edition of *America's Best Hospitals*. In its defense, Columbia/HCA points to surveys showing that customer satisfaction is very high.

In "Tommy" Frist, Columbia now has a CEO as likely to talk about patient care as profits—not withstanding his own substantial investment in the company. He says he is committed to bringing in new leadership, cooperating with government investigators,

and protecting the legacy of Hospital Corporation of America (HCA), the company built by his family and later bought by Columbia. But no one knows how much of Columbia's profits depended on illegal activities. "There was very much the flavor of a go-go 1980 savings and loan about this enterprise," says Goldsmith.

If Columbia ends up paying heavy penalties to settle the criminal case, it will join a number of other for-profit health care companies alleged to have exploited Medicare. They include National Medical Enterprises (NME), a chain accused of keeping psychiatric patients hospitalized until their insurance ran out, and Humana, Inc., investigated for overbilling insurers for items such as $7 Tylenol tablets. (Ironically, Humana was later absorbed by Columbia, and NME became Tenet Healthcare Corp., which has considered merging with Columbia.)

If proven, the alleged transgressions of the nation's largest health care provider may raise a larger question: How much of Columbia's alleged offenses are commonplace in the health care industry? So far, it's hard to tell whether Columbia was a maverick or just aggressive at doing what many other companies in the field do more quietly.

## The Rise and Fall of Columbia/HCA

Following a decade of extraordinary growth in which it became the nation's largest for-profit hospital chain, Columbia finds itself

facing executive resignations and charges of Medicare fraud.

**September 1988.** Richard Scott, a Texas mergers and acquisitions lawyer, founds Columbia Hospital Corp. with $125,000 and help from financier Richard Rainwater. Scott's previous holdings had consisted of two doughnut shops.

**Spring 1993.** An internal study by the Florida Agency for Health Care Administration suggests that doctors may be "skimming off" well-insured patients for two Columbia hospitals, while letting charity cases go elsewhere.

**September 1993.** Columbia merges with Galen Health Care Inc., the former hospital wing of health care conglomerate Humana Inc.

**October 1993.** One month after Galen merger, Columbia acquires Hospital Corp. of America (HCA) for $5.7 billion.

**November 1995.** In a lawsuit, Dr. James Thompson claims Columbia wooed him with vacations, half-price office rent, and a 1,000 percent return on a $19,000 investment.

**May 1997.** Members of the Gray Panthers protest Columbia's efforts to buy the Roger Williams Medical Center in Providence and turn it into Rhode Island's first for-profit hospital.

**July 1997.** Scott steps down as CEO of Columbia, and three other executives are indicted for alleged Medicare fraud. Columbia's stock value has fallen by 20 percent since February.

 **Article Review Form at end of book.**

What is the dilemma of "right vs. right"? Give some examples of this problem other than those mentioned in the reading.

# Right vs. Right and You're in the Middle

## Perry Pascarella

*Perry Pascarella is the former editor-in-chief of* Industry Week *and the author of six books—the most recent of which is* Leveraging People and Profit: The Hard Work of Soft Management *(Butterworth-Heinemann, 1997).*

## Abstract

*Managers are often faced with the dilemma on how to integrate ethics with some management techniques. The real business ethics battles dwell on the fields of right versus right and not just right as against wrong. The book* Defining Moment: When Managers Must Choose between Right and Right *by Joseph L. Badaracco, Jr. illuminates the so-called 'defining moments' in the lives of managers. The decisions often reveal managers' basic values, strength of commitment and sense of conviction.*

The more ethical you are, the more you will face difficult situations in management. When you work for the good of the company, you risk hurting an individual. When you try to be fair to an individual worker, you risk offending and undermining that person's boss. When you try to serve customers who want your new product, you encounter protests from environmentalists or other interest groups.

For a manager, right-or-wrong issues are relatively easy to deal with. It's the right-vs.-right conflicts that keep you awake at night.

In this era of more "open" business where everything a manager does can be challenged by practically everyone, management is drawn more and more into the ethics arena. This raises two challenges: knowing what you really believe in and finding the means to get others to do things your way without beating them over the head.

Because I have seen how uncomfortable managers are in this arena, I jumped right into the page proofs of a new book, *Defining Moments* by Joseph Badaracco. Then I talked with him about what I see as a surge of interest in ethics. But immediately he threw me a curveball by countering with his opinion that interest in traditional approaches to teaching ethics to businesspeople "plateaued a couple of years ago." Earlier scandals prompted schools to either launch or beef up ethics programs, and many

companies developed credos and mission statements. Much of this effort was predicated on the notion of the company as family with long-term commitments. But then the word loyalty went into decline. "The idea of the company's values and long-term commitments isn't as powerful. A more individualistic approach to ethics is replacing the 'here are our values, join the family' approach. I think interest has shifted to 'my ethics and my values' rather than the corporation's," says Joe.

Well, his curveball was still in the strike zone. I think it's that individualistic approach to ethics that is causing more and more emotional turmoil in the hearts of managers. As a manager I have more ethical decisions to make than ever before. People in all quarters demand more fairness and honesty. The real ethics battles are on the fields of right vs. right, not just right vs. wrong. That's what makes Joe's book timely and helpful.

These seemingly "no-win" or "dirty-hands" decisions can be what Joe calls "defining moments"—those decisions that reveal a manager's and sometimes an organization's basic values, test the strength of commitment to those values and cast a shadow forward, shaping the character of the person and the organization.

In his book, Joe intertwines the ethical dilemmas of several real managers with the moral philosophies of Aristotle, Machiavelli, Nietzsche and William James to help us learn how we can guide ourselves through defining moments. He is well-aware of the hard realities in which managers have to make decisions, and he stresses the accountability managers have to others for their decisions.

## Sleep Test

"Many people believe they have found a simple, user-friendly alternative to moral philosophy, corporate law and company mission statements. . . . Instead of relying on objective external principles, they look for answers within themselves, in their moral intuitions and instincts, and practice what can be called sleep-test ethics," Joe writes.

Whoa! Is this going to be a book about me-ism—tailoring ethics to oneself, in the absence of training? Are there no absolutes? Should we just do what feels good?

Through the course of the book, Joe straightened me out. What he is really trying to help us deal with are situations in which we get caught between two absolutes. Joe brings Aristotle to the rescue. "Aristotle said that people could trust their instincts once they had the right character and experience." In his book, he points out that Aristotle believes four great virtues—courage, jus-

tice, prudence and temperance—should govern behavior. None of them are found in me-ism.

Joe suggests asking four important questions when faced with "dirty-hands" decisions: "How do my feelings and instincts define the dilemma? Which of the responsibilities and values in conflict have the deepest roots in my life and in communities I care about? Looking to the future, what is my way? And how can expediency and shrewdness, along with imagination and boldness, move me toward the goals I care about most strongly?"

## Play to Win

Traditional teaching about business ethics can sensitize people to what's right and wrong and what they really believe in, but that's not enough, Joe believes. It's the action and accountability phases that put the rubber on the road.

If you really care about certain values, play to win. Deal with people in terms they can buy into. We've all worked with ethical people who prefer to sit back and complain, "I'm right and they're wrong," but don't get their hands dirty.

In order to win, start by defining what winning is for you. "That's got to be a combination of two things," says Joe. "One, the practical objectives. Two, how you will win; what values are you unwilling to sacrifice in order to achieve your practical objectives?

"Playing to win means I am doing everything I can within the limits of my values to achieve my goals. Am I really looking at my adversaries and examining how they're playing? Am I blocking

them or looking for opportunities to work with them? Seeing the world as it is might mean playing hardball in some cases."

He adds, "You've got to be even cleverer and shrewder and more realistic because in a sense you've already handicapped yourself since you care about these values and you've got constraints on what you can do that other people may not have. It takes a lot of pragmatism and cleverness to find ways to be effective without compromising your values or those of your organization."

That's why Joe delves more deeply into James Burke (of Johnson & Johnson). "He's often interpreted in the Tylenol episode as saying simply 'let's just do the right thing.' I think he brought a lot of skill and shrewdness, street-smarts, and media savvy to his effort to do the right thing. He's an extraordinarily effective manager, which means he's got a kind of instinctive talent for how he expresses himself and for understanding the politics of a situation and then making the right moves within it."

## Accountability

Action has to be matched with explanation. Joe believes, "There are two important facets to that. One comes back to the problem of pure intuition or me-ism. If you're a manager, you're accountable to other people and you can't just say 'it fits my values.' You've got to explain and persuade other people that this is the right course.

"The world being what it is, however, I'm not sure you're responsible for explaining everything," he says. "I like the

Venetian saying, 'The truth, but not to everyone.' It says the truth matters and you ought to figure out what's right and wrong. Then there's the realistic element—'not to everyone.' Sometimes you can't explain in real time and in complete candor to everybody why you are doing something."

For example, you may argue for the ethically right thing but offer economic reasons such as "it will help our finances, it will help the brand," or "it will keep us from being sued." Don't say, "We ought to do it because it's ethically the right thing." People will feel insulted if they feel you view them as unethical because they disagree.

"Ethics often ends up sort of cross-dressing as economics," Joe adds. "But the world's a better place because some managers do the right thing even if only (or so they say) for economic reasons. Of course, there are limits on how much of this cross-dressing you want to do." Sometimes, too, a manager has to compromise at the end of negotiations with conflicting parties. But, he advises, compromise "as little as you can as late as you can."

**The Thinker:** Joseph L. Badaracco Jr. Professor of Business Ethics

**Home Base:** Harvard Business School

**Latest Book:** *Defining Moments: When Managers Must Choose between Right and Right,* (Harvard Business School Press, 1997)

**Key Ideas:**

- A manager who has strong values finds that they sometimes conflict with one another.
- Right-vs.-right decisions can reveal the priorities of your values and those of your organization.
- The question is not whether you should rely on your ethical intuitions but how to do so.
- If you care about certain values, you must be clever enough to get where you want to go without compromising them.

In an academic setting, ethics may seem pure and simple. But Joe is one academician who knows that in the real world, there's often no straight line to the truth.

 **Article Review Form at end of book.**

# WiseGuide Wrap-Up

- Management is inherently about values. Since managers make decisions and can control organizational rewards and punishments, everything they do has an ethical-moral implication.

- Managers must work to maximize organizational outcomes while also being concerned with what happens to people. Doing what is best for the organization often may require making decisions that have significant impact on the lives of others. Managers need both a personal and organizational ethos to guide them as they confront these dilemmas.

- The most difficult ethical decisions of managers usually do not involve a choice between wrong or right, but a choice between two things, neither of which is inherently wrong, but either of which will cause pain or hardship for someone.

## R.E.A.L. Sites

This list provides a print preview of typical **Coursewise** R.E.A.L. sites. (There are over 100 such sites at the **Courselinks**™ site.) The danger in printing URLs is that web sites can change overnight. As we went to press, these sites were functional using the URLs provided. If you come across one that isn't, please let us know via email to: webmaster@coursewise.com. Use your Passport to access the most current list of R.E.A.L. sites at the **Courselinks** site.

**Site name:** American Psychological Association
**URL:** http://www.apa.org/
**Why is it R.E.A.L.?** This homepage of the American Psychological Association offers a variety of free information.
**Key topic:** women in management
**Try this:** Review five articles at this site, and summarize significant issues facing women in management.

**Site name:** The Society for Human Resource Management
**URL:** http://www.shrm.org
**Why is it R.E.A.L.?** The Society for Human Resource Management is comprised of more than 85,000 professional human resource practitioners and student members. The organization provides a forum for dialogue about human resource issues among its members. It also offers information services, publications, and conferences to further the profession of human resource management.
**Key topics:** diversity, future management trends
**Try this:** Review current and back issues of *Diversity Today,* and create a list of what you feel are the most compelling issues facing managers trying to make diversity an asset for their organizations.

**Site name:** Business Ethics Resources on the WWW
**URL:** http://www.ethics.ubc.ca/resources/business/
**Why is it R.E.A.L.?** This site, maintained by the Center for Applied Ethics (Canada), lists a number of organizations' stances on ethical activities in business.
**Key topics:** management ethics, research reports
**Try this:** Find and summarize an article on managerial ethics.

# section

# 4

- Describe the current managerial orthodoxy in terms of organizational design

- Compare and contrast the advantages and disadvantages of horizontal organizations as compared to more traditional hierarchies.

- Explain how organizations are likely to be designed in the twenty-first century.

# Getting Organized to Accomplish Work

 **WiseGuide Intro**

Organization is typically cited as one of the essential elements of managerial responsibility. Traditionally, managers have created organizational structures to serve common purposes, to provide mechanisms for control, and to deal with environmental complexity.

In his Pulitzer Prize-winning book on the history of management, *The Visible Hand,* business historian Alfred Chandler cites the advent of the railroads as the seminal event in the development of modern management structures. The first transcontinental railroads needed to manage multiple operations at distant locations. This created the need for management layers with decision-making responsibility—what we now call middle managers.

As commerce and society have matured and grown more complex, organizations have as well. Often, this organizational complexity, created by well-intentioned managers to maintain control and accomplish enterprise objectives, is cited as the source of organizational dysfunction.

The current management orthodoxy seems to be that managers should seek to make organizations flatter and less hierarchical. The rationale for this notion is that if top managers are closer to the operating surfaces of the organization and, therefore, to the consequences of their decisions, the result will be more effective decisions. In theory, reducing the layers of management and pushing more decision-making responsibility down into the interstices of an organization will result in organization members feeling more involved and committed to organizational goals. Ironically, however, most academic business programs prepare students to do middle management work and then advise them to reduce the size of middle management in their organizations. Still, the general logic of this proposition is intuitively satisfying, and many leaner, less bureaucratic organizations enjoy enormous success in the competitive marketplace.

Some observers of the economy cite the willingness of U.S. organizations to create these sleek, less complex, less expensive organizations as a key element of the sustained economic growth of the 1990s. As you might imagine, however, these relatively simple propositions sometimes have somewhat more complex implications in practice. The four readings in this section can help you understand the implications of current organizational practices and the challenges for managers.

In Reading 16, Andrew Kessler presents examples of how these new-form horizontal organizations have enjoyed success in the marketplace. Reading 17, by Bennett Harrison, provides a much less sanguine view of the move to this leaner organizational form. Harrison details the human consequences of flatter organizations that eliminate jobs and reduce job security for managers and workers. Readings 18 and 19, the final two articles in this section, provide different perspectives on how the current organizational design imperatives will manifest themselves in the future.

## ? Questions ?

**Reading 16.** What is meant by a "horizontal" organization? Would you describe your university as horizontal?

**Reading 17.** How does being "flexible" reduce fixed costs in an organization, and what are the potential ethical implications of this situation?

**Reading 18.** Are large companies inherently at a disadvantage in terms of their operational agility? Why or why not?

**Reading 19.** How will prototypical future organizations likely be similar to and different from those that currently characterize commerce?

What is meant by a "horizontal" organization? Would you describe your university as horizontal?

# Get Horizontal:

## Horizontal Firms Like Intel vs Vertically Integrated Firms Like General Motors

**Andrew J. Kessler**

### Parameters

I had a college roommate who, after taking business classes, would come back to our house, pound a few beers, proclaim, "Dude, when in doubt, get horizontal"—and then proceed to pass out in front of the TV.

It's probably not what he had in mind, but his maxim has great applicability to business. Horizontal firms like Intel that dominate one element of goods production do well. Vertically integrated firms like General Motors are not doing well.

The old IBM was vertical. It made everything in the computer but the squeak: the chips, the software, the box—and the sticker with the number to call for repair service.

The whole thing was copied from the GM model implemented by Alfred Sloan, a model that is starting to unwind today. Digital Equipment Corp. was in the same vertical mold, selling everything

from alpha chips to the VMS operating system.

In 1987, when DEC's stock was close to $200, Kenneth Olsen declared DEC's only constraint to growth was the number of sales representatives it had. He was right, but not in the way he meant. Instead of hiring 25,000 more sellers, he should have been firing them all—and getting horizontal.

AT&T was another vertically integrated monster. While working there I learned about "transfer pricing," the fictitious accounting used inside a vertical company in order to assign profits to divisions. Result: Each division could show a profit even if the end products were selling at a loss.

The chip division would charge $10 a chip—or whatever price included a profit, a huge R&D budget and massive overhead. The manufacturing division would buy 20 of these chips for $10 each, assemble them on a board with a power supply, put it in a box and sell it to the sales division for $400 as a modem.

The markup covered lots of cool new robotic assembly toys the engineers wanted to play with, and of course the annual management meeting in Laguna. The sales division would try to sell the modems at $600, but had trouble moving them when competitors were selling the same thing for $299.

The PC almost toppled these vertical manufacturers. In a hurry to compete with Apple Computer, IBM used Intel microprocessors, Microsoft software, Western Digital disk controllers and so on. Then Compaq came along with hardly more than an assembly line and a sales channel and beat IBM to market with a new 386 PC. Next Dell asked, Who needs a sales channel? We'll assemble these things and sell direct.

What started with a few horizontal specialties has spread to at least a dozen, each with its own leader, producing the various peripherals, parts and software that go into the PC on your desk. With the exception of the somewhat artificial pricing in horizontal segments led by near-monopolists (Intel, Microsoft), pricing in the vertically disintegrated computer business is competitive and efficient. You don't see delusional transfer pricing that hides inefficiencies.

This horizontalizing of electronics is spreading. The data networking industry, for example, was dominated by vertically integrated players like Cisco. But lately Cisco has learned the lesson of the PC market, and it now buys components outside—for example, chips from MMC Networks for its Ethernet and asynchronous transfer mode switches.

Internet firms are getting horizontal at a blinding pace. Yahoo! started as a search engine and built a portal business around it. Recently it outsourced its search capabilities to Inktomi. The Inktomi service is run out of Exodus Communications, a specialist in so-called Web hosting. (Please note that my firm has stakes in both Inktomi and Exodus.) Exodus buys bulk data lines from telecom companies like Qwest Communications and Sprint and resells them to publishers of Web pages who locate their Web servers at Exodus' hosting locations. In short, you have at least three specialist service providers inserting themselves into the communications chain that connects a computer user to the page he wants to look at.

The early part of this century was marked by a powerful movement toward integration. The next century will begin with a movement the other way.

 **Article Review Form at end of book.**

How does being "flexible" reduce fixed costs in an organization, and what are the potential ethical implications of this situation?

# The Dark Side of Business Flexibility

Small is not necessarily beautiful, argues this author. The competitive pressure for big corporations to become more flexible is taking a toll on workers' wages.

## Bennett Harrison

*Bennett Harrison is professor of urban political economy at the Milano Graduate School of Management and Urban Policy, New School for Social Research. This article is adapted from the new edition of* Lean and Mean *(New York: Guilford Press, 1997). Reprinted with permission.*

During the policy debates about economic development and the rise of the theory of flexible specialization during the 1980s, I became discontented with the extent to which the proposition was being repeated that new developments in competition and technology were systematically privileging smaller forms of business enterprise. But these were seriously theorized arguments, so I tried to accord them the respect they were due, in the course of offering my critique.

Less deserving of respectful treatment were the seemingly endless repetitions of the line, originating with David Birch, that "nearly x percent of all new jobs are created by [small, medium-sized, "gazelle-like"—take your pick] firms," a statement in which

x was sometimes said to be "50," sometimes "75," sometimes "90," sometimes even "virtually 100." Policymakers, including governors and mayors, repeated these assertions, and drew upon them as "evidence" that policies should systematically favor these small business "job generators." Much of this was, of course, traditional rank ideology. But much of it really did take the "research" as providing an objective rationale or basis for such policy designs as across-the-board tax breaks or environmental pollution variances for small businesses. This, even though a number of first-rate technical critiques of the Small Business Administration-based data and Birch-like analyses have been published, of late, that come to the same conclusions that I did.[1]

Even confronted with the revived merger and acquisition wave of the 1990s, the believers that small is both inherently beautiful and on the rise have stuck to their guns. (Item: With the recent merger of the Boeing Company and McDonnell Douglas, there are

now effectively only two producers of commercial aircraft in the entire world, Boeing-McDonnell and the European Airbus Industrie Consortium. Another recent aerospace merger, between Lockheed and Martin Marietta, is devoting itself entirely to manufacturing planes for the military and to managing a variety of what used to be publicly provided services, as recipients of government privatization contracts.) Concentration is on the rise even in the traditionally fragmented retail sector, both among discount chains like K-Mart and among the specialty retailers.

Many policymakers who casually use these numbers and repeat the conventional wisdom like a mantra fail to distinguish between individual sites of business—that is, establishments—and whole companies, or enterprises. A majority of all businesses have only one site of operation; they are truly small. But the minority that do have multiple facilities in different locations account for a disproportionate share of all

Table 1 Enterprise Employment and Sales Size Distributions in U.S. Private Sector

| | Firms with 100 Workers | | | Firms with < 500 Workers | | | Firms with 500+ Workers | | |
|---|---|---|---|---|---|---|---|---|---|
| | Share of All Firms (%) | Share of Employment (%) | Share of Sales (%) | Share of All Firms (%) | Share of Employment (%) | Share of Sales (%) | Share of All Firms (%) | Share of Employment (%) | Share of Sales (%) |
| All private industry | 98.4 | 38.6 | 34.3 | 99.7 | 63.0 | 47.0 | 0.3 | 47.0 | 53.0 |
| Manufacturing | 93.7 | 22.0 | 14.6 | 98.6 | 38.2 | 27.9 | 1.3 | 61.8 | 72.1 |
| Finance | 97.8 | 30.8 | 17.9 | 99.3 | 42.9 | 27.7 | 0.7 | 57.1 | 72.3 |

Source: Bureau of the Census, U.S. Department of Commerce, *Statistics of U.S. Businesses: 1992* (Washington, D.C.: U.S. Government Printing Office, 1994).

jobs, sales, and profits, in both manufacturing and the rest of the economy. I present a statistical accounting of this distinction in Table 1.

For the economy as a whole, firms with fewer than 100 employees (including the many sole proprietors who have no one on their payrolls at all) accounted for fully 98.4 percent of all companies in the United States in 1992. But that mass of businesses was responsible for only 38.6 percent of all jobs and received just 34.3 percent of all sales revenues. At the other end of the size distribution, companies that were so large as to employ 500 or more workers made up only three-tenths of 1 percent of all businesses, but that tiny fraction of the business community employed 47 percent of all workers and raked in 53 percent of all sales dollars. As Table 1 shows, the gaps were even more vast in the manufacturing and financial sectors.

Let me spell this out. In the finance sector (which, in the official definition of the Census Bureau, includes insurance and real estate, two industries that are popularly conceived to be dominated by the little guys), small firms accounted for almost 98 percent of the total number of businesses, but for less than one of every three jobs and fewer than a fifth of all sales revenues. By contrast, finance, insurance, and real estate companies employing 500 or more employees in 1992 made up only seven-tenths of 1 percent of all such businesses, but this tiny group accounted for 57 percent of all jobs in the sector and 72.3 percent of all sales. To repeat: this overwhelming dominance of the big firms is not new news in modern American economic life—and that is precisely my point. This, at least, has not changed.

## The Dark Side to Flexibility

What has changed, however, is that large corporations must now be more flexible in order to compete. This means that they must reduce their fixed costs, and this has had a serious impact on the security of jobs and worker remuneration. For the moment, the consequences have been disguised by the business cycle. Now, well into the seventh year of an economic upturn, it is not surprising that declining unem-

ployment, tightening labor markets, and expanding consumption and investment demand are finally conjoining to begin to raise average real wages after years of stagnation. That the Europeans may finally be recovering from their own (very different) experiences of stagnation only adds to the much-awaited improvement in domestic earnings. After adjusting for inflation using the new chain-weighted price index for consumer spending, the U.S. Department of Labor estimates that real average wages, which were falling at an annual rate of 1 percent in the last business cycle peak year of 1989, are now rising at an annual rate of a bit over 1 percent. This is not much growth, but is growth nonetheless.

Equally important, it now appears that this tightening of labor markets in the aggregate and in particular regions of the country is finally beginning to bring up the wage rate that low-skilled (or, at any rate, poorly paid) workers are able to command. With this development, the gap between high-paid and low-paid workers—that much-cited worsening earnings inequality— appears to be narrowing at last. Economists Rebecca Blank and

David Card estimate that, all other things being equal, a 1 percent drop in the jobless rate produces a 3.7 percent rise in annual earnings (mainly through increased hours of employment) for the lowest fifth of the work force, whereas the top fifth's gain is just 1.4 percent.

Welcome as they are, these are macroeconomic developments, subject to the usual ups and downs of the business cycle, with the associated tightening and loosening of labor markets. What about long-run trends? What about structural developments that go beyond (and across) cycles? Far-ranging changes are under way in how companies organize work: How they produce, where they locate the work to be done, and whom they hire to do the work. A central feature of these changes is what now appears to be a long-run ("secular" as opposed to periodic or "cyclical") move away from what, at least for the most profitable operations of the biggest, more visible, and most influential firms and agencies, constituted the dominant (if never universal) employment system of the post-World War II era.

To recapitulate: In the quarter century after 1945, with job tasks substantially standardized and broken down into a finely grained division of labor, managers commonly hired new young workers at the bottom of job ladders, trained them on the job, promoted people within the organization, and paid wages more in accord with seniority and experience than with individual productivity or current firm performance. While few companies ever formally committed themselves to literally "lifetime" employment, there was widespread expectation that (at least for white men, but gradually for others as well) there would be a high degree of long-term job security, with occasional disruptions in work triggering the receipt of unemployment insurance and other forms of temporary income maintenance. Seniority systems were promoted by unions, and within the civil service, as a means of achieving fairness. Business came to support them because, by according greater job security to more experienced employees, business could expect in return that senior employees would more willingly train and otherwise teach skills to and share know-how with younger workers within the organization.

Whether there is a well-defined, coherent new "system" of work coming into existence—one accommodating to globalization, deregulation, the shortened shelf lives of products, the enhanced capability of more and more competitors to quickly erode the advantages of (play catch-up with) the innovators through "reverse engineering," and generally heightened competition—is still an open question. But there is a growing consensus among scholars that the old system is coming apart. This is not the place to examine all of the many aspects of this "devolution" of internal labor markets, the growth of "flexible" forms of work organization, and the implications for training and economic development. But I can at least sketch the main features of what a number of researchers believe is happening to how work and labor markets are coming to be reorganized.

The changes are motivated by a complex of reasons: deregulation, greater actual or potential competition from abroad, growing numbers of corporate hostile takeover attempts and other signals from stockholders that put a premium on short-term firm performance. All of this has made managers increasingly conscious of short-term fixed (or, as economists like to describe the wages of workers on long-term implicit contracts, "quasi-fixed") costs, and committed to reducing them whenever and as much as possible. First with IBM, then with Xerox, most recently with AT&T and the big banks, the stock market has instantly rewarded companies that cut costs through consolidations, mass layoffs, and wage and benefit rollbacks by bidding up share values, which only further encourages this sort of management behavior. Even as progressive voices—from the former U.S. secretaries of labor Ray Marshall and Robert Reich, to labor economist Richard Freeman, to political theorist and activist Joel Rogers—were advocating that more companies should take (and stick to) the "high road" in labor policy, the business community has been organizing itself (e.g., through the Labor Policy Association) to advocate for, and legitimate, greater "flexibility" and management discretion in work arrangements.

What this amounts to, in practice, is a proliferation of different forms of work organization, blurring the traditional distinctions between "core" and "periphery," "permanent" and "contingent," "inside" and "outside" employees and between "primary" and "secondary" labor markets. Thus managers employ some workers in more or less routine wage and salary positions inside the firm or agency. But then they also hire temporary help agencies, management consulting firms, and other contractors to provide employees (ranging from specialized computer programmers to janitors and clerical personnel) to work along-side the "regular" people but on short-term assignments and under the management of the contractor. Companies, colleges, and hospitals outsource work formerly performed in-house to outside suppliers, here and abroad. They also shift some work from full-time to part-time schedules, in part to avoid federal labor regulations covering wages and benefits that have been interpreted by the courts as not covering "leased" workers. The "temp" agencies and other contractors are being used increasingly by managers in the "focal" firm as a mechanism for screening potential regular employees, with candidates serving their "probation" on the payrolls of the contractor before moving into the focal company or agency. This creates the possibility for further inequities, since two persons working side by side for an outside contractor may be equally competent, yet one will eventually be absorbed into a full-time job while the other remains bouncing from one temporary assignment to another.

Two concrete expressions of this growing heterogeneity in work organization and practices, both among and within particular employers, are declining employment security and more uncertain wage and salary prospects over time. Surveys conducted by the American Management Association show that managers increasingly regard layoffs as "strategic or structural in nature," rather than as a response to short-term, temporary business conditions. The fraction of laid-off workers who can expect recall to their old jobs has been lower in the post-1991 recovery than in the previous four national business cycles, while those who do get re-employed somewhere are more

likely than before to land in part-time jobs.[2]

Flatter organizational structures—yet another workplace "innovation" whose introduction in recent years has been responsible for the layoffs of so many middle-level managers—contribute to reduced promotion opportunities within the surviving internal labor markets of companies and agencies. More generally, the payoff to seniority, as measured by age-earnings profiles, is shrinking over time, both across the workforce and, more precisely, over the careers of specific individuals, including those who stay with the same employer. The flattening of average age-earnings profiles is suggestive, but longitudinal studies on specific workers or on cohorts are more definitive. There is now considerable evidence that younger workers cannot expect the same rate of pay increases over time that their parents received. For example, a new study from the Employee Benefit Research Institute reports that, between 1991 and 1996, median job tenure for men aged 25 to 64 fell by nearly 20 percent, which means that people don't remain in a particular job long enough to move up to the same extent as did earlier cohorts.[3]

Two researchers affiliated with the National Bureau of Economic Research have measured declining upward mobility more directly. Studying the U.S. Department of Labor's National Longitudinal Surveys for Youth, they found that, among younger men and women since 1979, there has been a significant increase in immobility over time within each quintile of the earnings distribution, with the degree of growth in immobility greatest for the bottom quintiles. More generally, what these researchers have

found is a convergence over time in interquintile transition probabilities toward the diagonal. That is "econospeak" for saying that people are increasingly likely to stay from one period to the next within their original position in the earnings distribution than to move up or down in position. This is a major discovery. Moreover, these estimates control for personal differences in schooling and other factors relating to skill. The overall conclusion, therefore, is that there has been, in the authors' own words, a sharp decrease in mobility over time, across all skill groups.

And there is more. Compared to expectations formed in earlier periods (such as the early 1970s) or to the average earnings profile for their age group, workers in the 1980s and 1990s may now be facing increasingly fluctuating earnings from one year to the next. The jury is still out on the relative magnitudes of the transitory (unexpectedly fluctuating) versus permanent (long-term, predictable) components of annual increases in wage inequality. Economists Peter Gottschalk and Robert Moffitt were the first to report a large transitory component.[4] Annette Bernhardt and her colleagues are finding the permanent component to be relatively larger, which, while not evidence for "fluctuation," certainly confirms the growing structural trend toward inequality. In their words, we are witnessing the very real possibility that the structure of mobility opportunity for young workers has changed, and that this change has been for the worse. . . . The recent cohort has substantially more workers who experience both low and high wage [permanent, as distinct from "transitory"] growth. In short, . . . what we are potentially looking at is a rise in the inequality of opportunity.[5]

Researchers are vigorously comparing notes and methodologies on the question of the relative importance of increasingly fluctuating earnings. Stay tuned; this is important. Quite apart from questions of "fairness," Cappelli and others are questioning the long-run implications of any growing instability in earnings streams for the continued smooth functioning of a consumer economy built on households borrowing against future income and having to make small regular payments over time for everything from housing and cars to their children's education.

In sum, the mix of types of jobs and work schedules is becoming more diverse. According to Cappelli's careful and sober formulation, "[T]here is a continuum between 'pure' internalized arrangements and complete market determination along which employers are moving, and the argument here is that, on average,

practices are shifting along that continuum," from the former in the direction of the latter.[6] If this were mostly a voluntary development, serving the needs of a greater share of the population, that would be one thing. But all serious researchers agree that these changes are being initiated mainly on the "demand side" of the labor market, with managers seeking to reduce their exposure to long-term fixed obligations. It appears that a growing fraction of pay is becoming "contingent"—on individual job performance, on the fortunes of the employer, on the current state of the "animal spirits" in the stock market, or on what the company thinks it can get for its money by turning to suppliers in other, lower-cost locations. Whatever the causes, the results are stagnating long-run average wages, declining personal mobility over time, and (possibly) increasing uncertainty in what a person's earnings next year will be.

This is all part of what I have called the dark side of the era of flexible accumulation.

## Notes

1. E.g., David Hirschberg, "Small Business Blarney: What Does It Take to Kill a Bad Number?" posed on *Slate,* the on-line magazine from Microsoft, on October 18, 1996.
2. For such evidence, see Dave Marcotte, "Evidence of a Fall in the Wage Premium of Job Security," Center for Governmental Studies, Northern Illinois University, 1994; Barry Bluestone and Stephen Rose, "Overworked and Underemployed," *American Prospect* (March-April 1997); and Stephen Rose, "The Decline of Employment Stability in the 1980s," National Commission on Employment Policy, Washington, DC, 1995.
3. Cited in *Business Week,* January 27, 1997, p. 20.
4. Peter Gottschalk and Robert Moffitt, "The Growth of Earnings Instability in the U.S. Labor Market," Brookings Papers on Economic Activity, no. 2 (1994). Some of this increasing volatility may be due to the growing incidence of performance-based pay and bonuses and, as such, is built into the new work systems by design.
5. Annette Bernhard, Martina Morris, Mark Handcock, and Marc Scott, "Job Instability and Wage Inequality: Preliminary Results from Two NLS Cohorts," Institute on Education and the Economy, Teachers College, Columbia University, February 11, 1997, p. 15.
6. Peter Cappelli et al., *Change at Work* (New York: Oxford University Press, 1997), p. 12.

 **Article Review Form at end of book.**

Are large companies inherently at a disadvantage in terms of their operational agility? Why or why not?

# Organizational Design in the 21st Century

Is "nimble behemoth" an oxymoron? Not necessarily, says one consultant.

Everybody seems to agree that the command-and-control model of corporate organization will not survive into the next century, and a number of new models have been suggested as replacements. One such model has been devised by Bruce A. Pasternack and Albert J. Viscio, the founding partners of Booz Allen & Hamilton's Strategic Leadership Practice.

Unlike other management thinkers, Pasternack and Viscio do not believe that only small companies will have the agility to compete in the coming century. Their model considers the advantage of size and is based on people, knowledge, and coherence. It is built around a global core, which provides strategic leadership, helps distribute and provide access to the company's capabilities and knowledge, creates the corporate identity, ensures access to low-cost capital, and exerts control over the enterprise as a whole.

JBS recently spoke with Mr. Viscio about the "centerless" corporation, which he and his co-author described in *The Centerless Corporation: A New Model for*

*Transforming Your Organization for Growth and Prosperity* (Simon & Schuster, 1998).

**JBS** You define the centerless corporation as a distributed business in which business units act autonomously. But you point out that there is also a need to cohere and to communicate across business unit boundaries. How do you reconcile those two needs?

**Viscio** Historically, there has been tension in organizations between providing direction from the top but also pushing accountability down into the ranks. The question they ask is, should we centralize or decentralize? We think that's the wrong question. You want to treat the company as a system just as your own body is a system—each part is a contributor, acts on its own, but yet there's overall direction and maintenance at the system level.

After all, what's the sense of being big if you can't use your size? In fact, we decided to write this book because we think that companies can be big and still grow and be profitable, and that the stagnation that one sees at

some big companies occurs simply because they're too hierarchical and really haven't developed a systems approach to the business. The top doesn't let go and empower employees and doesn't focus on the key things the company has at the system level—namely its people, what it knows, and what ties that together. Achieving this focus is the real mission of senior management.

**JBS** In the organization you describe, it's essential that people cooperate with each other. But cooperation is an unnatural thing, as you point out in your book. How can companies ensure the necessary unity?

**Viscio** The model for the centerless corporation is a cooperative model—people must be willing to participate as part of a team to make it effective. That's a mindset change. That's a leadership challenge. The leaders have to ensure that the system has cohesion by making sure people understand not only what the corporation is trying to do but also that each person must contribute to those goals.

If we look at the performance of big companies, say the Fortune 100, we see they've shed a million-and-a-half jobs. That's not a very successful model. But if you take a look at the economy, it's creating jobs like gangbusters. This suggests the Fortune 100 are not taking advantage of their size. So companies now are working to create more cooperative models. They look at the benefits they can derive from sharing services and coordinating purchases to take advantage of their size and leverage.

Companies that have done this well have forced change. Let's take Wal-Mart, for example. Wal-Mart will tell Procter & Gamble, "I'm not going to deal with 100 people in your sales organization, I want a single point of contact." So P&G might have to reorganize in order to provide that point of contact. But the benefits flow to both. The improved process reduces inventory and makes ordering more efficient, which means both partners enjoy lower costs, higher profits, greater stability, and greater flexibility.

Centerless companies are really tearing the business apart and saying, "We have to focus on the two or three things that are creating the value." Everything else you can share or do outside the company and just focus on the key things that are important.

It's unlike the old-fashioned company, which would do everything itself. Most old-fashioned companies are fortresses, and they're inward-looking. But the need to build coherence forces companies to be outward looking. And once they start looking out, they see market opportunities and potential links with other companies.

**JBS** What companies do you think are closest to being centerless corporations?

**Viscio** At the top of my list are GE and Hewlett Packard, because they're very coherent companies. People know what the company is up to. Both GE and HP have unique systems for developing people and pushing the frontiers of performance. They have cultures that don't tolerate any bad performance and do encourage innovation. But they do it different ways. Jack Welch charges ahead, saying, "Here's what we're going to do," and he gets people to follow him. HP accomplishes the same thing through its culture—the HP Way.

**JBS** Does it take a special kind of leadership talent to run centerless corporation? And how prevalent do you think that talent is?

**Viscio** Nowhere near prevalent enough. People are trained at early career levels to be managers, which means you're given a task and you execute the task. What's required in the future is more leadership—you see what has to be done and you initiate it and get it done. Now the challenge for any large corporation is to create a cascading of leadership, so that there's leadership at the top, but also leadership down at the bottom, and all the leaders are marching to the same tune.

The real job of the CEO is to build that kind of leadership throughout the organization. That's why we're seeing more and more companies worried about executive development, people development, giving greater accountability. You have to empower people to get leadership; you need greater coaching to get leadership. And not all companies have the ability to do that effectively. Over time more will.

**JBS** How do you build a deep bench in an era of downsizing when the middle management ranks, out of which you would get your future leaders, are now decimated?

**Viscio** You need different roles at different levels. You need to create leaders not at middle management levels but early on. You need to train people to be leaders, leaders of tasks. And once you start building and creating leadership skills from early on, there's not much of a role for this traditional middle management anyway. Middle management should be a networking function, tying different pieces of the company together, coaching. It's not hierarchical, where you had seven layers of middle management. That's just not going to fly.

**JBS** How would you sum up the leader's role in the centerless corporation?

**Viscio** A leader's role is really to serve the people. And a leader has to come up with a vision that makes people say, "I want to follow that. I believe it. I think it's valuable. It's the kind of life that I want to live. I want to work in this company because I like its values, I like the opportunity it affords me, it's career enriching."

We find in our own experience if our staff are not happy, they go someplace else. Why work someplace if you're unhappy? Motorola, for example, in its performance reviews, asks people, "Do you have an enriching job? Are you happy with what you do?"

So part of the leader's role is to provide that vision, the meaning in the work environment. Part of the leader's role is to knock down barriers blocking the vision. And part of a leader's role is to empower people to work toward it.

I don't think this is especially hard to do; I just think the talent for that kind of leadership wasn't often cultivated in corporations in the past. But now companies are looking for people who can work across the network and see opportunities outside the boundaries, the emphasis is on being more creative and feeling there are opportunities there. That means you need to promote the people with the attributes that you want.

This is not something that you're going to turn on a dime. You're really changing the role of senior management, and these people have to become leaders in a very different sense. The really good companies are already doing that.

 **Article Review Form at end of book.**

How will prototypical future organizations likely be similar to and different from those that currently characterize commerce?

# The Struggle to Create an Organization for the 21st Century

**Rahul Jacob**

In the manic rush to devise principles by which to manage and motivate companies, it is increasingly difficult to tell the big idea from the fashionable quick fix. An idea, reengineering, say, is hailed as the new cure-all. A herd of companies tears around chanting the new mantra, often without clear strategic objectives. Then the rush to judgment begins: "The best thing we ever did!" "No, an utter flop!" And so it goes.

Take heart: That rare thing, a consensus, is beginning to evolve around a model corporation for perhaps the next 50 years—the horizontal corporation. After more than half a century during which the functional hierarchy was the dominant—really the only—model for organizational design, we are on the cusp of a fundamental transition, suggests David Robinson, president of CSC Index: "Changes in operating models are the tectonic shifts of the business world. They don't happen often, but when they do, they flatten the unprepared." In Robinson's opin-

ion, just such a change is under way: "It's a shift from [competing on] what we make to how we make it." American Express Financial Advisors, which is moving toward a more horizontal organization, sells financial products—insurance and mutual funds, for example. But its organizational redesign focuses on how its financial planners sell these products, emphasizing building relationships with customers.

The horizontal corporation includes these potent elements: Teams will provide the foundation of organizational design. They will not be set up inside departments, like marketing, but around core processes, such as new-product development. Process owners, not department heads, will be the top managers, and they may sport wonderfully weird titles; GE Medical Systems has a "vice president of global sourcing and order to remittance."

Rather than focusing single-mindedly on financial objectives or functional goals, the horizontal organization emphasizes customer satisfaction. Work is simplified and hierarchy flattened by com-

bining related tasks—for example, an account-management process that subsumes the sales, billing, and service functions—and eliminating work that does not add value. Information zips along an internal superhighway: The knowledge worker analyzes it, and technology moves it quickly across the corporation instead of up and down, speeding up and improving decision-making.

Okay, so some of this is derivative; the obsession with process, for example, dates back to Total Quality Management. Part of the beauty of the horizontal corporation is that it distills much of what we know about what works in managing today. Its advocates call it an "actionable model"—jargon for a plan you can work with—that allows companies to use ideas like teams, supplier-customer integration, and empowerment in ways that reinforce each other. A key virtue, says Pat Hoye, dealer-service support manager at Ford Motor, is that the horizontal corporation is the kind of company a customer would design. The customer, after all, doesn't care about the service department's goals or the dealer's sales targets; he just wants his car fixed right and on time—so the organization makes those objectives paramount. In most cases, a horizontal organization requires some employees to be organized functionally where their expertise is considered critical, as in human resources or finance. But those departments are often pared down and judiciously melded into a design where the real authority runs along process lines. Done right, says Frank Ostroff, a McKinsey consultant who with former colleague Douglas Smith devised a clear, coherent architecture for the new model in 1992, "the horizontal corporation can take you from 100 horsepower to 500 horsepower."

As never before, management will make all the difference. Getting from here (the vertical, functional organization) to there (the horizontal, process-based one) is quite possibly the greatest management challenge of our time. Unraveling lines of authority and laying out new ones can entangle a company as quickly as a kitten will get tied up with a ball of wool. It is critical, experts say, that processes be defined with adequate breadth, which ensures that they span the company and include customers and suppliers. The challenge, almost by definition, is an epic one; you can't timidly test it in one corner of the organization. Says Mercer Management Consulting's David Miron: "That's like building a house one room at a time without a master plan. You never engage management in thinking about all the customer accountabilities and all of the suppliers in the process flow." Yet ever larger legions of companies are taking up the challenge. Four organizations that have started down this road show how long and hazardous it can be. They're well on their way—but not there yet.

## American Express Financial Advisors

When a company is basking in the glow of 21% annual earnings growth over the past five years, it takes a special nerve to turn it inside out. American Express Financial Advisors, based in Minneapolis, contributed a hefty $428 million to its parent company's profit of $1.4 billion in 1994. But these rosy earnings disguised a thorny problem: heavy attrition of its 8,000 planners—independent contractors who exclusively sell middle-class Americans an array of AEFA financial products like mutual funds, insurance, and investment certificates for a commission. Only 30% of the planners stayed for four years. Another problem: Selling on commission may be the norm in the industry, but people at AEFA believe it leaves them vulnerable to tomorrow's competitors.

Like whom, precisely? Like Bill Gates, replies Douglas Lennick, an executive vice president, referring to Microsoft's yet-to-be-approved acquisition of Intuit, maker of Quicken software, which allows users to pay bills, manage finances, and track investments online from their PCs. Says Lennick: "The marketplace does not want cold calling and adversarial tactics. Unless the industry responds better to clients, they'll turn to the equivalent of the automatic teller machine. Quicken is an emerging torpedo boat." By year-end AEFA intends to put an end to cold calling and to award planners—and managers—bonuses for scoring well on client-satisfaction surveys. The goals of the redesign are explicit: a 95% client-retention rate, 80% planner retention after four years, and annual revenue growth of 18%.

To reach these goals, AEFA knew it could not content itself with installing teams at the front line and giving extra training and software support to planners, though it is doing both of those. More important, AEFA brought elements of the horizontal corporation into its gracious 29th-floor executive offices in 1994. The position of general sales manager was dropped; those responsibilities are now shared by seven executives. Each has a vertical responsibility, usually regional, and "owns" a process that horizontally spans the organization—a process like client satisfaction or account management. Below the senior managers, 180 divisions have been reconfigured into 45 clusters led by group vice presidents, who own processes like new planner integration.

Organizing by process calls for a difficult and time-consuming hand-over of power, something you don't hear much about amid all the hosannas when companies reorganize. Says Lennick: "This creates a lot of trauma. People are saying, 'How can you take my district away from me?' " Simply defining what job belongs in which process can be confusing. "One of the beauties of the vertical, functional organization is that who you report to and who's the boss is very, very clear. The new system creates ambiguity for everybody," says Barry Murphy, AEFA's animated vice president of client service. For example, the executive team initially made client acquisition part of the marketing process. Later the team decided it was more appropriately Murphy's job, since satisfying the client begins at the very beginning.

Because AEFA is a successful company with strong leadership, the strategic vision of the redesign seems to be shared across the company, which improves its chances of success. Marilyn Pierson, a senior financial adviser in the Cleveland office, has taken to the new client-satisfaction she recently received back from her clients: "It's very valuable. If we want long-term clients, this is how we go about it."

Is going horizontal a euphemism for being spread too thin? Worries Brij Singh, a region director based in Cleveland: "There is a lot going on. My concern is that something could fall through the cracks." AEFA's single-minded focus on its horizontal design may also have hobbled its ability to take advantage of opportunities. While CEO Harvey Golub is pushing American Express to think more globally, AEFA has made few moves to capitalize on the growth of a large middle class in Asia and Latin America. This is a characteristic weakness of the horizontal corporation, argues Boston Consulting Group's Philippe Amouyal, who attacked the concept in a provocative article he co-authored. An organization obsessed with satisfying today's customer is prone to miss tomorrow's. The focus on process, he says, is not enough. A corporation must continually be replenished by its core, functional disciplines—"the professional excellence that elevates a company's processes from best practices to competitive breakthroughs."

## Ford Motors Customer Service Division

If proof were needed that the horizontal, process-based corporation has widespread appeal, here it is: Even Detroit is among the disciples. Ford's 6,200-employee customer service division is ripping up its organization chart to focus on increasing customer satisfaction, a yardstick by which it trails not only the Japanese but even General Motors. Says Ronald Goldsberry, the mildly theatrical division general manager: "We looked to see if anywhere in the division we had a quantifiable goal of 'fix it right the first time.' We couldn't find one. It shocked us."

After a 2½-year study, Ford announced last fall that it was organizing around four key processes that create customer satisfaction on the service side of the business: Fixing it right the first time on time, supporting dealers and handling customers, engineering cars with ease of service in mind, and developing service fixes quicker. Like most companies going horizontal, Ford elected to keep some employees organized in functions like employee relations or the controller's office, where specialized expertise was deemed critical. The division has stopped selling parts to independent repair shops directly, even though this was profitable, because it didn't contribute to customer satisfaction and customer retention, the new touchstones.

That's the right way to think about something as fundamental as the transition from a functional organization to a horizontal one, says McKinsey's Ostroff: "This is not just about efficiency. It starts from 'Where do we want to be in

ten years? What business do we want to be in? What are the processes that drive that?" Ford made building easy-to-repair cars one of its core processes, and so rather than pinching pennies, it has doubled staffing in upstream engineering.

Dealer support is a second core process. Dealers are independent businessmen, but obviously Ford's effort to improve service would be a nonstarter without their cooperation. To enlist it, Ford is simplifying the way it works with dealers by reducing the battery of functional experts—parts specialists, marketing incentive specialists, and many, many more—dealers routinely dealt with.

Ford has abandoned its functional organization in pilot projects in Minneapolis and the Washington, D.C., area. There, field teams to serve dealers are making a promising debut. Teams are staffed by a divisional operations manager, a field engineer, and a customer service representative—three people, vs. 25 in the old, hierarchical field office. Says Dick Strauss, a Ford dealer in Richmond: "It removes several layers of hierarchy we had to go through for official recognition of a customer problem. Now we make decisions on the spot in out-of-warranty situations, and the customer service rep backs us up." Despite widespread support from dealers, the pilots, which started in the summer of 1993, will not be evaluated till the summer of this year, when Ford will decide whether they will be rolled out across the country.

This raises a nagging question: Is Ford moving fast enough? The company is just beginning to experiment with systems that complement the horizontal organizational design, like 360-degree performance reviews. Budgets are still drawn up on departmental lines. Says Marshall Roe, who heads the division's business strategy and communications: "There are things we have to solve before we pull the trigger. In the past if we got close enough, we'd pull the trigger and pick up the pieces later."

Still, managers who once competed for resources now work in teams alongside finance folk and are actually putting money they think they won't need back on the table. Dealers seem excited. The division has its new structure in place. It has defined comprehensive core processes. It has set the bold stretch target of increasing customer retention—the percentage of Ford owners whose next car is also a Ford—from 60% to 80%. Each additional percentage point is worth a staggering $100 million in profits, Ford estimates.

Trouble is, consumer perception is a stubborn beast to ride. As it tools down the horizontal highway, Ford will have its work cut out for it staying abreast of competitors, who are also focusing on after-sales service as never before. Says Ford's Donald Sparkman: "If you take too long, you could miss the market." Which may explain why some industry veterans aren't impressed. "They've set themselves a pretty big challenge. It's a noble goal," says Jake Kelderman, executive director for industry affairs for the National Auto Dealers Association, making a game effort to stifle his skepticism: "In this industry we hear a lot of talk about doing things differently. The minute the objectives are not achieved, people are off to something else."

## GE Medical Systems, Milwaukee

Imagine a manufacturing operation where the manager in charge confesses he can't evaluate his three direct reports because he sees too little of them. Go down two layers to a production associate, a union steward to boot, who says he won't talk to his manager unless there is a problem because his manager has plenty on his plate. (He does check for E-mail messages daily, though.) Chaotic, you wonder? Far from it. This is a plant that has cut the time it takes for its order-to-remittance process—the period from when an order is received through shipment to payment—by 40% over the past three years.

GE Medical Systems is a tale of delayering run riot. In the Eighties, Frank Waltz took over the Milwaukee plant that makes magnetic resonance imaging machines. The managers of the nearby X-ray and CT scanner facilities moved to other positions in the past four years, so Waltz has assumed those jobs as well. Over the past six years two layers beneath him have been torn out altogether. In the X-ray facility, for instance, only a production manager stands between him and 170 people on the factory floor. Says Waltz: "Every year the organization changes. I would expect it to change next year."

Bet on it: His boss, Serge Huot, a direct French Canadian who is vice president of global sourcing and order to remittance, wonders in all seriousness if the organization is delayering fast enough: "In a big organization each layer slows down the process. By delayering you are giving people the power to change. Too many companies

spend too much time thinking about this. By the time they do it, the train's passed them."

When you're as flat as GE Medical is in Milwaukee, a lot of what some companies see as the niceties of the horizontal corporation are revealed to be necessities. Waltz is perfectly matter-of-fact about why production associates routinely visit GE facilities in Europe: "They see things the managers don't see." Elsewhere, people use 360-degree appraisals to shift employee focus—for example, to get employees to pay attention to more than pleasing the boss. Waltz has a more basic reason: "When it comes to evaluating managers who report to me, I can't do it alone. I see them for a few minutes a week sometimes. I don't know how they are doing their jobs."

Quite nicely, it turns out. At the X-ray facility, a team of engineers, production associates, and sourcing staff reduced the time needed to install complex X-ray machines at customer sites from 350 hours a couple of years ago to a third of that today. They did this in part by letting production associates perform calibration and radiation tests that used to be done by field engineers. The CT scanner facility hasn't missed a delivery since the first quarter of 1994.

Is this, then, the perfect organization? "You haven't asked me about the stress," says Bob Claudio, a production group leader in testing. We're all ears, Bob. There's plenty, he confirms: Most days after work he goes home, lies down, and listens to music for an hour to recoup. Barb Barras, who started out at the plant 23 years ago in an entry-level position in subassembly production, says her colleagues' response to the delayering is mixed; people like the greater responsibility, but some dislike the accountability that goes with it. In her current position she uses CAD systems to plot the production process flow, a job reserved for engineers until a couple of years ago. Says Barras: "Twenty years ago you came in, you punched a clock. Nobody came and asked you whether there was a better way to do this."

## Karolinska Hospital

Like many state-funded hospitals in Europe, prestigious Karolinska Hospital in Stockholm faced financial difficulties in 1992, in its case a reduction of funding by about 20%. Karolinska's then chief executive, Jan Lindsten, dreaded the prospect: He felt the hospital had already cut as much as it could without impairing the quality of care. When he turned to the hospital's professional advisory board, which includes the CEOs of companies like Volvo, they suggested trying Boston Consulting Group's Time Based Management methods to radically change the way work was done. BCG promptly set about reorganizing work at the hospital around patient flow. Instead of bouncing a patient from department to department, BCG advised, look at illness to recovery as a process with pit stops in admission, surgery, and a recovery ward.

What this means in practice is that patients now meet a surgeon and a doctor of internal medicine together, for instance, rather than separately, which results in better care and fewer hospital visits. Says Mikael Lovgren, a BCG consultant who worked with Karolinska: "Hospitals don't think along the patient dimen-

sion. They think only in terms of specializations"—not unlike many companies that manage only their functions and thereby obscure their line of vision to customers.

Karolinska's problems as it began to transform itself into a horizontal organization were compounded by the fact that it had recently been through a major decentralization, which had created 47 departments marching to their own drums. Tribalism is the human condition, it seems, within hospitals as well as corporations. Lindsten had brought the number down to 11, but coordination was still woefully haphazard. Patients had to scale the high walls between functions, often making multiple all-day visits to the hospital for tests. A patient with an enlarged prostate gland spent, on average, an astounding 255 days after his first contact with the hospital before it was treated; only 2% of that time involved actual treatment—the rest was passed waiting for appointments, shuttling between departments, and so on.

To manage patient flow, most departments in the hospital created a new position, that of "nurse coordinator," whose responsibilities include minimizing the number of visits a patient must make. Nurse coordinators— one might call them "process doctors"—look for situations where the baton is dropped in the handoff between or within departments. The position has also created a career track for nurses, who can aspire to become administrative heads of various departments. Departments have a medical chief as well, who is responsible for the professional expertise that is so obviously important in a hospital. Says

Sonia Wallin, a nurse coordinator, who has worked at Karolinska since 1981: "I report to a nurse who is over the doctors. A few years ago that would have been impossible."

Not all the doctors are entirely comfortable reporting to nurses, even on purely administrative matters. The new structure has been sold to physicians as a way to free them from scheduling and other drudgery. They can concentrate instead on their clinical work and research. Some departments at Karolinska have taken to the concept of patient flow faster than others— orthopedic and plastic surgery share a ward, for example—yet hospital managers are sanguine. Says Einar Areklett, a senior manager: "Running a hospital is like running an opera house. You have a lot of Pavarottis. It takes a few years before you have everyone with you."

One of the clear lessons managers involved in similar transitions can take away from Karolinska is the need for what Reengineering Management author James Champy calls "honest eloquence." Lindsten, who has since left to take charge of a similar redesign of a hospital in Copenhagen, consistently framed his exhortations for change in the context of the hostile external environment the hospital faced. Staff moved quickly from disbelief to action. Waiting times for surgery have been cut from six or eight months to three weeks. Three of 15 operating theaters have been closed, yet 3,000 more operations are performed annually, a 25% increase. Says Dr. Sten Lindahl, head of the department of anesthesiology and intensive care: "We would hate to go back to the lazy days."

That's the funny thing about newly horizontal companies. People get positively proprietary about them. Take John Vanderpoel, a team leader in AEFA's back office, who took his 20-member team out to dinner to celebrate five good months. A rare but rich pleasure; he wasn't able to spend time with the entire team as often as he would like, he said.

Across the hall sits Sandy Weeks, a service associate in the new business section. She began ten years ago in a department that only performed address changes on accounts, an example of Taylorism gone crazy. She exudes a quiet pride in her work, though she confesses that she sometimes finds her increased responsibilities daunting. To help her in those times, she's tacked a quotation from Machiavelli's *The Prince* onto a wall in her cubicle. Because it addresses the anxieties of anyone caught in the throes of organizational change and illustrates how one woman has embraced the challenge, some of it seems worth reproducing:

It must be considered that there is nothing more difficult to carry out, nor more doubtful of success, nor more dangerous to handle, than to initiate a new order of things.

 **Article Review Form at end of book.**

# WiseGuide Wrap-Up

- Managers have a responsibility to create organizational structures that facilitate the accomplishment of enterprise objectives. The range of possible ways to organize work is infinite; clearly, however, there is no one best way to organize.

- The "best" organizational structure or form is one that matches the organization's capabilities to its environment so as to accomplish organizational goals.

- The current business orthodoxy advocates flatter, less hierarchical organizations. In many instances, these organizational forms create more responsive, more economical structures; however, there are implementation issues and consequences for organization members.

## R.E.A.L. Sites

This list provides a print preview of typical **Coursewise** R.E.A.L. sites. (There are over 100 such sites at the **Courselinks**™ site.) The danger in printing URLs is that web sites can change overnight. As we went to press, these sites were functional using the URLs provided. If you come across one that isn't, please let us know via email to: webmaster@coursewise.com. Use your Passport to access the most current list of R.E.A.L. sites at the **Courselinks** site.

**Site name:** Gareth Morgan: Research and Writings

**URL:** http://www.yorku.ca/faculty/academic/gmorgan/index.html

**Why is it R.E.A.L.?** This site provides useful information and materials from an influential and provocative source on organizational theory. Professor Morgan has some of the most interesting ideas regarding organizations and our lives in them.

**Key topics:** management of change, organizational development, organizational control

**Try this:** Find some metaphors for organizations and their management that you consider particularly apt.

**Site name:** Organized Change

**URL:** http://www.organizedchange.com/index2.html

**Why is it R.E.A.L.?** This is the homepage for a group of organizational change consultants.

**Key topics:** organizational change, organizational development

**Try this:** Provide advice on decisions that must be made before undertaking planned organizational change.

**Site name:** Growing an Ownership Culture

**URL:** http://www.nceo.org/columns/ci1.html

**Why is it R.E.A.L.?** How do newly "empowered" employees react when their suggestions are not immediately acted on?

**Key topics:** organizational design, organizational development

**Try this:** How could a university create an "ownership culture"?

**Site name:** Center for Creative Leadership

**URL:** http://www.ccl.org/

**Why is it R.E.A.L.?** Founded in 1970, the Center for Creative Leadership is a nonprofit, international educational institution dedicated to furthering effective leadership.

**Key topics:** nature of management, organizational development, research reports

**Try this:** Find and summarize an article on the management of change in organizations.

# section
# 5

Sometimes, management is defined or operationalized as decision making. Certainly, a preeminent function of managers is to develop and choose among alternatives—in other words, to make decisions. And commercial marketplaces tend to provide managers with relatively quick and unambiguous feedback regarding the efficacy of their decisions.

As your text and professor have no doubt advised you, classic decision making is a process in which you define a problem, articulate and evaluate alternative courses of action, and decide which course of action to implement. While this concept sounds relatively simple and logical, your personal experience has probably shown that it can be considerably more complicated and ambiguous in practice.

Most postsecondary business schools require students to take advanced mathematics courses as a part of their education. At least part of the rationale for this math requirement is that studying mathematics helps management students develop logical, rational reasoning processes. But are the problems confronting managers logical and rational? Can managers rationalize their decisions using quantitative methods? A good philosophical argument can ensue from these questions and would likely not end with a definitive answer.

Most students and management practitioners would agree, however, that resolutions to real problems in the world of work are decided on the basis of incomplete information—there is not enough time to get the information, or the matter at hand is not important enough to collect every bit of relevant information. Decisions have to be made with the information that *is* available and on the basis of what Herbert Simon called "bounded rationality." In Reading 20, Jeffrey Seglin makes this point regarding incomplete and inadequate information, and offers his perspective on the ethical implications of deciding on the basis of company survival.

Reading 21 offers an interesting perspective on the extent to which management theory in general, and game theory in particular, can help managers divine the intentions of their competitors. A great deal of management theory has developed around efforts to use quantitative methods to help capture the complexity of decisions and evaluate alternatives. In Reading 22, Art Hammer makes the point that managers should use mathematical considerations to determine their decisions.

The dawning of the new millennium has provoked a variety of lists of greatest people, greatest events, and so forth. Not to leave the field of management out, this section offers Reading 23, which lists and describes the seventy-five greatest management decisions ever made.

As a bit of a counterpoint to Reading 21, the authors of Reading 24—Mary Crossan, Roderick White, Henry Lane, and Leo Klus— provide a perspective on the necessity for managerial innovation and creativity to deal with the complexity and ambiguity of modern organizational circumstances.

- Describe the limits to rationality in managerial decision making.

- Identify the characteristics of problems that make them amenable to solutions utilizing quantitative methods.

- Analyze managerial decisions and be able to describe qualities that lead to success or failure.

- Explain how flexibility can facilitate organizational success.

# ? Questions ?

**Reading 20.** How does the availability, or paucity, of information impact the ethical implications of a business decision?

**Reading 21.** How can management theory assist in ascertaining the intention of business competitors?

**Reading 22.** Describe the sorts of management problems that can best be solved through the use of quantitative methods and how those methods can best be used.

**Reading 23.** Which decisions were you most surprised to find on the list of the 75 greatest management decisions?

**Reading 24.** To what extent do you believe that the use of a jazz metaphor to describe managerial work is appropriate and accurate? Why?

How does the availability, or paucity, of information impact the ethical implications of a business decision?

# Black and White

**Jeffrey L. Seglin**

*Jeffrey L. Seglin is an executive director at Inc.*

"I'm at my board meeting," begins the CEO of a $20-million company that repairs aircraft engines, "and I get this fax from the airline saying that eight aircraft my company had repaired engine parts for were on the ground. They were not going to let the jets fly because the turbines went kaput. And they were saying that our parts had caused the problem.

"Within a couple of hours," he continues, "I get another call saying that another aircraft is downed by another airline in another country for the same reason. Then an hour later, another call. And then another. In all, 11 planes were grounded because of what they were saying were our parts." If the airlines ultimately needed to lease aircraft to cover those routes—and if his company was indeed found negligent—this CEO was looking at a $40-million tab. Put delicately, his company would be ruined.

In decades as an engine-repair manufacturer, he'd amassed a stellar reputation for quality. His company, which worked with 15 airlines, had also been ap-

proved as a supplier by the Federal Aviation Administration and by all the major aircraft-engine manufacturers. "Oh, sure, I'd had incidents in the past," he says, "but nothing to this extent."

By the time he'd first heard about the problem, FAA had already been notified by the airline and had started an investigation out of its local office. "If they wanted to," says the CEO, "the FAA could have decided to close not only the factory where those specific parts were repaired but all of our factories to scrutinize us, check our procedures, check all our people. Of course, that's what you want when you fly. You want to make absolutely 100% certain that the engines are safe. But for us as a business, such a companywide inspection would have been the end." And he could only imagine what might happen once word of such an investigation reached all of his lenders. "I had short-term loans with about eight banks for an amount of money equal to my equity in the business," he says. "They could have pulled those loans."

But—so far, anyway—the FAA hadn't notified his company of any such drastic impending ac-

tion. And as much as the airline may have pointed the finger at his business as the likely culprit, the company's name had managed to stay out of the press accounts. As a result, the CEO reasoned that there was no compelling need for him to do anything but remain in a holding pattern until more details emerged. As a strategy, at least for the short term, it sounded workable. If not, that is, for an unfortunate accident of timing.

The company, it so happened, was in the midst of an annual audit. As part of that process, the chief executive officer and the chief financial officer must sign a letter assuring the auditors that they have been informed about any outstanding circumstances that more than likely could have a negative financial impact. "The document was sitting on my desk waiting for my signature," says the CEO. "I was going to have to decide whether or not to sign it or to tell the auditors about the extent of our problem."

The stakes couldn't have gotten any higher: coming clean on the audit statement about the exact details he had in hand would have likely set off a chain reaction that would have left his company in shards. But given the state of what he knew—wildly incomplete—it seemed premature to put the life of his company, and the livelihood of hundreds of employees, in serious peril. It was frustrating. "In my industry there's a very tight code of ethics about the use of drugs or alcohol by a manufacturer's employees," he says. "But there's nothing that tells you how you're supposed to deal with reporting information like this."

So there he was, with few guidelines to follow and a set of audit papers awaiting his signature. What should he do?

These days, of course, it's not all that unusual to have to make crucial business decisions based on information that ranges from incomplete (at best) to woefully inadequate. A fast-moving economy puts a premium on those who can act with a decisiveness that gains speed in proportion to the skimpiness of the information at hand. To take advantage of opportunities, you need to think and act fast. So, for example, do you risk going into new markets when you're not sure you have the capital to back you up if you fail? Do you bring on new employees before that new market is fully developed? Do you increase overhead further by leasing office space to accommodate those employees without really knowing if the new market opportunities are as sure a thing as you told your board or your investors or your employees they were? And so on.

This CEO, facing a monumental decision, wanted to do what he believed to be the right thing. The lens through which he naturally scrutinized the situation was the one he'd used over all the years he'd been running a business: How do I do what I need to do to keep my company alive and thriving and, at the same time, minimize my financial and legal exposure?

First he asked his board, with whom he had been meeting when that original fax came in. "My directors advised against doing anything that would raise more alarm that we were out of control about the issue than necessary," he says. Aside from talking to his own lawyers, he also hired lawyers and consultants who specialized in FAA investigations. From their input he fashioned a delicate response.

"When it came time," he reflects back now, "to sign the representation letter from the auditors asking if I had any unreported information that would affect the financial performance of the company, I withheld the information. I consulted my lawyers and wrote that we had a problem and that we were on top of that problem. I didn't get any more specific about it. And they didn't ask."

In a pending investigation like this one, such a disclosure is not all that peculiar, according to Lynford Graham, director of audit policy at the New York City office of BDO Seidman LLP. (BDO Seidman was not the audit firm representing this CEO.) "Since the investigation had just been started and no responsibility had been assumed by the company, it's pretty unlikely that anything more needed to be disclosed at that point," says Graham. It's not unusual, he says, for such broad statements to be included in a company's financial statements, particularly if the situation doesn't affect the finances for the year's books being audited. Such language has become almost boiler-

plate to cover the multitude of possible adverse conditions a company may face that aren't accounted for anywhere else.

But even though he was able to use the elusive language that was standard operating procedure in dealings like this—and tantamount to not saying anything about anything—the CEO was still grappling with having to make a decision without knowing all that he needed to know. "I was frustrated that we weren't in control of the problem," he says. "It was in control of us. It was far beyond us, far beyond us. One of my biggest fears was that the groundings wouldn't stop with those 11 planes and that it would spread to all the airlines. After a while I knew this wasn't likely to happen, but it was a real fear, and it still ate away at me."

But that was not reason enough for him to risk his company and disclose everything he did know. "If you have a business that's going to react to remote possibilities, then everybody's going to be nervous, and nobody's going to be able to do anything," says BDO Seidman's Graham. It's certainly true that the CEO's actions kept the company in operation. "I didn't inform everybody about everything," the CEO says. "Of course, the situation would have been different if an engine had exploded in air."

Not that that was likely to happen—or was it? At the time, press reports pointed out that there was the remote yet daunting possibility that engine fragments could break off, hit the fuselage, and cause a crash. A critical factor to consider, you would think, yet one the CEO admits he chose to ignore. Yes, he weighed the consequences of having his bankers and employees know. But as he tells it now, several years later, he never considered the lives that could be at stake. While he was valiantly fighting to save the jobs of his employees, shouldn't he have weighed his responsibility to passengers boarding other possibly defective planes? That, he claims, was the FAA's burden.

This CEO was concerned about the impact his decision would have on some of his constituencies—his bankers, his employees—but he neglected to consider the constituency with potentially the most to lose: airline passengers. As a frequent flier, a user of headache remedies, a driver of cars, a consumer of meals, I'd like to believe that standard ethical behavior calls for companies—and certainly the people at the top—to always consider the vulnerability of consumers in their decisions. Had he acknowledged that angle, would it have changed what he told his auditors? Not likely, and that, as it turns out, might have been appropriate, since the FAA exonerated his company of direct responsibility for the groundings and even concluded that passengers were never in danger. But safety should have been among his considerations before he signed that auditor's statement.

It's natural for leaders of fast-growing companies to become desensitized to certain outgrowths of their actions. But CEOs shouldn't allow themselves to become so numb that they can ignore situations in which the consequences are of potentially vast proportions.

Looking at every issue through the lens of a seasoned business owner who's conditioned to do what's necessary to keep a company alive and thriving, a CEO like this one can all too easily hide behind the regulator's responsibility, or boilerplate language, or standard operating procedures, and forget that sometimes there are much bigger issues to weigh in the equation. "What do I know about engines?" he asks now, by way of defending his reasoning. "As a businessman, I was looking at this in terms of my survival."

 **Article Review Form at end of book.**

How can management theory assist in ascertaining the intention of business competitors?

# Movers and Shakers

If you want to stay ahead of your competitors, it pays to know what they are thinking. Can management theory help?

When Square D's competitors learned of the firm's new strategy, they ridiculed the idea. The plan, leaked to an industry trade journal, was to shrink the time needed to deliver its circuit boards and other customised components used in commercial buildings. At the time (the late 1980s), the typical delivery took from ten to 12 weeks. Square D's plan was to slash that to a week, by holding higher inventories and getting its employees to work overtime. But this seemed ludicrous in an industry that demanded customisation and skilled labour. Fortunately, Square D had one thing going for it: the story was not true.

In fact, the entire tale had been fabricated by Square D to throw competitors off the scent. The firm, which has since been acquired, had discovered that customers would indeed pay a substantial premium for faster delivery, and it had devised an entirely new system of order-taking, product-design and assembly to satisfy this unmet demand. But Square D needed time, both to switch to the new methods and to find distributors who could implement the new approach.

Convincing competitors that it was heading in the wrong direction helped Square D gain the headstart it needed.

This kind of gamesmanship is common in the business world—and is one of the main reasons why economists often fail to be useful to businessmen. In many industries, firms bear little resemblance to the passive bodies portrayed in the traditional economics textbook. Instead managers try to anticipate the actions of others—whether they be competitors, suppliers or customers—and influence those actions to their advantage.

## Anyone for Chess?

Part of the task is assiduous routine fact-finding. In the 1990s, firms that offer "business intelligence" services have grown rapidly: the revenues of one, Kroll Associates, have tripled in the past three years. But it is hard for managers to create a clear picture of competitors from the fragmented images flashed before them. Information from salespeople, technical experts and the business press are sketchy—and often seem contradictory.

That is where game theory comes in. Its chief insight is simple: if a firm makes decisions based only on the current business environment, it will fail. In the real world, firms respond to threats and the environment changes. By analysing the others' potential responses, game theory adds another dimension to a firm's sleuthing. Instead of simply asking what another party is planning to do, game theory encourages managers to ask what is in the other's best interest.

This often involves the cut and thrust of competition. A well-timed investment, or price cut, can cause others to think twice before invading your patch. Only last week, for example, Boeing announced that it would make a new regional jet—a move that seems designed to undermine Airbus's attempts to design an aircraft for the same market.

But game theory is not only about intimidating competitors. In many cases, it illuminates the importance of winning people's trust. When Intel was trying to establish its chip as a standard, it had to convince PC makers that they would not be held hostage. By licensing its technology to others, it assured buyers of a competitive supply. Once Intel chips had become standard, and PCs were widely adopted, the firm stopped the practice.

However, Adam Brandenburger,* an economist at Harvard Business School, argues that game theory can also do something far more powerful. Through elaborate scenarios, it can help managers imagine how their industry would evolve if they were not part of it. This makes them aware of what it is that they in particular have to offer, while reminding them of other firms' strengths.

This, Mr. Brandenburger argues, is the secret of making money in many new sectors. By working together, firms can make a new sector grow more rapidly. Yet to obtain these advantages, firms must often give up some bargaining power. Striking a balance between co-operation and competition can be one of the

---
*Some of these ideas are summarised in "The Added Value Theory of Business," by Adam Brandenburger and Barry Nalebuff, in *Strategy & Business*, published by Booz, Allen & Hamilton, fourth quarter 1997.

manager's hardest tasks. The choice is often between dominating a small market or assuming a humbler role in a huge one.

By allowing Microsoft to license its operating system so that other firms could make PCs, IBM enabled the personal computer to grow far more rapidly than it would have if IBM had gone off on its own. Even though IBM itself missed many of the gains—which have been captured by Microsoft, Intel and rival PC makers—it still does a thriving business thanks to the PC market's sheer size. By contrast, Apple tried to hold on to its monopoly in the Macintosh market by refusing for many years to grant licenses.

Such co-operative rivalry, which has been given the ugly name of "co-opetition" by Ray Noorda, the founder of Novell, a software firm, crops up time and again in rapidly evolving industries. It is easy to see why Oracle, Netscape and Sun are together promoting the Java language, since the success of the network computer would create a bigger market for all three. Similarly, the

growth of defined-contribution pensions—in which employers offer a range of mutual funds to their workers, and make it easy for them to manage their investments—helps several different kinds of firm, from fund houses to custody providers to providers of information systems. By collaborating, these firms can help the industry take off.

The hallmark of such industries is confusion. From one moment to the next, firms cannot tell their allies from their rivals. Should Fidelity co-operate with other mutual funds by selling them through its "supermarket," or should it try to crush them by leaving them out? Should Microsoft try to prop up Apple, or drive it out of business?

These choices naturally lend themselves to game theory. This does not always mean that firms will triumph—merely that they can make the most of their opportunities. In business, as in other games, firms can only do as well as the hand they have been dealt.

 **Article Review Form at end of book.**

Describe the sorts of management problems that can best be solved through the use of quantitative methods and how those methods can best be used.

# The Numbers Man

Should managers consult algebra before they redesign their factory or launch a product? A mathematician from Tennessee thinks so.

In action films there is usually a moment when a fast-talking boffin is summoned from the depths of the CIA to explain exactly why Bruce Willis has to retrieve the multiversatile decoder (or whatever). Art Hammer is a little burly for the boffin part; and his southern accent is a little thick. But he has the right qualifications (a spell in nuclear-weapons design), and some engaging eccentricities (his office is in Tennessee, but he lives in Idaho and the Philippines). As for explaining complicated algebra quickly, he is hard to beat. He scribbles formulae upside down on a piece of paper on his lap in a convincingly logical way that only in retrospect seems, well, slightly incomprehensible.

Mathematicians are now commonplace in dealing rooms, but Mr. Hammer is applying algebra to "normal" business questions, such as "How should I change my factory?" or "What is the best way to sell my products?" He helps to run QualPro, a small consultancy started by another Cold-War mathematician,

Charles Holland. Mr. Hammer has aided companies such as Du Pont and Monsanto to redesign chemical plants, helped long-distance telephone firms to improve their marketing and even told the *National Enquirer* what to put on its cover.

These are precisely the sort of examples managers give to demonstrate that they practise an instinctive art, rather than a logical science. Yet they are too hasty. The modelling of real-world situations (such as, say, the conversion of climate change into numbers) is now commonplace in laboratories. And number-crunching exercises such as "data mining" (sifting through customer information) are on the rise in business too.

Anyhow, the "instinctive" way of taking decisions actually involves much trial and guesswork. A manager might be able to think of 30 plausible ways to speed up an assembly line. In practice, he will guess which handful matter most, play with them and see what happens. He will not experiment with more

variables, because it would be too time-consuming.

Mr. Hammer's "multivariable testing" (MVT) allows a more systematic approach. To demonstrate it, he shows how the managers of a hospital-products firm thought they might improve sales of surgical trays. To find the best possible combination for the seven options they identified, one should run 128 experiments (or 2 to the power of 7). However, Mr. Hammer's technique, based on maths that was invented in the 1930s and was first to work out how to shoot down German aircraft, requires only seven trials. Three variables are changed each time (shown in the table by ticks)* and the average effect of each variable is then calculated; in an eighth trial, for comparison, none of the options is attempted. MVT offers a way to combine variables and deduce a result.

Here the maths suggested that only training, cash commissions and holiday incentives would have much effect on sales. The employees' pet suggestion—

*Not included in this publication.

tailoring the tray to each customer—actually cut sales. The company duly increased holiday and commissions, increased training and ditched a plan to customise the trays. Sales soared.

Mr. Hammer claims that if a firm uses MVT alone, its tests will show about 70% of the theoretically possible improvements. So he suggests that, having used MVT to find the two or three main variables, clients should fine-tune the process by concentrating on all the combinations that involve those.

Some of Mr. Hammer's "optimum solutions" look obvious. Even when they do not, he never tries to explain why a variable matters. Such mathematical impartiality conveniently allows him to work for competitors; but he also claims that those who know a business well (like the sales people at the hospital-product firm) still get it wrong three times out of four.

## Under the Slide Rule

Mathematical testing has long been used in the military installations where Mr. Hammer used to work; it has also been used on the research side of agribusiness, to test the effect of pesticides. Many of QualPro's first clients were big chemical firms tinkering with their manufacturing. This year, however, most of Mr. Hammer's work is no longer about manufacturing processes such as producing better ethylene, but about selling services.

Surely guessing what consumers want has always been something of an art—more of an art, indeed, than stimulating sales of surgical trays? In reply, Mr. Hammer says that his maths has helped the *National Enquirer,* at a cost of hundreds of thousands of dollars, to examine more than 500 variables for the design of its covers and decide which would work best.

Despite such successes a doubt remains: consumers vary so much that deductive number crunching runs the risk of missing something. Above all, it can test only what is there, not what might be there. Often consumers say they do not want a product, but when it is offered to them, they discover its charms. The robotic techniques of Mr. Hammer and other number-crunchers may make some management decisions more logical. On the other hand, if such methods become widely used, they will increase the value of people who have an instinct for something surprising. Far from fearing the ascent of Mr. Hammer and his like, mavericks should welcome it; they will rise with him.

 **Article Review Form at end of book.**

Which decisions were you most surprised to find on the list of the 75 greatest management decisions?

# The 75 Greatest Management Decisions Ever Made

As the AMA celebrates its 75th year, Management Review presents as many decisions that have helped define the very nature of management.

## Stuart Crainer

*Stuart Crainer is a business writer based near Oxford, England. He contributes to* The Times *(London),* The Financial Times *and many other publications. He is the editor of* The Financial Times Handbook of Management *and the author of numerous books, including a biography of Tom Peters. His most recent book is* The Ultimate Book of Business Gums *(AMACOM, 1998). E-mail: stuart.crainer@virgin.net*

Amid the fanfare being prepared for the new millennium, there are numerous listings and rankings of the great and the good. Most of these listings feature scientists, writers, artists, sports personalities, media stars and entertainers. Their achievements, inspirations and personalities are pored over and celebrated. Managers are conspicuous by their absence. Yet management is one of the great triumphs of our age. In the 20th century, humanity discovered management as a discipline, a profession and sometimes even a calling.

In celebration of this enduring discipline, *Management Review* asked experts for their nominations of the 75 greatest management decisions ever made. The resulting list is as eclectic and eccentric as one would expect. The link between the 75 decisions is simply that they were successful and had a major impact.

## Through the Ages

Management is nothing new, of course. Napoleon was exercising management skills when he deployed his forces. The ancient Egyptians practiced management when they built the pyramids. The teams of gardeners cultivating the Hanging Gardens of Babylon did not simply do whatever first came to mind; they were managed.

And, as a steady stream of books attest, Jesus Christ was a manager (witness the book, *Jesus CEO*). "Jesus taught many great principles," says Charles Manz, author of *The Leadership Wisdom of Jesus* (Berrett-Koehler, 1998). "A good actual decision was when he told anyone who had not sinned to throw the first stone [at] a woman caught in adultery. In doing so, [they would] choose not to condemn but to forgive."

Indeed, the bible is a ready source of management decisions. "By deciding to divide people into their tens, hundreds and thousands, Moses was the first to establish a hierarchy, a chain of command," observes Warren Bennis of the University of Southern California. Think of Noah, the project manager, making weighty logistical decisions to meet a tight and immovable deadline. "Could we include

Joseph's advice to the Pharoah on planting wheat to store for seven years?" asked Philip Kotler of Northwestern's Kellogg School when the question of nominating a decision was put to him. "Or Jesus' choice of his 12 disciples (except the blunder of Judas)? One could play with the question for years."

## Every Decision We Make

The more you look for great management decisions, the more you see. None of the great monuments of history would exist if it weren't for management. The Italian Renaissance painters may have been artistic geniuses, but they were also shrewd managers able to take advantage of delegation. The teams of laborers who helped build London's St. Paul's Cathedral did not gather spontaneously—they were recruited and managed.

Inevitably, some monuments are a testament to bad management. The Leaning Tower of Pisa would not attract tourists if it were perfectly vertical. For this we can thank a 13th century Italian building supervisor, a manager by any other title.

The somewhat daunting reality is that virtually all the decisions we make are managerial in nature. Decisions usually concern people (human resources); money (budgeting); buying and selling (marketing); how to do things (operations); or how to do things in the future (strategy and planning). The obvious exceptions are emotional decisions—though some sad creatures actually bring analysis to bear on their choice of partner.

While management is a truly human science, it is interesting

that people-related decisions generally are not the ones that remain strongly imprinted in our minds. Indeed, great decision makers such as Henry Ford and Bill Gates are not exactly renowned for their people management skills. Instead, people remember decisions that change businesses, industries and history.

## The Heart of Management

Although management is eternal and all-embracing, debate continues to rage about what actually constitutes the discipline. (It should be noted that the debate usually rages in academia and not on factory floors.) The host of definitions now available cannot cloud the central fact that management is about decision making.

"Decisions are the essence of management," says Des Dearlove, author of *Key Management Decisions* (FT/Pitman, 1997). "Management without decision making is a vacuum. Of course, that does not mean that every decision a manager makes is important or that they always make the right decisions. The vast majority of decisions made by managers are completely unimportant. And often the decisions they make are the wrong ones."

Managers are not perfect, but who said that management was about perfection? The reality is that it's a combination of following inexplicable hunches, getting lucky, working hard and taking risks. Often managers fall on their faces. That's part of the job. Managers may run all of the data through the latest regression analysis software and still screw it up. For every great decision, there are hundreds that didn't quite work out.

There is a wafer-thin line between success and failure in management decisions. The division is often barely discernible: Will Apple go down in history as the company that invented an industry, or as a glorious failure with a fantastic product but not the foresight to build long-term success?

## Whence Success

The roots of successful decisions often lie in obscure places. Peter Cohan, author of *Technology Leaders* (Jossey-Bass, 1997), cites the example of Hewlett-Packard's entry into the inkjet printer business. In the late 1970s, H-P's Vancouver division was in trouble. It had few products, and management was considering whether to fold it into another division.

An engineer working in a converted janitor's closet, however, had discovered that heating metal in a specific way caused it to splatter all over the room. The engineers realized this process might lead to a new method of spraying ink onto a page. Richard Hackborn, an H-P executive, told the division manager that exploiting this discovery was his last chance to save the division. H-P's first inkjet printer reached the market in 1984. Over the next decade, H-P's share of the U.S. printer market rose from 2 percent to 55 percent.

Success also can emerge from apparent failure. Our list includes examples of companies that recovered from catastrophic problems. Writer and bookseller Ted Kinni cites Johnson & Johnson's 1982 decision to pull Tylenol from store shelves following a poisoning episode as a classic recovery. "They put customer safety before corporate profit," says Kinni. (Warren Bennis provides another interesting slant: "Johnson & Johnson CEO Jim Burke was the first corporate leader to recognize the significance of the media. Tylenol was about being totally up-front and public.")

Sometimes, perhaps once or twice in their careers, managers get it gloriously right. In 1950, Frank McNamara found himself in a restaurant with no money. After calling his wife for help, McNamara came up with the idea of the Diners Club Card, which was launched in 27 Manhattan restaurants. Within a year, the card had 42,000 members and the credit card was born.

Getting it right usually has nothing to do with the use of a decision-making software package. Bill Gates didn't need software when he ceded control of the license to use MS/DOS for the IBM PC while remaining in control of the license for all non-IBM PCs. When Compaq, Dell, Hewlett-Packard and Gateway took over the PC market from IBM, Gates had locked in the foundation on which his wealth is built. Great decision, Bill.

The truly great decisions happen. They arise from spur-of-the-moment phone calls and from crazy ideas you try when you're desperate. They emerge from the corporate ether. Forget about strategy. Even the strategy gurus will admit that strategy is fatally flawed by the messiness of reality.

"I am a professor of strategy and oftentimes I am ashamed to admit it," confesses Gary Hamel, co-author of *Competing for the Future* (Harvard Business School Press, 1996), "because there is a dirty secret: We know a great strategy when we see one. In business schools we teach them and pin them to the wall. They are

specimens. Most of our smart students raise their hands and say, 'Wait a minute. Was that luck or foresight?' " They're partly right. We don't have a theory of strategy creation. There is no foundation beneath the multibillion-dollar strategy industry. Strategy is lucky foresight. It comes from a serendipitous cocktail."

## Our Lifeblood

At their moment of triumph—as the serendipity kicks in and everything turns rosy—it is unlikely that managers break into euphoric shouts during board meetings. Nor do they crack open a bottle of champagne and slide down the office banisters naked whistling "Stairway to Heaven."

Managers tend not to celebrate when decisions are gloriously justified for two reasons. First, getting it right is part of the job. Managers are paid to do the right thing (and, according to Dilbert, blame others if they fail to do so). If the product launch is screwed up in Estonia and Latvia, it seems excessive to celebrate a perfect entry into the Finnish market.

Second, managers do not celebrate getting it right because they usually do not realize they did so. The fact is, perfect decisions usually are perfect only in retrospect. Henry Ford did not sprint around Detroit announcing the arrival of mass production. Queen Isabella of Spain did not immediately proclaim her wisdom when she sponsored the voyage of Columbus. She sensibly kept quiet. (The corollary of this is to be aware of people who trumpet the perfection of their decisions. If Queen Isabella had handed out a press release announcing the imminent

discovery of America, you can be sure America would still lie undiscovered.)

Managerial decisions are risks. Looking back, they may seem obvious. Of course Intel had to get out of the memory business. International Business Machines? Bound to be globally successful. Mickey? Great name for a cartoon mouse. But did Walt Disney know he would make many millions of dollars from the mouse? Did he know it was an important decision? I don't think so. It wasn't a foolproof, get-rich-quick scheme, just a decision that worked.

Great decisions change things. Some do so by setting standards and creating models for behavior. "I would nominate the decision by Aaron Feuerstein of Malden Mills in 1995 to keep his business open in the wake of a major fire that destroyed most of his company," says book author Manz. Feuerstein kept his entire workforce of 2,400 people on the payroll and paid them out of his own pocket.

"Most people would've been happy at their 70th birthday to take the insurance money and go to Florida, but I don't want to do that" Feuerstein says. It appeared to be bad business at the time even though it was highly moral. In the end, Malden Mills was back to virtually full capacity within 90 days. The committed and grateful employees worked so well that productivity shot up. Feuerstein says that the employees paid him back nearly tenfold.

Such a decision has everything: high risk, strong ethics, humanity and a business payoff. It is proof that decision making is not only the heart of management; it is the heartbeat of life.

# The Greatest Management Decisions Ever Made

Some are well-known choices, others might be controversial. Still others are surprises. Herewith, in random order, are 75 compelling decisions that shaped the human endeavor of management through the ages.

1. Walt Disney listened to his wife, Lillian, and named his cartoon mouse Mickey instead of Mortimer. Entertainment was never the same after Mickey and Minnie debuted in Steamboat Willie in 1928.

2. As Ambassador to France in the 1780s, Benjamin Franklin spent his time encouraging the emigration of skilled workers to the United States—an early instance of poaching staff.

3. In desolate post-World War II Japan, Toyota listened to an obscure American statistician, W. Edwards Deming, who arrived unheralded in 1947. Deming introduced Toyota to quality techniques, and it conquered the world.

4. Around 59 B.C., Julius Caesar kept people up-to-date with handwritten sheets that were distributed in Rome and, it is suspected, with fly posters that were placed around the city. The greatness of leaders has been partly measured ever since by their ability to communicate.

5. In 1950, Frank McNamara found himself in a restaurant with no money and came up with the idea of the Diners Club Card. The first credit card changed the nature of buying and selling throughout the world.

6. The Middle Kingdom in Egypt, stretching from 2052 B.C. to 1786 B.C., was long enough—if papyrus records are to be believed—for the Egyptians to introduce the subdivision of labor into factories. Work was never the same again, though it was a little better organized.

7. The 1962 decision by IBM's Thomas Watson Jr. to develop the System/360 family of computers cost the company $5 billion—more than the development costs of the atomic bomb. Although IBM's market research suggested it would sell only two units world-wide, the result was the first mainframe computer.

8. In the early 1960s, Philip Morris repositioned Marlboro as a man's cigarette. This positioning, and the Marlboro cowboy, helped create one of the world's most successful and durable brands.

9. During the 1920s, Matsushita was a struggling young business and its latest product, a bicycle light, was initially unsuccessful. Then Konosuke Matsushita ordered salespeople to leave a working light in each store. The working model changed perceptions. Sales took off and so did the company.

10. Ignoring market research, Ted Turner launched the Cable News Network in 1980. No one thought a 24-hour news network would work. It did.

11. The founding of the Society of Jesus, also known as the Jesuits, in 1540 by Ignatius de Loyola provided an organizational model with an emphasis on practical work rather than contemplation. It became, according to Peter Drucker, "the most successful staff organization in the world."

12. During WWII, Robert Woodruff, president of Coca-Cola, committed to selling bottles of Coke to members of the armed services for a nickel a bottle. Customer loyalty never came cheaper.

13. Richard Arkwright, an 18th century English inventor and one of the founding fathers of the Industrial Revolution, licensed his technology, confident that he could innovate to stay ahead. His decision brought in the then fantastic sum of [pounds]200,000.

14. Honda arrived in America in 1959 to launch its big motorbikes. Customers weren't keen on their problematic performance, but they admired the little Supercub bikes Honda's managers used. Honda bravely changed direction, thus transforming the motorbike business virtually overnight.

15. In 1924, Thomas Watson Sr. changed the name of the Computing-Tabulating-Recording Company to International Business Machines. The company had no international operations, but it was a bold statement of ambitions.

16. As the Incas expanded their empire during the 15th century, they realized that communication and logistics are vital to any large, dispersed organization. They decided to create a network of administrative centers and warehouses for food, along with thousands of miles of roads.

17. The second Vatican Council (1962–65) called by Pope John Paul XXIII, launched one of the biggest change management programs in history. It altered the shape of the Catholic Church into a decentralized, low-hierarchy management model that has stood the test of time.

18. When Masaru Ibuka and Akito Morita established the Tokyo Tsushin Kogyo company after the end of WWII, the first thing they did was to write down the company's philosophy. Its initial products—radio parts and a rice cooker—didn't last, but Sony's philosophy did.

19. In Thebes in 1000 B.C., someone lost a slave named Shem. He decided to post an advertisement offering a whole gold coin for the slave's return. This is the oldest existing ad and the precursor of the modern advertising merry-go-round.

20. In 1961, Jean Nidetch was put on a diet by the Obesity Clinic at the New York Department of Health. She invited six dieting friends to meet in her Queens apartment every week. The decision created Weight Watchers and the slimming industry.

21. In 1981, Bill Gates decided to license MS/DOS to IBM, while IBM ceded control of the license for all non-IBM PCs. This laid the foundation for Microsoft's huge success and IBM's fall from grace.

22. The Chinese Qin Dynasty (221–206 B.C.) produced the Great Wall—a fantastic feat of both management and engineering. They also developed what is reputed to be the first reliable system of weights and measures, thereby aiding commercial development.

23. In April 1978, John Larson of McKinsey & Co. asked colleague Tom Peters to step in at the last minute to do a presentation on some research

he'd done. The presentation led to *In Search of Excellence,* which changed the business book market and created the management guru industry.

24. When ITT named Harold Geneen CEO in 1959, the company had sales of $765 million. When Geneen retired in 1979, ITT had revenues of nearly $12 billion and was the largest conglomerate in the world. Geneen created a working model of rational, data-driven management.

25. In 1979, a Hewlett-Packard engineer found that heating metal in a specific way caused it to splatter. The decision to exploit this discovery launched the inkjet printer business and became the impetus for more than $6 billion in H-P revenues.

26. Sony chief Akito Morita noticed that young people liked listening to music wherever they went. He and the company developed what became the Walkman, first made in 1980. There was no need for market research. "The public does not know what is possible. We do," said Morita.

27. In 1947, the Haloid Co. in Rochester, N.Y., acquired the license to basic xerographic patents taken out by Chester Carlson. In 1949, the first xerographic copier, the Model A, was introduced. In 1960, the company was renamed Xerox Corp.

28. In the 1920s, the cofounders of retailer Marks and Spencer decided they had a better handle on customers' needs than did manufacturers. So they turned the tables in the merchant business and called on manufacturers to meet the specifications of the products they designed.

29. In the 19th century, Andrew Carnegie decided to import British steel and steel-making processes to America to build railway bridges made of steel instead of wood. The imported skills ignited the U.S. steel industry and Carnegie became a steel baron.

30. Apple decided to chase the prize for the first sellable PC, creating an industry. The Apple I led to the Apple II, then VisiCalc and finally the Mac, first shipped in 1984. (It also drew a veil over Xerox's decision not to go ahead with development after its PARC team had made a vital breakthrough in PC technology.)

31. Henry Luce's creation of Fortune in 1929 spawned the Fortune 500, which provided the corporate benchmark for the 20th century—and became a clever marketing gimmick for the magazine.

32. In 1892, Henry Heinz decided that the H.J. Heinz company needed a slogan. He came up with "57 varieties" to describe the company's foods. This was one of the few cases of successful underselling. Heinz produced 60 products then, but the slogan has stood the test of time.

33. In 1072–73, the Italian cities of Venice and Genoa entered into a partnership to fund commercial voyages. The joint venture was born.

34. Thomas Coutts, an 18th century British banker, wrote off the royal family's gambling debts to keep them as customers. It was a great loss-leading strategy. Coutts thrives as "the top people's bank" to this day. Her Majesty the Queen is a customer.

35. When the Wilson family of Memphis went on a motoring vacation, they discovered it was not much fun to stay in motels that were either too expensive or too slovenly. So Kemmons Wilson built his own. The first Holiday Inn opened in Memphis in 1952.

36. Henry Ford's decision to start his own company in 1903 led to the first mass-production line, created a mass market for automobiles, launched a corporate giant, changed perceptions of travel, led to the establishment of various industries, and provided a blueprint for industrial production.

37. Queen Isabella of Spain decided to sponsor Columbus' voyage to the New World in 1492. The ultimate in R&D.

38. In 1965, Giuliana Benetton decided to knit a brightly colored sweater. More than 30 years later, Giuliana and her three brothers have a global retail chain of 7,000 stores in 120 countries selling brightly colored sweaters.

39. The two offices of consulting firm McKinsey & Co. went their separate ways in 1939. A.T. Kearney launched his own firm in Chicago. Marvin Bower kept the McKinsey name in New York, correctly deciding that the use of his name would lead clients to expect his involvement in every assignment. McKinsey became The Firm.

40. In 1905, Sears, Roebuck and Co. opened its Chicago mail-order plant. The Sears catalog made goods available to an entirely new audience. The Sears operation also provided a model for mass production.

41. In 1970, Spencer Sylver of 3M invented the Post-It note. But it took Arthur Fry to recognize the opportunity in 1979. The Post-It remains a ubiquitous money-spinner.

42. In the manner of a modem CEO, Emperor Hadrian (76–138) managed the vast Roman Empire by traveling addictively. In an early example of managing by walking around, he saw that the miners needed bath houses and ordered that they be built. Unfortunately, enlightened management of human resources remained exceptional.

43. Before 1000 B.C., a decision was made in China to manage buying and selling by using a cowry shell as currency. It was bigger than a dollar and equally important. Without this decision, there would have been no Adam Smith or Gordon Ghekko.

44. In 1987, Percy Barnevik surprised commentators with his decision to create the world's largest cross-border merger between Sweden's ASEA and Switzerland's Brown Boveri. The $30 billion giant that resulted, Asea Brown Boveri, is now lauded as the organizational model for our times.

45. During 1943, Paul Garrett of General Motors asked a young Austrian teacher and writer, Peter Drucker, to study the company. The career of the century's foremost management thinker was launched.

46. In 1896, Boron Pierre de Coubertin, a French educator, decided to reinstitute the Olympic Games, modeled on the competition that began in Athens in 776 B.C. His decision produced a phenomenon that rivals the United Nations in its internationalism.

*(continued on next page)*

47. After Warner Brothers produced the first "talkie" movie in 1927, others joined the fray. But studios weren't soundproofed so filming took time. Sam Jaffee of RKO suggested that the studio should film at night when it was quiet. It did so and stole a march on its rivals.

48. When Lou Gerstner became CEO of IBM in 1993, he decided not to split the company—something the previous CEO, John Akers, had been prepared to do. The company's revitalization owes a great deal to this decision.

49. After WWII, General Douglas MacArthur committed to rebuilding the Japanese economy. Such was the success of this decision that 30 years later the Japanese were breathing down the necks of corporate America.

50. In 1982, Johnson & Johnson pulled Tylenol from store shelves after capsules were found to be poisoned. It put customer safety before corporate profit, and CEO Jim Burke provided a lesson in media openness.

51. During the 1970s, Japanese giant Matsushita developed VHS video and decided to license the technology. Sony developed the immeasurably better Betamax but failed to license it. The world standard is VHS, and Betamax is consigned to history.

52. In the 1930s, Motorola was performing indifferently. CEO Paul Galvin was encouraged to misrepresent how well the company was doing. He refused: "Tell them the truth, first because it is the right thing to do and second they'll find out anyway."

53. Napoleon made some rash moves (Russia in winter), but he was also the first leader to create a meritocracy in which competency was more important than breeding.

54. Before the 1862 Battle of Antietam in the U.S. Civil War, two Union soldiers found the confederate battle plan of General Robert E. Lee and decided to take it to General McClellan, who was leading the Union forces. McClellan failed to take advantage as the battle degenerated into a costly draw, but the decision of the soldiers was right and brave.

55. The farsighted William Hoover saw that automobiles would soon kill his business, which made leather accessories for horse-drawn carriages. He started the Electric Suction Sweeper Co. in 1908, which created the mass-market vacuum cleaner and provided a (largely ignored) blueprint of how to move with the times.

56. In 1979, Ernest Thomke developed the Swatch watch. Almost overnight, the dormant Swiss watch industry was revived as the humble timepiece became a fashion accessory. The Swiss market share of the watch industry rose from 15 percent to more than 50 percent.

57. General Motors' William Durant dismissed Alfred P. Sloan's ideas on how to manage the automaker. When Pierre du Pont took control in 1920, he decided to follow Sloan's planned reorganization: The dominant corporate form of our times—federal decentralization—emerged.

58. Ray Kroc liked Mac and Dick McDonald's stand in San Bernardino, Calif., selling hamburgers, fries and milkshakes so much, that he opened his own franchised restaurant in 1955 and formed McDonald's Corp. Kroc went on to create a huge global company and a vast market for fast food.

59. In 1968, the Carr family, owners of the UK newspaper *News of the World*, decided to go into partnership with a then unknown Australian, Rupert Murdoch, to ensure that Robert Maxwell didn't take over the newspaper. The partnership worked. Murdoch later cast off the Carrs and reached for the media skies.

60. In 1850, Julius Reuter used carrier pigeons to communicate share prices between the end of the Belgian telegraph line in Brussels and the end of the German line in Aachen. It was the beginning of the news and information business.

61. An aggressive marketing campaign by Bayer, a German drug company, in the 1910s changed the nature of the U.S. pharmaceutical industry. Amid opposition from the American Medical Association, the company forged ahead with its plan to advertise the link between its hallmark product, aspirin, and the brand name, Bayer.

62. In 1798, the U.S. government decided to give a contract to make 10,000 guns to Eli Whitney. The production was supposed to take two years but eventually took eight. Along the way, Whitney developed the basic techniques of mass production.

63. In 1930, Messrs Eugene Ltd. of London decided to use closed-circuit television to advertise their permanent hairwaving technique at the Hairdressing Fair of Fashion. The television ad was born.

64. In 1948, the world's first instant camera, the Polaroid Land Camera Model 95, was demonstrated. Management bravely decided to price it at $89.75 against Kodak's Baby Brownie, priced at $2.75. The entire initial stock of 56 was sold on the first day, and Polaroid was launched.

65. The Miletus region in Ancient Greece (around 500 B.C.) may have been the cradle of philosophy, but it also was keenly commercial. It decided to specialize in wool and associated products, thus serving as a distant prototype for Silicon Valley.

66. In 1931, Procter & Gamble introduced its brand management system, which elevated brands to center stage and provided a blueprint its management has followed ever since.

67. Wallace Dohan, dean of Harvard Business School, oversaw the 1922 launch of the *Harvard Business Review*. "The effect of hedging upon flour mill control" hardly set the pulse racing, but it was the beginning of a publishing success story and a prestigious addition to the Harvard brand.

68. In 1914, Henry Ford paid his workers $5 a day. It was a great leap forward in HR management, but it was not a totally altruistic decision. Ford effectively created the market for his own product by ensuring his workers could afford to buy a car.

69. Pierre du Pont decided that the DuPont company needed financial management. During his tenure with the company (1902–40), he developed modern corporate accounting, including concepts such as

double-entry accounting, financial forecasting and return on capital invested.

70. In the mid-13th century, a number of cities in Northern Germany entered into an association to promote their commercial interests. The Hanseatic League eventually had approximately 40 members with representatives throughout Europe.

71. Businessman Cyrus McCormick is best known for developing the mechanical harvester. But fierce competition in the 1850s led to his decision to develop some of the fundamentals of marketing, such as deferred payments and guarantees.

72. Publisher P.T. Barnum decided to promote a woman who claimed to be George Washington's nurse in the late 1830s. Barnum became a master of promotion, sowing the seeds for the growth of popular entertainment and promotional skills.

73. Michael Dell decided to sell PCs direct and built to order. Now everybody in the industry is trying to imitate Dell Computer's strategy. Too late?

74. After Montgomery Ward rejected his idea of moving into retailing, Robert E. Wood was hired by Sears, Roebuck and Co. In 1924, Julius Rosenwald liked the idea, and Sears opened its first retail store in 1925. It proceeded to become the world's largest general merchandiser.

75. In 1981, Jan Carlzon, new chief of airline SAS, sent 10,000 front-line managers to two-day service seminars and 25,000 managers for three-week courses. Within four months, SAS was the most punctual European airline and its service levels were rejuvenated.

Sources: A wide variety of opinions were canvassed to collect these decisions. *Management Review* is grateful to all who participated. In particular to Philip Kotler of Northwestern, Don Sull, Costas Markides and Gerry Griffin of London Business School; Chris Lederer and Sam Hill of Helios Consulting; Peter Cohan; Alex Knight and Phil Hodgson of Ashridge Management College; Des Dearlove; David Arnold of Harvard Business School; Warren Bennis and Jay Conger of the University of Southern California; Charles Manz; Randy White of RPW Executive Development; William E. Halal of George Washington University; Daniel Wren of the University of Oklahoma; Ann Marucheck and Allison Adams of Kenan-Flagler. Other sources include Peter Drucker's *On the Profession of Management* (Harvard Business School Press, 1998) and Charles C. Mann and Mark L. Plummer's *The Aspirin Wars* (Harvard Business School Press, 1993).

**Article Review Form at end of book.**

To what extent do you believe that the use of a jazz metaphor to describe managerial work is appropriate and accurate? Why?

# The Improvising Organization:

## Where Planning Meets Opportunity

If the future is uncertain, best learn to improvise. Find out how by looking at how actors and jazz musicians do it.

**Mary M. Crossan, Roderick E. White, Henry W. Lane, and Leo Klus**

The best companies distinguish themselves from all others by their ability to adapt to and capitalize on a rapidly changing, often unpredictable environment. Consider, for example, IBM. During the period when mainframes dominated computing and IBM dominated the computer industry, the company embraced a radical new concept—the personal computer—that directly threatened its primary business. Despite predictions that its innovation would never last, IBM went on to dominate the hardware side of the personal computer market.

However, that adaptive ability did not survive. As leadership in the PC industry moved away from the equipment manufacturers, Microsoft, Intel, and other computer suppliers proved to be more nimble. But now with new management, reorganization, cost cutting, and the purchase of Lotus, IBM begins to show signs of adapting once again.

Many large companies have fallen on hard times because they were unable to innovate and renew themselves. In addition, as the IBM example pointedly shows, meeting a challenge once is no guarantee of successfully repeating the feat. Such failures to adapt are rarely, if ever, the result of a lack of planning. These companies typically employ legions of internal planners and external planning consultants. No matter how many times managers have been told by the likes of Henry Mintzberg and Tom Peters that they cannot plan their way into the future, they retain a powerful corporate planning and control mind-set. Their overriding assumptions about the future business environment remain: it is largely predictable, and control of the firm's performance in that environment is possible.

Executives still believe, or at least behave as if they believe, that success depends on their ability to predict environmental change and develop tactical strategic plans to deal with that change. Managers cling to conventional techniques such as vision statements, long-term plans, and strategic benchmarking, in the hope that they will enable the organization to successfully chart its way into the future. Why do managers continue to rely on this limited tool kit? In large part, because they have nothing to replace or supplement traditional forms of planning. If they cannot forecast and plan, then what can they do?

We propose that improvisation can be harnessed as a managerial technique for coping with the new reality of rapidly changing business environments.

Lessons can be learned from improvisation, both in theater and music, for application to business. In addition, training exercises from the performing arts can be used to convey the principles of improvisation in corporate settings.

## The Environment: Knowable? Yes! . . . Predictable? No!

The business environment is one of the most discussed topics in business schools and board rooms. Indeed, appreciating the complex interactions between companies and their customers, competitors and government, as well as the implications of rapid changes in technology, is important. Unfortunately, managers place too much emphasis on projecting or predicting future conditions, and on developing strategies and actions to meet those predictions. This approach stems from a widely held belief that the business environment is an arena that is knowable, hence predictable, and thus controllable by managers. However, that is not the case. As Rosabeth Moss Kanter described in *When Giants Learn to Dance:*

To some companies, the context in which they are now entered seems increasingly less like baseball or other traditional games and more like the croquet game in Alice in Wonderland—a game that compels the player to deal with constant change. In that fictional game, nothing remains stable for very long, because everything is alive and changing around the player—an all-too-real condition for many managers. The mallet Alice uses is a flamingo, which tends to lift its head and face in another direction just as Alice tries to hit the ball. The ball, in turn, is a hedgehog, another creature with a mind of its own. Instead of lying there waiting for Alice to hit it, the hedgehog unrolls, gets up, moves to another part of the court, and sits down again. The wickets are card soldiers, ordered around by the Queen of Hearts, who changes the structure of the game seemingly at whim by barking out an order to the wickets to reposition themselves around the court.

Managers might relate to the continuous change in Alice's fictional world. However, they believe that their own situations are far more predictable than Alice's, and try to gain control over their own environments through ever more detailed analysis, prediction, and sophisticated planning. Most likely, they do not have the tools or training to function in any other way. Additionally, they might interpret assumptions about the unpredictability of the environment as negative, counterproductive, and even job threatening.

The powerful new paradigm called "chaos theory" provides insights into uncertain conditions by illustrating the inherent unpredictability of dynamic, complex systems—like Alice's world. Such systems may exhibit periods of relative calmness and stability, but even these periods are unpredictable. Take weather patterns, for example. The theory holds that this complex system exhibits elements of chaos within broader, recognizable patterns, such as the seasons. However, forecasters now accept that they cannot predict specific weather systems with any accuracy much beyond a week. Thus, chaos theory has had a significant impact on the ability of scientists to understand and explain, although not accurately predict, previously unexplainable phenomena.

Chaos theory also makes a profound point that corporate executives need to internalize: beyond a certain point, increased knowledge of complex, dynamic systems does little to improve our ability to extend the horizon of predictability for those systems. No matter how much we know about the weather, no matter how powerful the computers are, specific long-range predictions are not feasible. We can know, but we cannot predict.

Business systems, like weather systems, are characterized by thousands of interacting effects. As a result, we can anticipate the broader recognizable patterns such as sales seasonality and business cycles, but we cannot predict the specifics, such as what product will be hot this year, with any reliability. In fact, as companies increasingly face "hypercompetition"—rapid technological change, rapidly shifting consumers tastes, and seemingly continuous new product offerings by competitors— some experts advocate improvisation as a technique for new product development.

Consider the phenomenal popularity of the Internet as an example of the inability of large corporations to predict the future. When telephone companies, cable companies, movie studios, and computer companies were busy creating alliances to construct the information superhighway and take it into the homes of millions of Americans, they dismissed the Internet entirely. It was a medium for academics and hackers—too awkward and complex to be the superhighway. Even Microsoft initially missed its potential. Meanwhile, Internet use expanded rapidly, spawning an industry with a multitude of new and different competitors.

Even if managers recognize the inherent unpredictability of their environment, they have few existing techniques to cope with it. We see improvisation as a potential link between the need to plan for the predictable and the ability to respond simultaneously to the unpredictable.

## A Different Perspective: The Improvising Organization

Whether because of belief in the predictability of the environment, or lack of appropriate techniques, managers continue to apply traditional forecasting and planning practices to new problems. Following the traditional paradigm, they assume that the environment is predictable and manageable through the use of the correct combination of processes and practices, and that sustainable success results from accurate and rigorous analysis through which they formulate and implement both short- and long-term plans.

We are not saying that traditional planning tools are of no value to organizations, or that they should be discarded. Many of these practices permit the development of sound business analyses, and improve knowledge and awareness of the environment. However, though these tools can serve a useful function, they are not enough. The danger arises when managers rely too much on planning in new and different business conditions. In effect, the reach of planning exceeds its grasp.

In contrast, the new assumptions suggest that significant parts of the business environment are largely unpredictable, and that the key task for managers is to explore and innovate in chaotic conditions. Essentially, an organization must be flexible enough to adapt, creative enough to innovate, and responsive enough to learn

The classic case studies describing Honda's entry during the early 1960s into the U.S. motorcycle market illustrate the tension between planning and improvisation. Honda quite logically planned to use its bigger, more powerful motorcycles to spearhead its entry into the U.S. market, beginning with California. But unanticipated events intervened. The more demanding driving conditions caused unexpected engine failure, effectively curtailing sales of the big bikes. However, the Honda people had also brought with them some of the smaller 50-cc Supercubs. Believing there was no U.S. market for these smaller motorcycles, Honda's U.S.-based managers had been using them for personal transport. As the somewhat apocryphal story goes, a Honda executive riding his Supercub encountered a Sears buyer in a supermarket parking lot. A conversation ensued, interest was expressed, and the rest is motorcycle (and eventually automotive) history.

The Supercub and Honda's subsequent development of the motorcycle market changed the image of motorcycling in America, radically altered the nature of motorcycle distribution, and accelerated Honda along the path to global dominance of the industry. Success flowed from a series of unlikely occurrences: the initial shipment of Supercubs to the U.S. even though conventional wisdom indicated it was a big-bike market; the chance meeting with the Sears buyer; the willingness of Honda's U.S. managers to pursue a serendipitous encounter. Honda's managers did not feel bound by their original plan; they were prepared to work with the situation they faced—in other words, to improvise.

Exhibit 1* summarizes what we refer to as the "old" and "new" assumptions about the environment, and the corresponding management tasks and tools for each set of assumptions. However, the new tools and the old tools are not mutually exclusive practices. Rather, they are based on completely different assumptions about the environment and how an organization can and should function within it.

## Improvisation: A New Management Technique

While conducting research on organizational renewal, we explored some novel approaches that organizations could employ, one of which was improvisation. Our pursuit of improvisation arose in response to a challenge that, contrary to popular belief, perhaps businesses should not renew themselves. Many businesses dedicate their physical, mental, and emotional assets to a particular strategy. How can they compete with new entries that can better target their stock of assets toward a new way of doing business? Examples abound of companies such as IBM and GM whose once successful strategic orientations have been buffeted by new entries better suited to the changing environment. In the bestseller *In Search of Excellence*, Peters and Waterman identified a number of companies as "state of the art." Within five years, two-thirds of those same companies

*Not included in this publication.

were no longer described as excellent; they didn't adapt.

We compared traditional theater, where plays seem to have a pre-determined life, with improvisational theater, which undergoes constant renewal. We wanted to see if we could learn something about this continually new and changing form of theater that might be applicable to business. Contrasting the traditional and improvisational modes led us to a better appreciation of the differences between the old approach of controlling the environment and the new approach of exploring it. We investigated improvisation by reading the classics in the field, by attending workshops presented by the Second City improvisation group, and by having members of Second City work with management groups.

In addition to contrasting theater methodologies, we considered the differences between the musical performances of a traditional symphony orchestra and a jazz quartet. A close analysis of the process of jazz improvisation resulted in insights about the relationship between practice and performance, the role of leadership, and the differing roles of individuals and the group. We also reached some conclusions about integrating old and new assumptions.

Our experiences dramatically altered our initial understanding of improvisation. We gained some insights that, we believe, make it applicable for use by management groups. Although it is not an exact science, neither is improvisation an art that only certain talented individuals can pursue. Instead of a random "anything that comes to the top of the head will do," improvisation is a disciplined craft. Its skills can be learned through continual practice and study, and applied to situations. As a team-based rather than an individual-based technique, improvisation offers a different method of approaching problems or challenges.

## Improvisation in Theater

Traditional theater begins with a specific script, which dictates the direction and life of the performance. The director selects a group of actors to fulfill prescribed roles, which are well defined and largely unalterable, and ensures that they deliver the script faithfully. The cast consists of these actors, who have been chosen for their age, appearance, capability, and gender. The set provides the necessary atmosphere to enhance the performance. Costumes further clarify and focus the situation and the actors' roles. In rare cases, such as Miss Saigon or The Phantom of the Opera in Toronto, Canada, the theater is even constructed specifically for the play.

Improvisation differs, first and foremost, in that there is no script. Interaction between the audience and the cast ignites the actors' imaginations. There are no sets, although minimal props and costumes can help accentuate the story line or assist the actors in their delivery. Instead of accurately following a prescribed role or a previously defined scene, the actors are free to determine their roles within the broad parameters set by the audience, unrestricted by factors such as age or gender. As a result, the director does not plan the action. Rather, the director helps the actors reflect on their actions in order to learn from their experiences.

Where the traditional play is by necessity focused and controlled, operating in a predetermined environment, improvisation is flexible, open, and unpredictable. In traditional theater, planning is the cornerstone to a successful performance as the script, director and actors control the environment: the acts are orchestrated and the interactions are rehearsed. In improvisation, the acts are spontaneous and the audience fuels the actors.

The contrast between these two methods of performance illustrates some fundamental differences between managing the environment and exploring it. As Viola Spolin, an influential writer on theater improvisation, writes:

Spontaneity creates an explosion that for the moment frees us from handed-down frames of reference, memory choked with old facts and information and undigested theories and techniques of other people's findings. Spontaneity is the moment of personal freedom when we are faced with a reality and see it, explore it and act accordingly. In this reality the bits and pieces of ourselves function as an organic whole. It is the time of discovery, of experiencing, of creative expression.

To us, this description of improvisation has the ring of "horizontal management," an organizational structure that many companies are adopting. Or maybe it is the other way around. Process teams and process owners that are close to customers and have significant interaction with them, and that make decisions and adapt to changing needs and conditions, seem to be improvising. If you add the attitudes, skills, and culture necessary for successful horizontal management, such as those suggested by Mercer Management Consulting, you have a prescription for successful improvisation. These shared characteristics include tolerance for change, initiative, and belief in teamwork and collaboration, as well as a culture of innovation, flexibility, risk-taking, and adaptive learning. In fact, we think training in improvisation could help prepare people for their new conditions and roles in horizontal management structures.

We can also make an analogy between traditional theater and business. A business operates under an overall corporate strategy and set of policies (script), which determines the nature of the business in terms of goals, products, markets, and competitive advantage (plot). Organizational structures delineate the function and scope of employees (actors), whose role is to operate within that strategy as specialists confined to a specific function. The CEO (director) plays an integral role in ensuring that the strategy unfolds as intended. Assets (sets) and in some cases uniforms (costumes) facilitate the delivery of the strategy. Like a traditional play, businesses tend to be stereotypical planning organizations, emphasizing focus and control. However, many businesses need to become more improvisational if they do not want to close like a play at the end of its run.

Intel's CEO, Andy Grove, recognized that the company's strategy or script, and he as the director, were impeding Intel's ability to compete in a changing environment. For two years, senior management had ignored signals from the competitive environment that were suggesting Intel could not be a leader in both memory chips and microprocessors. Grove recounts:

Management might have been fooled by our strategic rhetoric, but those on the front lines could see that we had to retreat from memory chips. . . . People formulate strategy with their fingertips. Our most significant strategic decision was made not in response to some clear-sighted corporate vision but by the marketing and investment decisions of front-line managers who really knew what was going on.

Some companies are putting the principles of improvisation into practice on a large scale. Ricardo Semler's Brazilian manufacturing conglomerate, SEMCO, is perhaps one of the largest "improvising" organizations. The company has a policy not to have policies. No one in the company really knows how many people it employs, because work moves between in-house production and company-supported satellite production. There are no organization charts because managers believe that "structure creates hierarchy and hierarchy creates constraints." In addition, SEMCO operates without dress codes or specific office hours, and employees set their own salaries.

Contrasting traditional theater with improvisation provides a powerful metaphor for organizations to examine the paradigm under which they operate. However, improvisation is more than a metaphor; it is a skill that participants can develop. An examination of improvisation in music reveals some of its salient characteristics.

## Improvisation in Music

Improvisation in music, specifically jazz, demonstrates the integration between traditional skills that musicians must master, and the less traditional skills they later develop. Moreover, two distinct yet integral phases of learning—the practice and the performance phases—are vital to the entire learning process at both the individual and the group levels. Through these two phases, the traditional skills and the improvisational skills blend to enable innovation.

### Individual Practice

A common but distorted view holds that musicians who improvise play notes randomly, or "make it up as they go along." In reality, a musician dedicated to the art of improvising undergoes a rigorous method of learning the skill of improvising, requiring the initial development of the primary music skills such as tone development, sight reading, and dexterity. Successful improvisation depends particularly on dexterity, which the musician can only develop through drills and the mastery of scales. In return, practicing the technical exercises often leads the musician into improvisation, and into creating new ideas to put into a personal "portfolio" for performance. Many times during performance, these ideas will emerge in new and creative ways not planned by the performer. Listening to other jazz performers as they improvise, as well as participating in jazz bands, also expands each musician's repertoire as he or she continues to develop new ideas while reinforcing old ones.

Thus, improvisation can be learned, but must be grounded in a traditional skill base. Only then can the performer look beyond the status quo for new ideas and continual personal reinvention. To improvise in an organizational setting, individuals must be highly trained before they can adapt the technique to management practice. Therefore, they must first develop the process skills—listening, communicating, coaching, and time management—along with the substantive skills of the particular trade. A group's improvising will be effective only if the individual members have good basic management and technical skills.

### Group Practice

Examining different groups of musicians, and contrasting those practicing in a symphony to those practicing in a jazz quartet, yields additional insights. Each symphony musician has to invest sufficient practice time to master the piece of music both technically and musically in order to understand what the composer intended. The lead violinist, for example, must ensure the violin section's quality by practicing with that section. Finally, all the musicians in all the sections follow the lead of the conductor who guides, develops, demands, and creates the mood of the piece. The conductor has a vision and works with the group to achieve it.

In contrast, the practice session of a jazz quartet is loose, unstructured, and experimental—a time when ideas are developed or discarded, and group cooperation is fostered. Instead of simply following a conductor's interpretation of a piece such as Duke Ellington's classic "In a Sentimental Mood," the group defines its cohesiveness and style by blending the individual styles of the members. The group need not play exactly what is written on paper. It might follow the basic underlying chord changes that define this song, but the quartet will experiment to create a fresh and dynamic sound unique to it. Individuals who have mastered the basic skills and are committed to this process of creativity must practice improvising together in preparation for performance.

Organizations can learn an important lesson from these elements of group practice. The coordinating and integrating mechanisms in the symphony are the musical score and the conductor. These musicians operate in a professional capacity, meaning, for most individuals, "they don't have to like one another." By contrast, jazz improvisation requires a high degree of trust and mutual respect; these musicians self-integrate and are often good friends.

If organizations want to improvise, they have to strip away the veneer of artificial integrating mechanisms, and rely on camaraderie, mutual trust, and respect. John Seely-Brown, vice president of research at Xerox, recognizes the importance of what he refers to as "communities of practice," where individuals self-select into groups that share ideas. They self-select, at least in part, on the basis of whom they like to work with, and whom they can learn from.

These elements of group practice also suggest some limits to size. To self-integrate, individuals need to be familiar with one another. Ricardo Semler developed a principle he calls "Divide and Prosper." For individuals to work at their potential, they need to know everyone around them. Therefore, the effective organization cannot be more than 150 people. Effective improvising within that group requires even smaller numbers. Most improvisational groups operate with only three to six members at a time.

### Leadership

In improvisation, leadership takes on a new meaning. Picture a jazz quartet about to perform "In a Sentimental Mood," beginning with a loosely defined musical theme (strategy), musicians (employees), audience (customers), and instruments (assets). The sax player (CEO) assumes the leadership role. As the group performs, its members have assurance and confidence gained from personal mastery of their respective instruments and many hours of rehearsal together. This confidence does not stem only from memorizing music or preset patterns, but from understanding the personalities, styles, and reactions of each member, and from practicing in an environment that has fostered the continual development of ideas together.

The musicians (employees), each of whom is committed to intense individual improvement, are integral parts of the unit. Assuming either leadership or support roles to play the song, improvise a solo, or underscore a soloist, the individuals must listen carefully and communicate clear ideas through their instruments. By contrast, the musicians in a symphony must follow specific roles; many of these are exclusively supportive. Although listening to the other musicians is crucial, the participants play in an environment that is not conducive to developing new ideas or individually responding to others' ideas.

As the jazz melody continues, the members of the quartet feel the energy of the audience (customers)—a continually changing environment. Thus, the musicians absorb the mood of the audience into their creative process. During a more traditional performance, the symphony defines the mood for the audience.

Then the piano player begins to play a solo, picks up on this energy, and leads the quartet with an exciting variation. The other players follow this lead and embellish, support, and experiment with the ideas. The sax player (CEO) follows an unorthodox leadership style and assumes many roles throughout the performance. Instead of conducting, directing, or even demanding, this musician supports and follows the leads of the other soloists' improvisations, listens to the ideas of the other members, interacts with the audience, and also participates in improvising a solo.

The sax player demonstrates a style of leadership referred to as the "servant-leader." Leaders who learn to serve first are more apt to pick up on the subtle nuances of client relations and employee behavior. A servant-leader also requires foresight: a sense for managing in an unknowable and unforeseeable environment. In these respects, the sax player is a servant-leader who intimately listened to and communicated with the other members of the band, assumed roles that benefitted the rest of the group, allowed others to lead and fully develop their ideas, and whose skill in listening and communicating enhanced the overall performance of the group.

Perhaps one of the most visible examples of this form of leadership is Ricardo Semler, who operates with five others as rotating CEOs of SEMCO. He prides himself on the self-sufficiency of the company and the fact that his office has been moved twice, without his knowledge, while he was away on a long trip.

## Practice and Performance

Some have suggested that most learning in any field takes place only in the practice phase. But practice and performance are both major components of the organizational learning process.

Key innovations at the individual and group levels take place in both phases, as well as in the reflection stage between the two. In jazz improvisation, the group defines the strategy of the song during practice. It creates a framework to perform within, in contrast to the established blueprint that the symphonic orchestra follows exactly.

We don't want to give the impression that improvisation is preferable to traditional practice and performance. Successful improvisation requires a strong skill base in traditional practice and performance skills. Indeed, the improvising journey is a more difficult one because of this reliance on both modes of learning—traditional and improvisational.

In turn, improvisation can enrich traditional performance. Many great solos played in an improvised performance setting are transcribed note for note so they are not lost. These new "institutionalized" solos can then be played by non-improvisers, who practice and perform them in the traditional manner. When this approach is followed, the group embeds the past individual and group learning from performance and practice sessions. On the one hand, the group has assured that the wonderful and creative aspects of the revised solo will be delivered during a subsequent performance. But on the other, when musicians institutionalize past learning to become the framework for future learning and interpretation, they risk undermining the very basis of their ingenuity: the loose, unstructured approach to performing every song.

Improvising in the arts has provided us with some important lessons. Successful improvisation

rests upon strong development of core skills, whether in theater, music, or business. Communication within a team and with the audience is the greatest asset improvisers have for spontaneous performance. This skill, developed through practice and performance, requires that the performer have a flexible attitude in order to adapt to the demands of the audience, fellow workers, and leader. It is not enough to listen to the customer, observe changes, and sense the potential; the performer must also respond, both in language and action, to those changes. Ultimately, the success of the group depends upon the skills of each individual.

## Management Application: Training for Serendipity

The gap between theory and application can be bridged through the use of a series of improvisation exercises, developed for theater training, which provide a basis for team training with management groups. These exercises develop skills in the areas of environment, story development (strategy), the cast (organization members), and ambiance (organizational culture). A word of caution first: It is not sufficient to read about improvisation; you must experience it to grasp the power of its effect. Experiencing is what improvisation is all about.

### The Environment

An organization could benefit from its members' ability to see familiar products, markets, and industries in different ways and through different eyes. However, some organizations make creative thinking difficult, where individuals are constrained not only by conventional mind-sets, but also by conventional policies and procedures that can create tunnel vision.

Improvisation requires individuals to explore and work with the environment (being "shaped" by it), rather than trying to manage or control it. As managers begin to understand the unpredictable nature of the business environment, their need to be shaped by it, to improvise, increases. In permitting your environment to shape you, you must minimize preconceptions and biases that tend to focus your attention on the familiar and expected. Tapping into right-brain intuitive capabilities helps to minimize the logical and rational, or left-brain, thinking that often drives out creativity.

The Second City improvisation group uses a variety of individual and group exercises designed to stimulate right-brain thinking. These exercises may seem simplistic and elementary. However, they are challenging, and are based on well-founded principles, particularly the importance of disengaging the rational thought process by emphasizing spontaneity through contradictory actions.

One exercise, Nonsense Naming, requires an individual to walk quickly around the room while simultaneously pointing at and naming an object. The only hitch is that he or she cannot call the object by its real name. In a group exercise called Clap and Point, one person calls out the name of another person while simultaneously clapping, looking, and pointing at someone else. The person whose name has been called then carries on the process. The participants quickly discover that it is very difficult to carry out conflicting actions. Furthermore, it is also difficult for participants to receive conflicting signals. Often the person who was pointed at starts to respond, rather than the person whose name was called.

A third exercise, Dubbing, requires two people to act according to the words spoken by two others. The rest of the group provides the context by defining their roles and the situation. Essentially, each of the two "actors" consists of a voice and a body located in different parts of the room. Each body finds it extremely difficult to be controlled by its voice, and the two voices find it difficult to provide the conversation for the bodies' movements. Eventually, the separate parts learn to coordinate their words and actions.

## Story Development (Business Strategy)

Story development teaches the creation of scenarios or stories by working with the cues provided by the setting and other people, then developing them in detail. In improvisation, actors develop stories in an incremental fashion. They feed off every subtle nuance or aspect of the situation, amplifying each one in a process that permits deeper exploration and more extensive development.

Although the incremental nature of story development seems to be at odds with the frequently cited need for transformational change, we suggest that the two are complementary. Underlying all transformational change are incremental changes in thinking at the individual level. An organizational transformation often occurs when bottlenecks in the incremental change process that had been dammed up for a long time get unblocked; action becomes possible. Improvisation develops incremental changes in both thought and action that eventually result in organizational transformation over time, rather than culminating at a time of crisis. Big leaps become necessary only if the organization has not been attuned to the incremental shifts in the environment.

Another exercise, Create a Story, requires a group of participants to build on each other's development of a story line. The non-active participants provide the group with the title of the story; for example, "A Lunar Western." One member orchestrates the development of the plot, pointing to an individual to provide a few opening sentences. At mid-sentence, another person is selected to continue the development of the story by adding a little more, and so on. Some individuals have their own ideas of what the story line should be and fail to build on what others have started. The stories then develop big, disjointed leaps from one theme and situation to another, not unlike the strategies of some organizations. Other individuals resist straying from the theme, in spite of the fact that the story has developed in a totally different, but possibly promising, direction.

Story development closely relates to strategy development. Managers must "manage what is on the plate" at a given point in time, by focusing on small, anticipatory developments as in the technique of continuous improvement, rather than by making large, reactive decisions. Unfortunately, our research indicates that many North American companies are looking for the "home run" rather than focusing on improving operations in an incremental fashion.

## The Cast
## (Organization Members)

The Create a Story exercise also focuses on another critical element of improvisation—relationships between cast members. When you relinquish control of a situation and you do not know exactly where you are heading, you must have trust in your fellow team members and in the process. Reciprocation is a critical ingredient in developing trust. It requires that you are able to give, receive, and acknowledge information and cues. Good chemistry in improvisation is fueled by individuals generously giving each other good material with which to work. Likewise, a study of professional hockey players demonstrated that, in teams with high levels of trust, puck passing from one member to another was more accurate and more effective, resulting in higher levels of scoring than in teams with lower levels of trust.

Many of the interactive team elements of improvisation are demonstrated in An Imaginary Tug of War. The members of the two separate teams need to read the cues and work as one to effectively manage the "give and take" required to make the image appear real. Each team takes the lead at different times. The teams must cooperate, while appearing to compete.

How can the cast's principles apply to managing and working with organizational members? First, establishing an environment that fosters trust helps creativity to flourish. Second, from the top down, employees as well as managers must learn the three aspects of reciprocation: giving, receiving, and acknowledging. Learning these skills will not only further trust, but will also aid in improving communications and in continuing the story or strategy development.

## Ambiance
## (Organizational Culture)

All improvisation activities need a positive ambiance or culture. To exercise improvisational muscles, and to improvise in real time, requires an environment that does not punish mistakes or criticize what might superficially look like foolishness. One of the prime reasons that individuals resort to what they know how to do, what has worked in the past, or what is in the plan in spite of the fact the environment has changed, is fear of reprisal or embarrassment. Guy Claxton identified the four "C's" that are barriers to learning: a desire to be confident, comfortable, consistent and competent. Unfortunately, exploring the unknown requires individuals to place these conditions aside. Doing so can either be exhilarating or extremely stressful.

The difference between exhilaration and stress lies in the strength of the safety nets in place. The feelings of setting the four "C's" aside are comparable to those of a trapeze artist who lets go of one bar and, suspended in the air, trusts that the next bar will be there. The performer who is confident that emotional and physical safety nets are in place can undertake what appear to be risky moves.

Organizations must consider what security factors to provide that will encourage members to put themselves at risk. Without trust, people won't commit, and without commitment, they won't take risks to reach beyond the status quo.

## Not a Finale

By juxtaposing traditional theater with improvisational performances, and traditional symphonies with improvisational jazz concerts, we have highlighted different modes of relating to and working within an environment. Traditional theater, characterized by scripts, sets, props, actors, costumes, and directors, delivers an experience to the audience in a relatively predictable, controllable, and predetermined way. When the play is over, the organization disbands.

In contrast, improvisation has few of the trappings of traditional theater, thereby providing the group with maximum flexibility to adapt to the demands of the audience. After each performance, the material changes, but the troupe remains and the organization persists. Although most businesses operate like traditional theater, managers are not like the director of a play, who knows that the production will have a limited run. As a result, many businesses try to extend their run beyond what the customers (audience) will support, and consequently, fail.

While we presented the example of different theater styles to underscore the differences between "old" and "new" assumptions about the environment, we used jazz improvisation to highlight the integration between the two. The specific skills that form the foundation for both improvised and traditional forms of music are like the "planning" side of business. However, good improvisors require an additional set of skills in order to take advantage of the opportunities that present themselves in the moment.

Exercises from theater improvisation are a practical way for managers to learn about improvisation in a business setting. These exercises can enhance individual and group practice and performance. But organizations also need to consider several questions if they are committed to building a process to seize opportunity that complements their planning process: Do the structures and systems of the organization encourage or discourage improvisation? Does the organization encourage experimentation without fear of reprisal? How do elements of practice and performance fit into daily activities? If an organization operates more like a theatrical play or symphony orchestra, the critical question is this: Should we disband when the play has run its course, or should we try to engage an improvisational process that may allow for ongoing renewal? An organization can extend its life by forming teams that are more improvisational. However, the organization has to be able to tolerate disruption, inconvenience, and occasional mistakes.

There are some situations in which superb planning is paramount, and others in which spontaneity is critical. Even improvisation groups like Second City have planned elements in their program. Second City uses its successful improvised pieces (only thirty percent in any given show) to provide the basis for ongoing program development. In each show, the actors have at least one set that they know has worked in the past. Similarly, there are companies such as 3M that have been extremely successful in nurturing an innovative culture for new product develop-ment. For example, the successful invention of "Post-It" notes shows how 3M has institutionalized improvisation.

So, it is possible that today's business environment requires both orientations simultaneously. Traditional management tools help build planning and execution capability. Improvisation can help to maximize opportunities. How effectively organization members are able to respond to opportunity depends to a large extent on their improvisation skills.

Simply reading this article will not allow an executive to transform a company into an improvising organization. Nevertheless, as Johnstone wrote, "Reading about spontaneity won't make you more spontaneous, but it may at least stop you heading off in the opposite direction." You need to start practicing, performing, and improvising.

## Selected Bibliography

Guy Claxton, in his book *Live and Learn: An Introduction to the Psychology of Growth and Change in Everyday Life* (Harper and Row, 1984), discusses a variety of aspects of learning, including the four "C's" that inhibit learning: the need to be comfortable, confident, consistent, and competent.

Robert Greenleaf coined the term "servant-leader" to describe a different kind of leadership style. Further discussion of his work can be found in "The Servant as Leader," an essay published by the Center for Applied Studies (1973).

Two excellent books on improvisation in theater are Keith Johnstone, *Impro: Improvisation and the Theater* (New York: Routledge, Chapman and Hall, 1991), and Viola Spolin, *Improvisation for the Theater* (Northwestern University Press, 1990).

Christine M. Moorman and Anne S. Miner, "Walking the Tightrope: Improvisation and Information Use in New Product Development" (Marketing Science Institute, Report No. 95-101, March 1995), supports the link between improvisation and new product development.

The *Alice in Wonderland* example was borrowed from Rosabeth Moss Kanter, *When Giants Learn to Dance* (New York: Simon and Schuster, 1989).

John Hanson and Christopher Myer, "Horizontal Management: Dismantling Organizational Barriers to Growth," *Mercer Management Journal*, No. 3, 1994, discusses horizontal management in greater detail. Ralph Stacey, *The Chaos Frontier: Creative Strategic Control for Business* (Boston: Butterworth Heinemann, 1991), discusses chaos theory as it applies to business.

Jaclyn Fireman, "Winning Ideas from Maverick Managers," *Fortune*, Feb. 6, 1995, provided the background for some of the examples provided. Background on SEMCO was derived from a presentation made by Ricardo Semler and from his book *Maverick* (New York: Warner Books, 1993).

The Intel example was drawn from Christopher Bartlett and Sumantra Ghoshal, "Changing the Role of Top Management: Beyond Strategy to Purpose," *Harvard Business Review*, November–December 1994. Richard Pascale, "Perspectives on Strategy: The Real Story Behind Honda's Success," *California Management Review*, Vol. XXVI, No. 3, Spring 1984, is the source for the story behind Honda's entry into the U.S. motorcycle market.

**Mary M. Crossan** is the F.W.P. Jones Faculty Fellow and assistant professor of strategic management at the Richard Ivey School of Business at the University of Western Ontario in London, Canada. She received her doctorate in business policy from the University of Western Ontario and has been on the faculty of the Richard Ivey School of Business since that time.

Professor Crossan's research, teaching, and consulting have provided her with exposure to a variety of companies and industries in North America, Europe, and Asia. As part of a research team at the Richard Ivey School of Business, she has done extensive research on organizational learning and strategic renewal, which is represented by her articles in the *Journal of Management Studies*, the *International Executive*, the *Business Quarterly*, several book chapters, and a monograph entitled *Learning in Organizations*. A more theoretical perspective on improvisation is forthcoming in *Advances in Strategic Management*.

**Henry W. Lane** is the Donald F. Hunter Professor of International Business in the Richard Ivey School of Business at the University of Western Ontario in London, Canada. He received his D.B.A. in organizational behavior from the Harvard Business School. Professor Lane's research interests include international business as well as organizational learning and strategic renewal. He teaches courses in cross-cultural management, valuing and managing diversity, and organizational renewal and change.

He has authored or co-authored four books and numerous articles. His most recent books are *International Management Behavior: From Policy to Practice and Border Crossings: Doing Business in the United States*, which uses strategic renewal concepts to understand why some companies fail in trying to enter foreign markets while competitors in the same industry succeed. It was nominated for Canada's National Business Book Award. His articles have appeared in the *Journal of International Business Studies, Management International Review,* and the *Journal of Business Ethics*. He is the associate editor of the *Journal of International Business Studies*.

Professor Lane is active as a consultant as well as a faculty member on executive education courses for universities and corporations, and has engaged in varied assignments around the world.

**Roderick E. White** is an associate professor in the business policy area at the Richard Ivey School of Business at the University of Western Ontario. His consulting activities and research interests include the functioning of top management teams and questions of business strategy-organization relationships within large, complex companies. Currently he is exploring how teams of managers learn, or fail to learn, and how this process contributes to organizational excellence and strategic renewal.

Professor White has authored or co-authored articles on these and other topics appearing in *Academy of Management Review,* *Harvard Business Review, Business Quarterly, Policy Options, Planning Review,* and the *Strategic Management Journal*. He was co-chair of the 1991 Strategic Management Society Conference and co-editor of *Building the Strategically Responsive Organization*. Professor White serves on the editorial board of the *Strategic Management Journal*. He is the director of the Western Business School's doctoral program. He received his D.B.A. and M.B.A. from Harvard University and his bachelors of arts in business with honors from the University of Western Ontario.

**Leo Klus** is a management consultant with the Toronto office of Mercer Management Consulting, one of the world's leading strategy consulting firms. Since joining the firm, he has worked on a number of projects throughout Europe, North America, and Asia in the financial services, transportation, and professional service firm industries.

 **Article Review Form at end of book.**

# WiseGuide Wrap-Up

- Decision making is an essential element of managerial work. Most problem-solving models suggest a rational process. However, the solutions to many, if not most, problems are reached under conditions of incomplete information and inadequate time for comprehensive consideration of all elements.

- Some, but not all, problems are amenable to the use of quantitative methods to discern and evaluate alternatives. The keys are to understand when quantitative methods will add value and not to overestimate their validity.

- The most important management decisions ever made involved various combinations of rationality and creativity.

## R.E.A.L. Sites

This list provides a print preview of typical **Coursewise** R.E.A.L. sites. (There are over 100 such sites at the **Courselinks**™ site.) The danger in printing URLs is that web sites can change overnight. As we went to press, these sites were functional using the URLs provided. If you come across one that isn't, please let us know via email to: webmaster@coursewise.com. Use your Passport to access the most current list of R.E.A.L. sites at the **Courselinks** site.

**Site name:** Logic and Feeling in Decision Analysis

**URL:** http://rowlficc.wwu.edu:8080/~market/tj/logic.html

**Why is it R.E.A.L.?** This site discusses the decision-making process and how it is both rational and irrational.

**Key topics:** decision making, nature of management

**Try this:** What are the relationships between logic and feeling in decision making?

---

**Site name:** Enchanted Mind

**URL:** http://www.enchantedmind.com/

**Why is it R.E.A.L.?** This rich information site combines humor, inspiration, fun, and puzzles to teach creativity.

**Key topics:** planning and decision making, managerial creativity

**Try this:** Summarize the advice at this web site for increasing creativity in management.

---

**Site name:** 3M Innovation Quiz

**URL:** http://rockford.mmm.com/quiz/

**Why is it R.E.A.L.?** Go to this site to take 3M's Innovation Quiz!

**Key topics:** managerial creativity, innovation

**Try this:** What accounts for 3M's success in new product development?

---

**Site name:** Mind Tools-Problem Solving and Analytical Techniques

**URL:** http://www.mindtools.com/page2.html

**Why is it R.E.A.L.?** This site describes different analytical and problem-solving techniques, such as brainstorming, critical path analysis, decision trees, force field analysis, PMI, etc.

**Key topic:** decision making

**Try this:** Review the various idea generation techniques described at this site, and select the one you feel would work best for leading a problem-solving session in a student organization.

---

# section 6

## Leading and Motivating Others to Accomplish Work

**WiseGuide Intro** In the late 1960s, the U.S. Supreme Court was grappling with its proper role in regulating pornography. At one point, the Court considered establishing some national standard for what was and was not obscene. For reasons of legal philosophy and because of the inherent difficulty of the task, the Court eventually sent the responsibility for deciding those matters back to the states and local communities. However, while the justices were still attempting to define a standard, they were necessarily required to view films, photographs, and other materials that were potentially obscene. At the height of the debate, someone asked Justice Potter Stewart if he could define pornography. He replied, "No, but I know it when I see it!"

A similar response is likely regarding the concept of leadership. Leadership has various definitions, and although most of us remain sure of its existence and importance, we sometimes have difficulty defining exactly what it is or is not. However, we know it when we see it. Ralph Stodgill, the great scholar and chronicler of research on leadership, once observed that, "There are as many different definitions of leadership as there are persons who have attempted to define the concept." Consensus is growing, however, that leadership can be described as an intentional social *influence* process that one person exerts to sway the behavior or attitudes of one or more others in regard to a goal. So every time you attempt to persuade a friend to accompany you to a certain place for lunch, or encourage someone to adopt a certain style of clothing, or persuade a fellow student to take a certain course, you are, in fact, exerting influence and therefore attempting to exercise leadership.

Sometimes, leadership is regarded as the province only of elected officials, company presidents, politicians, generals, and people who hold positions of power. To be sure, these individuals have considerable power at their disposal and can cause people to spring into action. However, is this really leadership? When followers comply with the requests or demands of the boss, are they responding to leadership or simply meeting the terms of their employment contracts?

Reading 25 is an interview with Professor Jeffrey Pfeffer, well known for his sometimes iconoclastic views on leadership and management. In this reading, Pfeffer advocates strongly for "people-centered" forms of leadership and points out impediments to these forms of leadership in modern business organizations. Pfeffer cites current research that tends to debunk the notion that merit pay can stimulate and support organizational productivity. The relationship of pay to individual motivation is an often-debated and complicated issue. In Reading 26, Geoffrey Colvin suggests that the relationship between pay and motivation is weak and that motivation in contemporary organizations emanates almost entirely from other sources.

Effective leadership behavior has been explained in a variety of different ways. Notable breakthroughs in the understanding of what constitutes effective leadership have included the Ohio State and University of Michigan studies on leadership behaviors, contingency theory (which showed that there is no single best way to lead and manage), and the concepts of charismatic and transformational leadership. The most recent revelations have occurred in the area of emotional intelligence. In Reading 27, Daniel Coleman reviews leadership in the context of the combination of skills and attributes that characterize exceptional leadership performance.

The final two readings in this section concern various aspects of how managers/leaders communicate with their constituencies. In Reading 28, Gillian Flynn describes how Pillsbury uses employee feedback systems to allow workers to contribute to the achievement of organizational goals. In Reading 29, Cheryl O'Donovan makes the point that the post–baby boom generation will demand the people-centered organizations suggested in Reading 25.

---

## ? Questions ?

**Reading 25.** Compare the relative importance of human resources to other things—like capital or strategy or organizational design—that are normally associated with enterprise success.

**Reading 26.** What is the relationship of pay to performance in contemporary organizations?

**Reading 27.** What exactly is emotional intelligence, and how does it impact managerial performance?

**Reading 28.** Describe some proven techniques for improving communications with employees.

**Reading 29.** What are some of the managerial implications of the sentiments and characteristics of the so-called "Generation X?"

---

Compare the relative importance of human resources to other things—like capital or strategy or organizational design—that are normally associated with enterprise success.

# Jeffrey Pfeffer:
# Putting People First

## Joanne Cole

*Joanne Cole is a freelance writer and president of New York City-based J. Cole Communications.*

Management expert and best-selling author Jeffrey Pfeffer has spent the past decade working with people and organizations in some 21 countries to gain insight into how traditional and nontraditional management systems work. His new book, *The Human Equation: Building Profits by Putting People First*, presents landmark research and evidence showing that people-centered management delivers greater productivity and profit, and that some traditional management practices are doomed to fail. Recently, *HR Focus* spoke with Pfeffer about his unorthodox, yet commonsense, theories.

**Q.** Your book debunks current thinking about what is required to succeed in today's competitive environment and contends, specifically, that merit pay systems can undermine company morale, discourage teamwork and shake a worker's faith in management. Is this as revolutionary as it sounds?

**Pfeffer:** Not at all. There is no doubt that the merit pay systems have a number of problems that are supported by numerous surveys. [This evidence] indicates that companies continue to be displeased with merit pay systems despite the fact that they continue to tinker with them. Research also supports the fact that moving away from a merit pay system can actually be better for business. Inherently, the traditional merit pay plan has nothing to do with merit. More likely, it is based on performance evaluations that are very often subjective and all too often reward those individuals with well-honed political skills.

**Q.** What are some of the proven alternatives to these, and other, traditional systems?

**Pfeffer:** Research at numerous companies, both in the U.S. and abroad, shows that systems which specifically reward what you want to encourage—which is organizational performance, not necessarily individual performance—work better. A good example would be the preponderance of CEOs in this country who get rich at the same time their company is going down the tube. Entrepreneurial and smart organizations are showing that a collective reward system, such as profit sharing, stock ownership and gainsharing, fosters more productivity and profit than the traditional merit pay system.

**Q.** What are some other management systems that have the potential to cause more harm than good?

**Pfeffer:** The new employment contract, the idea of employability and the idea that we should have a contingent workforce are three good examples. Think about it. Companies now have employees sign "at-will" contracts the first day of employment. These "at-will" contracts are a way of acknowledging that an employee can be fired at any time, for either good cause or no cause at all. Offering "employability," another in-vogue notion, is a way for companies to say, "we really owe you nothing in terms of long-term continuity; all we need to do is offer you the opportunity to get ready for your next job." Then, having done that, the companies are surprised that the employee takes his "employability skills" and leaves for another job. Additionally, "employability" as a management practice makes employees spend a disproportionate amount of time keeping resumes ready and keeping in touch with the job market. There are just so many hours in a workday, and it benefits management to have the undivided attention and effort of each employee.

**Q.** In theory, the "putting people first" strategy sounds good for business. What stops companies from applying these principles?

**Pfeffer:** In today's knowledge-based economy, companies will talk about putting people first because it's the fashionable thing to do. But talk is cheap. The reasons companies don't "walk the talk" are so numerous, so multifaceted and so important, a colleague and I have launched a new research project to try to understand why it is that companies don't do what they say, and more important, why it is that companies don't do what they know they ought to do.

One explanation I can provide is that we have come to venerate the "tough, mean" management style that Wall Street usually responds to positively in the short term, although not in the long term. Financial markets, at least, seem to value a management style that doesn't value putting people first. Also, managers today are not trained to think about people issues because managers who came out of business schools probably took no required courses in human resource management, took one course in organizational behavior and then took a ton of courses in finance, accounting and economics.

Another difficulty is the time horizon issue. It's very hard to change your culture and change how you manage people in a day or a week. Consequently, people tend to solve the easy problems, like changing the compensation system, instead of changing the hard problems that ought to be solved because they're the ones that provide more leverage.

**Q.** Do you think the companies that don't change will be hurt financially?

**Pfeffer:** Sure. The data from a number of studies proves it. These are studies that span industry and studies from within industries, ranging from integrated steel manufacturers to the famous worldwide motor vehicle study, to studies of the apparel industry, to studies of semiconductors to oil refineries. The list goes on and on.

These are methodologically sophisticated studies that are peer reviewed—many of them funded by the Sloan Foundation, and many of them enormously precise and enormously careful and enormously thoughtful. The evidence of these studies is very overwhelming. For instance, when a colleague was doing research on the effect of information and technology on organizational performance, he found almost no evidence, but then he added people management practices and got a return of about 40 percent—which is what all the studies show.

I'd like to say that if these were double-blind studies in medicine, you would have to stop the study because it's not ethical to give a placebo, given the differences in consequences being observed. These studies have found enormous differences in performance depending upon how you manage your people.

Given the evidence, it's hard to believe that companies that continue to manage in the old way, and therefore are 30 percent to 40 percent less productive than their counterparts who manage by putting people first, will survive over the long run.

**Q.** If you had to pick the most startling part of this evidence, what would it be?

**Pfeffer:** The enormity and the consistency of the returns you get when you put in place what some people call high-commitment or high-performance management practices. And, by the way, it's a set of practices, which is another reason why they're hard to apply, because it's not just "let's tinker with the compensation system," or "let's add some training or do this or do that." It's an interrelated set of practices.

All you have to do is look at some of the most profitable businesses today. People-centered management practices are putting a large number of different industries at the top, including such organizations as Wal-Mart, the Ritz Carlton, Whole Foods Market and ServiceMaster, to name a few.

**Q.** Smart organizations often do dumb things when it comes to how they recruit, manage and retain their people. What's one of the most foolish things you have seen a smart company do?

**Pfeffer:** My book outlines seven practices of successful organizations. And while all seven practices are important and interrelated, perhaps the one that is most controversial is the one on recruiting, which relates to your question.

Last week I met with a company in Silicon Valley that had just done a very good culture diagnosis along with a very good rationale of what they wanted their future culture to be. When we sat down to talk, I asked them what they were going to do to get there, because everyone thinks that culture changes by some mystical process. Then I posed a question to them. I said, "Suppose you were hiring someone, and you found this fabulously brilliant engineer. But you knew from the interview that this engineer had none of the attributes that fit your new culture. Would you hire them anyway?" This executive from this very smart company looked at me like I had just hit him with a two-by-four.

What I mean is, if culture is important, then you hire for cultural fit; you don't just hire for skills. There are many examples of smart organizations, including PeopleSoft, Hewlett-Packard, AES, Southwest Airlines, The Men's Wearhouse, and a bunch of others, that hire for cultural fit. The Men's Wearhouse, for instance—which is this lovely, low-tech retailer of men's clothing that is growing very fast—fired its best salesperson because he didn't fit the culture.

The point is, it takes a certain willingness to violate what everybody else is doing, and beyond that it requires tremendous courage to put people first. It takes tremendous courage to be who you say you are, and it takes tremendous courage to live your mission statement. It's easy to talk "people first"; it's a lot harder to put "people first."

**The Author:** Jeffrey Pfeffer

**The University:** Stanford Graduate School of Business

**The Book:** *The Human Equations: Building Profits by Putting People First* (Harvard Business School Press, 1999)

**The Message:** There is a direct, unassailable correlation between good people management and profits.

 **Article Review Form at end of book.**

What is the relationship of pay to performance in contemporary organizations?

# What Money Makes You Do

A lot, you say? Well, sure—everyone says that. But think again. If you're bringing Industrial Age attitudes about pay into the New Economy, you're in trouble.

## Geoffrey Colvin

Many people, including his wife, thought he was crazy. A few actually believed he was evil. All Rob Rodin knew for sure was that he was worried. He was about to do something extremely radical for the CEO of a large distribution company: He was going to wipe out all—truly all—individual incentives for his sales force. No commissions. No bonuses. No Alaskan cruises or Acapulco vacations or Hawaiian pig roasts or color TVs or plaques. Just a base salary plus the opportunity for profit sharing, which would be the same percent of salary for everyone, based on the whole company's performance.

In a few days Rodin will celebrate the sixth anniversary of that decision, and he hasn't looked back. He's CEO of Marshall Industries, a big distributor of electronic components based in El Monte, Calif. (1997 sales: $1.2 billion), and I asked him how his heretical move is working out. Pretty well, it seems: Productivity per person has almost tripled, he says, "and

the system is more right today than it was six years ago." He loves how the new system gets rid of distortions that used to mask real results—people shipping early to meet quotas, pushing costs from one quarter into the next to make budget, beating one another up over allocating the costs of computer systems, and a million others. Plus, he says, "look at the trust that develops when everyone's on profit sharing." Some doubters still tell him he's crazy; they insist salespeople just won't perform without incentives. But Rodin isn't changing the rules. "How do you design an incentive system robust enough to accommodate every change in every customer and every product and every market every day? You can't—you'd be designing it the rest of your life." The doubters will never stop, but Rodin realizes they are now just part of his life. "I have to explain this system to somebody every day," he says. "Except customers—they get it right away."

Rob Rodin is standing smack in the middle of one of the nastiest battle zones in modern

management, because in a dramatic, in-your-face way he has raised a highly contentious question: Does money motivate? Exactly what does and doesn't it do? These are ancient questions, but they're suddenly urgent. The infotech revolution is steadily taking away the drudgery of work, the adding of numbers, the typing of data, the reconciliation of accounts, even the tightening of bolts. That ought to be great news: It means humans don't have to do donkey work and can instead spend more time creating, judging, imagining—the things infotech can't do. But there's a problem. The New Economy demands that workers at every level be creative problem solvers, while many managers' attitudes about paying those employees are holdovers from the donkey-work era. "The workplace is demanding more innovation and creativity," says George Bailey, a consultant with Watson Wyatt. "That's a fundamental shift from five years ago, when the focus was on reengineering and efficiency. It's a lot easier to reward for efficiency."

We can go much further: Efficiency—of a certain type—is one of the very few things in this world you can motivate with pay. In an age when companies are desperate to make employees innovative, it has to be said that pay is an incredibly weak tool with which to build a high-performance organization.

Some people, mainly members of the behaviorist school of psychology, hate this kind of talk. "Let the Evidence Speak: Financial Incentives Are Effective!!" is what two of them called a recent article in a compensation trade journal. Okay, let the evidence speak. It shows that financial incentives will get people to do more of what they're doing. Not better, just more. Especially if it isn't very complicated. Give food to the pigeon when he pecks the bar, and he'll peck more. If you want to speed up the assembly line and you're not too particular about quality, workers will speed it up for a financial incentive. That's what the evidence shows.

But this is exactly what employers today don't want. If they want to speed up the assembly line, they rewrite the software. From employees they want imaginative thinking about how to solve problems that didn't exist yesterday. Can you get this kind of thinking by offering to pay for it?

What would you guess?

You're right, of course. Trying to pay for it gets you nowhere. The evidence on this is so overwhelming that it's amazing anyone thinks otherwise, but plenty of people do.

Start with the endlessly documented fact that money isn't what people are mainly working for. I'm looking now at a new survey of "drivers of work force commitment" from Aon Consulting; pay ranks 11th. Things like recog-

nition and responsibility always rank ahead of pay in these surveys. And by the way, money's weak motivational power is waning; my favorite recent factoid is that the impact of monetary rewards has declined significantly with the advent of direct deposit.

In addition, trying to pay for particular types of performance, even when it works, is loaded with perils. Pay customer-service reps to answer the phone on the first ring, and they'll answer it—and then put it down. Research on pay-for-performance plans shows that many employees suspect the criteria or outcomes are rigged.

Then realize that money is especially weak in driving the most innovative employees. Mihaly Csikszentmihalyi, a University of Chicago psychology professor whose name I have never once pronounced in 12 years of daily radio broadcasts, has long studied creative people. He writes: "They all love what they do. It is not the hope of achieving fame or making money that drives them; rather, it is the opportunity to do the work that they enjoy doing."

Top this off with the finding that paying people to do things they enjoy doing actually seems to reduce their interest in doing them. The psychological mechanism is complicated, but the result has been replicated many times.

I think we can take it as settled that you can't pay more to get more innovation and creativity, because they aren't about money in the first place. So if you can't pay for them, how do you get them?

First (small) piece of advice: Stop crushing them. "It's much easier to incent people not to be innovative and creative, and many companies are excellent at

it," says George Bailey of Watson Wyatt. Judith Bardwick, a psychiatrist and consultant whose latest book is *In Praise of Good Business*, adds, "Giving people permission to make reasonably small innovations is easy if there is no punishment for failure. But punishment is endemic."

Second (large) piece of advice: Look inside and outside your organization for employees who are naturally innovative and creative. Sounds obvious, but the implications are upsetting: You're acknowledging that some workers just aren't that way and never will be, and many people, especially Americans, don't like that idea. Too bad. It's reality, and you know it. No one can say where innovativeness comes from, but we all know some people have way more of it than others. So find those who have it.

Third (most radical) piece of advice: Give employees a stable, secure environment.

Huh? What about the burning platform, creating a crisis, getting workers alarmed and mobilized for major change? Well, that tactic has its uses. But it's the wrong way to encourage free-thinking imagineers. For insight into why, look to the fascinating new field of evolutionary psychology. Its commonsense premise: Humans evolved instincts and tendencies that helped us survive as hunter-gatherers 200,000 years ago, and, evolution being slow, those are the instincts and tendencies we carry around today. If we feel threatened, our instinct is not to be imaginative; it's to fight fiercely. "We thrive best as creative people under a stable plan we can comprehend," says Nigel Nicholson, professor of organizational behavior at the London Business School and a student of evolutionary psychology. "Space, safety, and support" are the optimal conditions for thinking creatively.

I told Nicholson his description reminded me strongly of the companies *Fortune* identified a few months ago as the 100 best to work for in America. These companies find dozens of ways to make employees' lives easier, richer, more secure; 18 of them have something you thought was extinct, a no-layoff policy. And they're winners: The publicly traded ones vastly outperformed the market last year, and they've done it again so far in 1998.

Nicholson laughs at the notion that these companies are some kind of new-wave organizations. Just the opposite: "They have unconsciously found something close to the model for which we were designed."

What's the best way to pay people in the New Economy? Alfie Kohn, a writer who is America's most biting critic of money as motivator, offers a three-point plan: Pay well, pay fairly, and then do everything you can to get money off people's minds. "Sounds right to me," says Nicholson. Sounded right to Rob Rodin. Sounds right to me too.

 **Article Review Form at end of book.**

What exactly is emotional intelligence, and how does it impact managerial performance?

# What Makes a Leader?

IQ and technical skills are important, but emotional intelligence is the sine qua non of leadership.

## Daniel Coleman

*Daniel Coleman is the author of* Emotional Intelligence *(Bantam, 1995) and* Working with Emotional Intelligence *(Bantam, 1998). He is co-chairman of the Consortium for Research on Emotional Intelligence in Organizations, which is based at Rutgers University's Graduate School of Applied and Professional Psychology in Piscataway, New Jersey.*

Every businessperson knows a story about a highly intelligent, highly skilled executive who was promoted into a leadership position only to fail at the job. And they also know a story about someone with solid—but not extraordinary—intellectual abilities and technical skills who was promoted into a similar position and then soared.

Such anecdotes support the widespread belief that identifying individuals with the "right stuff" to be leaders is more art than science. After all, the personal styles of superb leaders vary: some leaders are subdued and analytical; others shout their manifestos from the mountaintops. And just as important, different situations call for different types of leadership. Most mergers need a sensitive negotiator at the helm, whereas many turnarounds require a more forceful authority.

I have found, however, that the most effective leaders are alike in one crucial way: they all have a high degree of what has come to be known as emotional intelligence. It's not that IQ and technical skills are irrelevant. They do matter, but mainly as "threshold capabilities"; that is, they are the entry-level requirements for executive positions. But my research, along with other recent studies, clearly shows that emotional intelligence is the sine qua non of leadership. Without it, a person can have the best training in the world, an incisive, analytical mind, and an endless supply of smart ideas, but he still won't make a great leader.

In the course of the past year, my colleagues and I have focused on how emotional intelligence operates at work. We have examined the relationship between emotional intelligence and effective performance, especially in leaders. And we have observed how emotional intelligence shows itself on the job. How can you tell if someone has high emotional intelligence, for example, and how can you recognize it in yourself? In the following pages, we'll explore these questions, taking each of the components of emotional intelligence—self-awareness, self-regulation, motivation, empathy, and social skill—in turn.

## Evaluating Emotional Intelligence

Most large companies today have employed trained psychologists to develop what are known as "competency models" to aid them in identifying, training, and promoting likely stars in the leadership firmament. The psychologists have also developed such models for lower-level positions. And in recent years, I have analyzed competency models from 188 companies, most of which were large and global and included the likes of Lucent Technologies, British Airways, and Credit Suisse.

In carrying out this work, my objective was to determine which personal capabilities drove outstanding performance within these organizations, and to what degree they did so. I grouped capabilities into three categories:

purely technical skills like accounting and business planning; cognitive abilities like analytical reasoning; and competencies demonstrating emotional intelligence such as the ability to work with others and effectiveness in leading change.

To create some of the competency models, psychologists asked senior managers at the companies to identify the capabilities that typified the organization's most outstanding leaders. To create other models, the psychologists used objective criteria such as a division's profitability to differentiate the star performers at senior levels within their organizations from the average ones. Those individuals were then extensively interviewed and tested, and their capabilities were compared. This process resulted in the creation of lists of ingredients for highly effective leaders. The lists ranged in length from 7 to 15 items and included such ingredients as initiative and strategic vision.

When I analyzed all this data, I found dramatic results. To be sure, intellect was a driver of outstanding performance. Cognitive skills such as big-picture thinking and long-term vision were particularly important. But when I calculated the ratio of technical skills, IQ, and emotional intelligence as ingredients of excellent performance, emotional intelligence proved to be twice as important as the others for jobs at all levels.

Moreover, my analysis showed that emotional intelligence played an increasingly important role at the highest levels of the company, where differences in technical skills are of negligible importance. In other words, the higher the rank of a person considered to be a star performer, the

more emotional intelligence capabilities showed up as the reason for his or her effectiveness. When I compared star performers with average ones in senior leadership positions, nearly 90% of the difference in their profiles was attributable to emotional intelligence factors rather than cognitive abilities.

Other researchers have confirmed that emotional intelligence not only distinguishes outstanding leaders but can also be linked to strong performance. The findings of the late David McClelland, the renowned researcher in human and organizational behavior, are a good example. In a 1996 study of a global food and beverage company, McClelland found that when senior managers had a critical mass of emotional intelligence capabilities, their divisions outperformed yearly earnings goals by 20%. Meanwhile, division leaders without that critical mass underperformed by almost the same amount. McClelland's findings, interestingly, held as true in the company's U.S. divisions as in its divisions in Asia and Europe.

In short, the numbers are beginning to tell us a persuasive story about the link between a company's success and the emotional intelligence of its leaders. And just as important, research is also demonstrating that people can, if they take the right approach, develop their emotional intelligence. (See "Can Emotional Intelligence Be Learned?", p. 131.)

## Self-Awareness

Self-awareness is the first component of emotional intelligence—which makes sense when one considers that the Delphic oracle gave the advice to "know thyself"

thousands of years ago. Self-awareness means having a deep understanding of one's emotions, strengths, weaknesses, needs, and drives. People with strong self-awareness are neither overly critical nor unrealistically hopeful. Rather, they are honest—with themselves and with others.

People who have a high degree of self-awareness recognize how their feelings affect them, other people, and their job performance. Thus a self-aware person who knows that tight deadlines bring out the worst in him plans his time carefully and gets his work done well in advance. Another person with high self-awareness will be able to work with a demanding client. She will understand the client's impact on her moods and the deeper reasons for her frustration. "Their trivial demands take us away from the real work that needs to be done," she might explain. And she will go one step further and turn her anger into something constructive.

Self-awareness extends to a person's understanding of his or her values and goals. Someone who is highly self-aware knows where he is headed and why; so, for example, he will be able to be firm in turning down a job offer that is tempting financially but does not fit with his principles or long-term goals. A person who lacks self-awareness is apt to make decisions that bring on inner turmoil by treading on buried values. "The money looked good so I signed on," someone might say two years into a job, "but the work means so little to me that I'm constantly bored." The decisions of self-aware people mesh with their values; consequently, they often find work to be energizing.

How can one recognize self-awareness? First and foremost, it shows itself as candor and an ability to assess oneself realistically. People with high self-awareness are able to speak accurately and openly—although not necessarily effusively or confessionally—about their emotions and the impact they have on their work. For instance, one manager I know of was skeptical about a new personal-shopper service that her company, a major department-store chain, was about to introduce. Without prompting from her team or her boss, she offered them an explanation: "It's hard for me to get behind the rollout of this service," she admitted, "because I really wanted to run the project, but I wasn't selected. Bear with me while I deal with that." The manager did indeed examine her feelings; a week later, she was supporting the project fully.

Such self-knowledge often shows itself in the hiring process. Ask a candidate to describe a time he got carried away by his feelings and did something he later regretted. Self-aware candidates will be frank in admitting to failure—and will often tell their tales with a smile. One of the hallmarks of self-awareness is a self-deprecating sense of humor.

Self-awareness can also be identified during performance reviews. Self-aware people know—and are comfortable talking about—their limitations and strengths, and they often demonstrate a thirst for constructive criticism. By contrast, people with low self-awareness interpret the message that they need to improve as a threat or a sign of failure.

Self-aware people can also be recognized by their self-confidence. They have a firm grasp of their capabilities and are less likely to set themselves up to fail by, for example, overstretching on assignments. They know, too, when to ask for help. And the risks they take on the job are calculated. They won't ask for a challenge that they know they can't handle alone. They'll play to their strengths.

Consider the actions of a midlevel employee who was invited to sit in on a strategy meeting with her company's top executives. Although she was the most junior person in the room, she did not sit there quietly, listening in awestruck or fearful silence. She knew she had a head for clear logic and the skill to present ideas persuasively, and she offered cogent suggestions about the company's strategy. At the same time, her self-awareness stopped her from wandering into territory where she knew she was weak.

Despite the value of having self-aware people in the workplace, my research indicates that senior executives don't often give self-awareness the credit it deserves when they look for potential leaders. Many executives mistake candor about feelings for "wimpiness" and fail to give due respect to employees who openly acknowledge their shortcomings. Such people are too readily dismissed as "not tough enough" to lead others.

In fact, the opposite is true. In the first place, people generally admire and respect candor. Further, leaders are constantly required to make judgment calls that require a candid assessment of capabilities—their own and those of others. Do we have the management expertise to acquire a competitor? Can we launch a new product within six months? People who assess themselves honestly—that is, self-aware people—are well suited to do the same for the organizations they run.

## Self-Regulation

Biological impulses drive our emotions. We cannot do away with them—but we can do much to manage them. Self-regulation, which is like an ongoing inner conversation, is the component of emotional intelligence that frees us from being prisoners of our feelings. People engaged in such a conversation feel bad moods and emotional impulses just as everyone else does, but they find ways to control them and even to channel them in useful ways.

Imagine an executive who has just watched a team of his employees present a botched analysis to the company's board of directors. In the gloom that follows, the executive might find himself tempted to pound on the table in anger or kick over a chair. He could leap up and scream at the group. Or he might maintain a grim silence, glaring at everyone before stalking off.

But if he had a gift for self-regulation, he would choose a different approach. He would pick his words carefully, acknowledging the team's poor performance without rushing to any hasty judgment. He would then step back to consider the reasons for the failure. Are they personal—a lack of effort? Are there any mitigating factors? What was his role in the debacle? After considering these questions, he would call the team together, lay out the incident's consequences, and offer his feelings about it. He would then present his analysis of the problem and a well-considered solution.

Why does self-regulation matter so much for leaders? First of all, people who are in control of their feelings and impulses—that is, people who are reasonable—are able to create an environment of trust and fairness. In such an environment, politics and infighting are sharply reduced and productivity is high. Talented people flock to the organization and aren't tempted to leave. And self-regulation has a trickle-down effect. No one wants to be known as a hothead when the boss is known for her calm approach. Fewer bad moods at the top mean fewer throughout the organization.

Second, self-regulation is important for competitive reasons. Everyone knows that business today is rife with ambiguity and change. Companies merge and break apart regularly. Technology transforms work at a dizzying pace. People who have mastered their emotions are able to roll with the changes. When a new change program is announced, they don't panic; instead, they are able to suspend judgment, seek out information, and listen to executives explain the new program. As the initiative moves forward, they are able to move with it.

Sometimes they even lead the way. Consider the case of a manager at a large manufacturing company. Like her colleagues, she had used a certain software program for five years. The program drove how she collected and reported data and how she thought about the company's strategy. One day, senior executives announced that a new program was to be installed that would radically change how information was gathered and assessed within the organization. While many people in the company complained bitterly about how disruptive the change would be, the manager mulled over the reasons for the new program and was convinced of its potential to improve performance. She eagerly attended training sessions—some of her colleagues refused to do so—and was eventually promoted to run several divisions, in part because she used the new technology so effectively.

I want to push the importance of self-regulation to leadership even further and make the case that it enhances integrity, which is not only a personal virtue but also an organizational strength. Many of the bad things that happen in companies are a function of impulsive behavior. People rarely plan to exaggerate profits, pad expense accounts, dip into the till, or abuse power for selfish ends. Instead, an opportunity presents itself, and people with low impulse control just say yes.

By contrast, consider the behavior of the senior executive at a large food company. The executive was scrupulously honest in his negotiations with local distributors. He would routinely lay out his cost structure in detail, thereby giving the distributors a realistic understanding of the company's pricing. This approach meant the executive couldn't always drive a hard bargain. Now, on occasion, he felt the urge to increase profits by withholding information about the company's costs. But he challenged that impulse—he saw that it made more sense in the long run to counteract it. His emotional self-regulation paid off in strong, lasting relationships with distributors that benefited the company more than any short-term financial gains would have.

The signs of emotional self-regulation, therefore, are not hard to miss: a propensity for reflection and thoughtfulness; comfort with ambiguity and change; and integrity—an ability to say no to impulsive urges.

Like self-awareness, self-regulation often does not get its due. People who can master their emotions are sometimes seen as cold fish—their considered responses are taken as a lack of passion. People with fiery temperaments are frequently thought of as "classic" leaders—their outbursts are considered hallmarks of charisma and power. But when such people make it to the top, their impulsiveness often works against them. In my research, extreme displays of negative emotion have never emerged as a driver of good leadership.

## Motivation

If there is one trait that virtually all effective leaders have, it is motivation. They are driven to achieve beyond expectations—their own and everyone else's. The key word here is achieve. Plenty of people are motivated by external factors such as a big salary or the status that comes from having an impressive title or being part of a prestigious company. By contrast, those with leadership potential are motivated by a deeply embedded desire to achieve for the sake of achievement.

If you are looking for leaders, how can you identify people who are motivated by the drive to achieve rather than by external rewards? The first sign is a passion for the work itself—such people seek out creative challenges, love to learn, and take great pride in a job well done. They also display an unflagging energy to do things better. People with such energy often seem restless with the status quo. They are persistent with their questions about why things are done one way rather than another; they are eager to explore new approaches to their work.

A cosmetics company manager, for example, was frustrated that he had to wait two weeks to get sales results from people in the field. He finally tracked down an automated phone system that would beep each of his salespeople at 5 P.M. every day. An automated message then prompted them to punch in their numbers—how many calls and sales they had made that day. The system shortened the feedback time on sales results from weeks to hours.

That story illustrates two other common traits of people who are driven to achieve. They are forever raising the performance bar, and they like to keep score. Take the performance bar first. During performance reviews, people with high levels of motivation might ask to be "stretched" by their superiors. Of course, an employee who combines self-awareness with internal motivation will recognize her limits—but she won't settle for objectives that seem too easy to fulfill.

And it follows naturally that people who are driven to do better also want a way of tracking progress—their own, their team's, and their company's. Whereas people with low achievement motivation are often fuzzy about results, those with high achievement motivation often keep score by tracking such hard measures as profitability or market share. I know of a money manager who starts and ends his day on the Internet, gauging the performance of his stock fund against four industry-set benchmarks.

Interestingly, people with high motivation remain optimistic even when the score is against them. In such cases, self-regulation combines with achievement motivation to overcome the frustration and depression that

come after a setback or failure. Take the case of another portfolio manager at a large investment company. After several successful years, her fund tumbled for three consecutive quarters, leading three large institutional clients to shift their business elsewhere.

Some executives would have blamed the nosedive on circumstances outside their control; others might have seen the setback as evidence of personal failure. This portfolio manager, however, saw an opportunity to prove she could lead a turnaround. Two years later, when she was promoted to a very senior level in the company, she described the experience as "the best thing that ever happened to me; I learned so much from it."

Executives trying to recognize high levels of achievement motivation in their people can look for one last piece of evidence: commitment to the organization. When people love their job for the work itself, they often feel committed to the organizations that make that work possible. Committed employees are likely to stay with an organization even when they are pursued by headhunters waving money.

It's not difficult to understand how and why a motivation to achieve translates into strong leadership. If you set the performance bar high for yourself, you will do the same for the organization when you are in a position to do so. Likewise, a drive to surpass goals and an interest in keeping score can be contagious. Leaders with these traits can often build a team of managers around them with the same traits. And of course, optimism and organizational commitment are fundamental to leadership—just try to imagine running a company without them.

## Empathy

Of all the dimensions of emotional intelligence, empathy is the most easily recognized. We have all felt the empathy of a sensitive teacher or friend; we have all been struck by its absence in an unfeeling coach or boss. But when it comes to business, we rarely hear people praised, let alone rewarded, for their empathy. The very word seems unbusinesslike, out of place amid the tough realities of the marketplace.

But empathy doesn't mean a kind of "I'm okay, you're okay" mushiness. For a leader, that is, it doesn't mean adopting other people's emotions as one's own and trying to please everybody. That would be a nightmare—it would make action impossible. Rather, empathy means thoughtfully considering employees' feelings—along with other factors—in the process of making intelligent decisions.

For an example of empathy in action, consider what happened when two giant brokerage companies merged, creating redundant jobs in all their divisions. One division manager called his people together and gave a gloomy speech that emphasized the number of people who would soon be fired. The manager of another division gave his people a different kind of speech. He was upfront about his own worry and confusion, and he promised to keep people informed and to treat everyone fairly.

The difference between these two managers was empathy. The first manager was too worried about his own fate to consider the feelings of his anxiety-stricken colleagues. The second knew intuitively what his people were feeling, and he acknowledged their fears with his words. Is it any surprise that the first manager saw his division sink as many demoralized people, especially the most talented, departed? By contrast, the second manager continued to be a strong leader, his best people stayed, and his division remained as productive as ever.

Empathy is particularly important today as a component of leadership for at least three reasons: the increasing use of teams; the rapid pace of globalization; and the growing need to retain talent.

Consider the challenge of leading a team. As anyone who has ever been a part of one can attest, teams are cauldrons of bubbling emotions. They are often charged with reaching a consensus—hard enough with two people and much more difficult as the numbers increase. Even in groups with as few as four or five members, alliances form and clashing agendas get set. A team's leader must be able to sense and understand the viewpoints of everyone around the table.

That's exactly what a marketing manager at a large information technology company was able to do when she was appointed to lead a troubled team. The group was in turmoil, overloaded by work and missing deadlines. Tensions were high among the members. Tinkering with procedures was not enough to bring the group together and make it an effective part of the company.

So the manager took several steps. In a series of one-on-one sessions, she took the time to listen to everyone in the group—what was frustrating them, how they rated their colleagues, whether they felt they had been ignored. And then she directed the team in a way that brought it together: she encouraged people to speak more openly about their frustrations, and she helped people raise constructive complaints during meetings. In short, her empathy allowed her to understand her team's emotional makeup. The result was not just heightened collaboration among members but also added business, as the team was called on for help by a wider range of internal clients.

Globalization is another reason for the rising importance of empathy for business leaders. Cross-cultural dialogue can easily lead to miscues and misunderstandings. Empathy is an antidote. People who have it are attuned to subtleties in body language; they can hear the message beneath the words being spoken. Beyond that, they have a deep understanding of the existence and importance of cultural and ethnic differences.

Consider the case of an American consultant whose team had just pitched a project to a potential Japanese client. In its dealings with Americans, the team was accustomed to being bombarded with questions after such a proposal, but this time it was greeted with a long silence. Other members of the team, taking the silence as disapproval, were ready to pack and leave. The lead consultant gestured them to stop. Although he was not particularly familiar with Japanese culture, he read the client's face and posture and sensed not rejection but interest—even deep consideration. He was right: when the client finally spoke, it was to give the consulting firm the job.

Finally, empathy plays a key role in the retention of talent, particularly in today's information economy. Leaders have always needed empathy to develop and keep good people, but today the stakes are higher. When good people leave, they take the company's knowledge with them.

That's where coaching and mentoring come in. It has repeatedly been shown that coaching and mentoring pay off not just in better performance but also in increased job satisfaction and decreased turnover. But what makes coaching and mentoring work best is the nature of the relationship. Outstanding coaches and mentors get inside the heads of the people they are helping. They sense how to give effective feedback. They know when to push for better performance and when to hold back. In the way they motivate their proteges, they demonstrate empathy in action.

In what is probably sounding like a refrain, let me repeat that empathy doesn't get much respect in business. People wonder how leaders can make hard decisions if they are "feeling" for all the people who will be affected. But leaders with empathy do more than sympathize with people around them: they use their knowledge to improve their companies in subtle but important ways.

## Social Skill

The first three components of emotional intelligence are all self-management skills. The last two, empathy and social skill, concern a person's ability to manage relationships with others. As a component of emotional intelligence, social skill is not as simple as it sounds. It's not just a matter of friendliness, although people with high levels of social skill are rarely mean-spirited. Social skill, rather, is friendliness with a purpose: moving people in the direction you desire, whether that's agreement on a new marketing strategy or enthusiasm about a new product.

Socially skilled people tend to have a wide circle of acquaintances, and they have a knack for finding common ground with people of all kinds—a knack for building rapport. That doesn't mean they socialize continually; it means they work according to the assumption that nothing important gets done alone. Such people have a network in place when the time for action comes.

Social skill is the culmination of the other dimensions of emotional intelligence. People tend to be very effective at managing relationships when they can understand and control their own emotions and can empathize with the feelings of others. Even motivation contributes to social skill. Remember that people who are driven to achieve tend to be optimistic, even in the face of setbacks or failure. When people are upbeat, their "glow" is cast upon conversations and other social encounters. They are popular, and for good reason.

Because it is the outcome of the other dimensions of emotional intelligence, social skill is recognizable on the job in many ways that will by now sound familiar. Socially skilled people, for instance, are adept at managing teams—that's their empathy at work. Likewise, they are expert persuaders—a manifestation of self-awareness, self-regulation, and empathy combined. Given those skills, good persuaders know when to make an emotional plea, for instance, and when an appeal to reason will work better. And motivation, when publicly visible, makes such people excellent collabora-

tors; their passion for the work spreads to others, and they are driven to find solutions.

But sometimes social skill shows itself in ways the other emotional intelligence components do not. For instance, socially skilled people may at times appear not to be working while at work. They seem to be idly schmoozing—chatting in the hallways with colleagues or joking around with people who are not even connected to their "real" jobs. Socially skilled people, however, don't think it makes sense to arbitrarily limit the scope of their relationships. They build bonds widely because they know that in these fluid times, they may need help someday from people they are just getting to know today.

For example, consider the case of an executive in the strategy department of a global computer manufacturer. By 1993, he was convinced that the company's future lay with the Internet. Over the course of the next year, he found kindred spirits and used his social skill to stitch together a virtual community that cut across levels, divisions, and nations. He then used this de facto team to put up a corporate Web site, among the first by a major company. And, on his own initiative, with no budget or formal status, he signed up the company to participate in an annual Internet industry convention. Calling on his allies and persuading various divisions to donate funds, he recruited more than 50 people from a dozen different units to represent the company at the convention.

Management took notice: within a year of the conference, the executive's team formed the basis for the company's first

Internet division, and he was formally put in charge of it. To get there, the executive had ignored conventional boundaries, forging and maintaining connections with people in every corner of the organization.

Is social skill considered a key leadership capability in most companies? The answer is yes, especially when compared with the other components of emotional intelligence. People seem to know intuitively that leaders need to manage relationships effectively; no leader is an island. After all, the leader's task is to get work done through other people, and social skill makes that possible.

A leader who cannot express her empathy may as well not have it at all. And a leader's motivation will be useless if he cannot communicate his passion to the organization. Social skill allows leaders to put their emotional intelligence to work.

It would be foolish to assert that good-old-fashioned IQ and technical ability are not important ingredients in strong leadership. But the recipe would not be complete without emotional intelligence. It was once thought that the components of emotional intelligence were "nice to have" in business leaders. But now we know that, for the sake of performance, these are ingredients that leaders "need to have."

It is fortunate, then, that emotional intelligence can be learned. The process is not easy. It takes time and, most of all, commitment. But the benefits that come from having a well-developed emotional intelligence, both for the individual and for the organization, make it worth the effort.

## The Five Components of Emotional Intelligence at Work

| | **Definition** |
|---|---|
| **Self-Awareness** | The ability to recognize and understand your moods, emotions, and drives, as well as their effect on others |
| **Self-Regulation** | The ability to control or redirect disruptive impulses and moods |
| | The propensity to suspend judgment— to think before acting |
| **Motivation** | A passion to work for reasons that go beyond money or status |
| | A propensity to pursue goals with energy and persistence |
| **Empathy** | The ability to understand the emotional makeup of other people |
| | Skill in treating people according to their emotional reactions |
| **Social Skill** | Proficiency in managing relationships and building networks |
| | An ability to find common ground and build rapport |

| | **Hallmarks** |
|---|---|
| **Self-Awareness** | Self-confidence |
| | Realistic self-assessment |
| | Self-deprecating sense of humor |
| **Self-Regulation** | Trustworthiness and integrity |
| | Comfort with ambiguity |
| | Openness to change |
| **Motivation** | Strong drive to achieve |
| | Optimism, even in the face of failure |
| | Organizational commitment |
| **Empathy** | Expertise in building and retaining talent |
| | Cross-cultural sensitivity |
| | Service to clients and customers |
| **Social Skill** | Effectiveness in leading change |
| | Persuasiveness |
| | Expertise in building and leading team |

## Can Emotional Intelligence Be Learned?

For ages, people have debated if leaders are born or made. So too goes the debate about emotional intelligence. Are people born with certain levels of empathy, for example, or do they acquire empathy as a result of life's experiences? The answer is both.

Scientific inquiry strongly suggests that there is a genetic component to emotional intelligence. Psychological and developmental research indicates that nurture plays a role as well. How much of each perhaps will never be known, but research and practice clearly demonstrate that emotional intelligence can be learned.

One thing is certain: emotional intelligence increases with age. There is an old-fashioned word for the phenomenon: maturity. Yet even with maturity, some people still need training to enhance their emotional intelligence. Unfortunately, far too many training programs that intend to build leadership skills—including emotional intelligence—are a waste of time and money. The problem is simple: they focus on the wrong part of the brain.

Emotional intelligence is born largely in the neurotransmitters of the brain's limbic system, which governs feelings, impulses, and drives. Research indicates that the limbic system learns best through motivation, extended practice, and feedback. Compare this with the kind of learning that goes on in the neocortex, which governs analytical and technical ability. The neocortex grasps concepts and logic. It is the part of the brain that figures out how to use a computer or make a sales call by reading a book. Not surprisingly—but mistakenly—it is also the part of the brain targeted by most training programs aimed at enhancing emotional intelligence. When such programs take, in effect, a neocortical approach, my research with the Consortium for Research on Emotional Intelligence in Organizations has shown they can even have a negative impact on people's job performance.

To enhance emotional intelligence, organizations must refocus their training to include the limbic system. They must help people break old behavioral habits and establish new ones. That not only takes much more time than conventional training programs, it also requires an individualized approach.

Imagine an executive who is thought to be low on empathy by her colleagues. Part of that deficit shows itself as an inability to listen; she interrupts people and doesn't pay close attention to what they're saying. To fix the problem, the executive needs to be motivated to change, and then she needs practice and feedback from others in the company. A colleague or coach could be tapped to let the executive know when she has been observed failing to listen. She would then have to replay the incident and give a better response; that is, demonstrate her ability to absorb what others are saying. And the executive could be directed to observe certain executives who listen well and to mimic their behavior.

With persistence and practice, such a process can lead to lasting results. I know one Wall Street executive who sought to improve his empathy—specifically his ability to read people's reactions and see their perspectives. Before beginning his quest, the executive's subordinates were terrified of working with him. People even went so far as to hide bad news from him. Naturally, he was shocked when finally confronted with these facts. He went home and told his family—but they only confirmed what he had heard at work. When their opinions on any given subject did not mesh with his, they, too, were frightened of him.

Enlisting the help of a coach, the executive went to work to heighten his empathy through practice and feedback. His first step was to take a vacation to a foreign country where he did not speak the language. While there, he monitored his reactions to the unfamiliar and his openness to people who were different from him. When he returned home, humbled by his week abroad, the executive asked his coach to shadow him for parts of the day, several times a week, in order to critique how he treated people with new or different perspectives. At the same time, he consciously used on-the-job interactions as opportunities to practice "hearing" ideas that differed from his. Finally, the executive had himself videotaped in meetings and asked those who worked for and with him to critique his ability to acknowledge and understand the feelings of others. It took several months, but the executive's emotional intelligence did ultimately rise, and the improvement was reflected in his overall performance on the job.

It's important to emphasize that building one's emotional intelligence cannot—will not—happen without sincere desire and concerted effort. A brief seminar won't help; nor can one buy a how-to manual. It is much harder to learn to empathize—to internalize empathy as a natural response to people—than it is to become adept at regression analysis. But it can be done. "Nothing great was ever achieved without enthusiasm," wrote Ralph Waldo Emerson. If your goal is to become a real leader, these words can serve as a guidepost in your efforts to develop high emotional intelligence.

 **Article Review Form at end of book.**

Describe some proven techniques for improving communications with employees.

# Pillsbury's Recipe Is Candid Talk

**Company execs know exactly what's on their employees' minds.**

## Gillian Flynn

*Gillian Flynn is the editor-at-large for Workforce.*

The most important information a company can have is the kind it rarely gets: frank, unreserved, this-is-how-it-is feedback from employees. No matter how many rallying speeches managers give about how their doors are always open, about how they want employees to challenge them, that sliver of fear remains. Where's the line between offering constructive criticism and giving offense? How can anyone be sure today's pointed conversation won't influence tomorrow's performance review?

Minneapolis-based The Pillsbury Company has the answer. A unique employee-feedback tool, a hot line called InTouch, allows anyone to phone any time and talk about anything with the comfort of anonymity and the assurance that their issues will be addressed. The technology used isn't particularly innovative—but the way in which the company uses it is.

"Getting this feedback wasn't fun the first time out, and sometimes it still isn't," says Lou de Ocejo, senior vice president of HR and corporate affairs. "But the system does just what we need it to do."

Pillsbury finds a recipe for frank feedback. The early '90s were a confusing time at Pillsbury. Between 1990 and 1993, the food company experienced a major shakeup of senior management, had been acquired by British-based conglomerate Grand Metropolitan PLC, started growing globally and had massively restructured, tossing away functional silos.

The new management team, including de Ocejo, realized a new communications plan was in order. It introduced an employee newspaper and CEO luncheons with employees—anything to encourage employee interaction with top management. "It's easy for executives to talk a lot and assume they're having conversations," says de Ocejo. "And it's hard as hell to get employees to risk telling you what's really going on."

It's a nationwide problem, according to Market Facts' TeleNation, a Chicago-based independent research organization. In a 1997 poll of 638 employees, more than 90 percent said they had good ideas on how their companies could run more successfully. Yet more than 50 percent said a lack of management interest and lack of a good means for sharing those ideas prevented them from communicating their ideas to management.

While de Ocejo was looking for a better communication tool for his company, Peter Lilienthal was looking for clients for his sole product, InTouch. Lilienthal had started his Minneapolis company, Management Communications Systems Inc., thinking InTouch would be an easy sell. In his previous career as a corporate officer at several large corporations, Lilienthal had been reluctant to criticize his superiors. "I wondered how everyone else must feel," he said. "That gave me an idea on how to improve communications." That idea was the anonymous hot line InTouch, a toll-free, third-party voicemail messaging system through which employees could send comments straight to the top without fear of reprisal.

InTouch had one catch—Lilienthal couldn't give it away, literally. At a Society for Human

Resource Management convention, Lilienthal raffled off 10 free one-year subscriptions to his service. The winners all turned him down. "A lot of HR people are nervous about this," says Lilienthal. "They don't know what they're going to [hear] from employees. But if you're really interested in improving communications, you should want to know."

Lilienthal only had one client when he met de Ocejo at a dinner party in 1993. Over the evening's courses, de Ocejo explained Pillsbury's communications problem to Lilienthal, and Lilienthal explained to de Ocejo how InTouch could work at the company. Employees from all locations could dial a number around the clock and leave a message of up to four minutes. The outside service would transcribe the messages—no worries about the boss recognizing a voice or handwriting—and send them to Pillsbury executives. The system would only cost $3 per employee a year; a bargain, de Ocejo says, for unreserved comments.

De Ocejo decided Pillsbury should become Lilienthal's second client. He pitched it to the senior management team, who, he says, "gave me a quizzical look, but approved it." The next hurdle was, of course, getting employees to use it.

Seasoning to taste: Pillsbury adapts the system. Executives bombarded employees with information about InTouch. The workforce received stickers, business cards and magnets, inviting workers to "direct your opinions straight to Pillsbury management." Employees, says de Ocejo, were cynical. But they also, apparently, were desperate for a safe means of voicing themselves. The calls came pouring in.

Employees left messages about faulty work systems, ineffective supervisors and new product ideas.

Today, Karen Gustafson, director of employee communications, says InTouch is key to ensuring "senior managers [aren't] isolated from the rest of the company. It has strengthened our commitment to two-way communication."

In the four years since introducing InTouch, de Ocejo's main concern has been to tailor it to be useful to the company and employees, rather than seeing it degenerate into a depository for employees' gripes. When employees call, a recorded voice suggests they consider whether they want to remain anonymous, whether they'd like to receive a personal phone call and even if they want to address their message to a specific person. Each employee also receives an instruction sheet for InTouch, with questions such as "Is this a broad issue or should I be talking to my local manager?"

De Ocejo also constantly reminds the workforce that InTouch isn't a voting machine. Just because a large number of employees ask for a certain course of action doesn't mean they will get it.

What they will get is the knowledge that de Ocejo, CEO Paul Walsh and the company's general counsel review every transcript. The three receive weekly packets of transcripts—Walsh even has his faxed to him when he's on business trips.

If an employee leaves a name and requests contact (27 percent of callers do), someone will follow up, generally the line manager in whatever area the call concerns. If the caller simply leaves a complaint or a sugges-

tion, the executives decide whether it's valid and deserves more research. If a call concerns a specific area or plant—the hot line suggests employees name the area they're calling from—the executives will send the transcript on to the head of that area also. The general counsel and HR thoroughly vet questions or issues of a legal nature, although, because Pillsbury also has a whistle-blower hot line, these are few and far between.

De Ocejo sends out management letters answering questions and reporting changes made as a result of the hot line. Managers post responses on bulletin boards. Gustafson says the company never posts an actual letter, only a paraphrase, to ensure employees can't be identified through particular word choice or vernacular.

*Pillsbury Today,* the company's newsletter, prints monthly questions and answers elicited by InTouch. When an employee suggested returning the Pillsbury Doughboy as a Macy's Thanksgiving Day parade float, for example, the director for advertising was able to respond that he would consider the idea. When a caller left a compliment for a computer-assistance person, the newsletter printed it, giving the man some public recognition. An employee who asked for an ATM on the 31st floor of headquarters received a response from the facilities administrator about why the machine wouldn't generate enough business to justify its cost.

Still, says de Ocejo, not everyone's satisfied all the time. "I spend a lot of time and effort digging deep and finding [answers]. But I never promised I was going to give out lollipops."

Being "InTouch" makes a difference. Some big changes have been made as a result of the

## Great HR Starts with Great Business Skills

*Workforce* talked with Lou de Ocejo, senior vice president of human resources and corporate affairs, about HR. The highlights:

**Q:** How and why did you decide to get into HR?

**A:** I initially got into HR by chance. A great opportunity to be the manager of the benefits functions [came along]. Over time, I made a conscious decision that HR can and should play a major role in organizational performance. After all, it is all about people and financial resources.

**Q:** What's the best part of your job?

**A:** [Having the opportunity to] influence, shape and support the culture of the company, in support of our business strategy.

**Q:** What's the toughest part of your job?

**A:** For me, the toughest part of my job is identifying and then sticking to the right priorities.

**Q:** What are some of the best decisions you've made as an HR professional?

**A:** Selecting the right leaders. Unfortunately, this is also representative of some of my worst decisions.

**Q:** What advice do you have for people considering an HR career?

**A:** Early in your career focus on sound, core technical skills, such as compensation, benefits, selection, organization development and core

business skills, finance, marketing, manufacturing and so on.

**Q:** What advice do you have for other established HR professionals?

**A:** Become a broad business person who brings excellent functional skills to the table.

**Q:** What sorts of changes were going on when you started at Pillsbury?

**A:** A lot. I arrived in 1992, along with a number of other senior managers. The company got a new CEO in the fall of 1991, and he put together a group of us. Before I was a gleam in anyone's eye, we went through a fairly extensive structural change in how we run the business—we focused on competencies in food technology, brands marketing and that type of thing, and away from the old focus, which was on divisions within the company and functional silos.

**Q:** What effect did these changes have on the HR function?

**A:** Back then, human resources was considered a support function—and we support functions weren't doing well in those days in terms of being a player at the table. That changed in 1992. Business contributions came first, and functional contributions became a given. So as opposed to how it was before, when HR only had to do HR—that was tossed out. The mission became to attend to what drives the business first, and then [our

department] would just happen to be great at HR.

**Q:** Were there any other changes going on?

**A:** There was nothing but change in 1992. Work was starting to be done in cross-functional teams. When we made that change it was very traumatic. Philosophically it was a good idea, but the lines of authority got blurred, and new things became important. People became discombobulated—who's my boss? Where do I go? Couple that change with the fact that as a business we weren't growing—it was flat. Then we were a fundamentally U.S. business. So we put our stake in the ground saying we wanted to grow outside the United States. So all of a sudden this organization in which all roads began and ended in Minneapolis had to look at things differently. Roads were beginning and ending in Argentina or Bombay.

**Q:** What was communication within the company like?

**A:** Prior to 1992, there was very little place for communications. In 1992 we started a business-focused employee newspaper. We started having CEO luncheons every month, and communication meetings with all functions at least once a quarter. We tried to do a lot of things to tell people what this new age at Pillsbury was all about.

—GF

hot line. The more than 2,300 messages recorded since 1993 have prodded about 200 product and cost-savings ideas, including recommendations for new pizza toppings and recycling of surplus plant paper into packaging material. Pillsbury has streamlined the business-expense reimbursement system and speeded up the process for calculating pension benefits. And, a broadcast voice-mail now shoots automatically into everyone's voicemail in the case of a plant closing due to weather, courtesy of a caller's suggestion.

## At a Glance

**Organization**
The Pillsbury Company

**Industry**
Food industry

**Employees**
18,000

**HR Employees**
120 (U.S.)

**Challenge**
Pillsbury needed to strengthen two-way conversation in the wake of numerous corporate changes.

**Solution**
Management contracted with InTouch, a toll-free, third-party voicemail messaging system.

**Results**
More than 2,000 messages recorded since 1993 have prodded about 200 product and cost-saving ideas; everyday process problems, questions get handled quickly.

These big changes, however, aren't the crux of InTouch. De Ocejo says 99 percent of calls are about more mundane local matters that just need clearing up—the sales force isn't getting price lists on time, or a new delivery route isn't working. Thirty-six percent of calls concern benefits, followed by 18 percent concerning product and cost-savings ideas and 18 percent concerning organization and morale issues. Workplace and environment suggestions make up 7 percent of calls, as do policy and procedure suggestions. The remaining 4 percent is miscellaneous.

Lilienthal attributes In-Touch's success to its comfort zone of anonymity and to its convenience. "Most employee suggestion systems aren't necessarily easy to use. This [hot line] is. You don't even need to figure out whom to go to—the message goes right to the top."

As important as convenience is to Pillsbury's approach, Lilienthal says the company's follow-through efforts are what makes it really work.

Of course, de Ocejo admits the hot line will never be preferable to one-on-one frank conversation. But the hope is that employees will transfer the skill of talking candidly to in-person conversations and that managers will become better listeners and problem solvers for their workers.

As for employees, they're grateful. "It's things like this that make me work twice as hard . . . that re-motivate me," one caller said.

Someday, Corporate America may reach that nether world in which all employees can say anything to all managers. Until then, Pillsbury's hot line—and HR's involvement with it—is a major ingredient to the company's success.

 **Article Review Form at end of book.**

What are some of the managerial implications of the sentiments and characteristics of the so-called "Generation X?"

# The X Styles

## Cheryl O'Donovan

*Cheryl O'Donovan, a creative consultant, recently launched her own consulting firm, O'Donovan Creative Consulting, Schaumburg, Ill.*

Generation X resents limits, hypocrisy and anyone defining them. "Generation X," those 44.5 million born between 1965 and 1976, are individuals, not a category. Some researchers call them "Busters," because the 11-year span was a blazing contrast with the U.S. Baby Boom of 1946–1964, when 77 million children entered the world.

Xers are now 21, with un-lined faces and most with college diplomas, or 32 and fed up with corporate antics. Their impatience leads the more swashbuckling Xers to forge their own "virtual" online businesses to conquer the Internet. Many Xers did not attend college—or were serial students, attending school after school. Xers don't climb ladders, as one *Fortune* article suggested, but dangle across a jungle gym, making shrewd moves that broaden their skills. They are sponges, soaking up technical knowledge that eclipses their Boomer predecessors. Xers crave constant stimulus. They love fun. They hate routine.

The label "Generation X" originated with Canadian Douglas Coupland, whose wry 1991 novel talked about "McJobs" and lowered expectations. Media hyperbole portrays Generation X as petulant "slackers" who refuse to leave the nest, with toddler-like attention spans. Twenty-somethings deserve a closer look, starting with their family origins. Most Xers weren't raised by stay-at-home moms. Their parents were probably divorced. The first "latch-key" kids, Xers went to day care and returned to an empty home after school. They turned to friends or a video game to ease their loneliness. Television imprinted this generation—starting with the children's TV show "Sesame Street" and then on to darker cable fare, including violence. Many have used a computer since they were six years old. Xers were also saturated with ad slogans and brands. Ergo, they want variety. Options. Brevity.

Several outcomes sprung from these early experiences. One, Xers grew up quickly. They mastered self-reliance. Some experts contend the reason why Xers postpone leaving home: They didn't have their parents' attention as children, and want to compensate. Other Xers concede it is too late, and freely admit their parents weren't influences. One young man credited his peers and the media in fortifying his work ethic, not his mother or father. Says Michael, a technical programmer, "They weren't around much to reinforce any habits."

Parental leniency and indifference also led to Xers' issue with authority—taking orders, for example. Interestingly, Xers demand respect, yet expect elders to earn theirs. Also, Xers tend to be vocal. "They always ask 'why' they have to do something," grouses a 39-year old finance manager, who's never seen any Xer employee stay after five. "I never asked 'why.' I just bit the bullet and did it."

Part of the communication rupture is because of Xer perceptions. Xers want it real. They loathe hypocrisy. And Boomers, feel many Xers, drip with hypocrisy. Boomers bemoan the Xer work ethic, yet waste time politicking. Remember the hazy footage of Boomers swarming

Woodstock and protesting the Vietnam War? They didn't miss a beat in trading in those love beads and idealism for BMWs and the boardroom, and have largely preserved corporate hierarchies. Xers are struck by the double-talk. They heard about "quality time" when they seldom saw their vagabond parents. Mission statements that preach "teamwork" and "time management" defy those glib Boomers who try to outdo each other, or who apply layer after layer of procedures and standards.

The U.S. Congress and White House display those same fissures. "Leadership lacks decision-making," says Michael, 29, who's helping fine-tune a voice response system. "No one is firm on their positions. 'Pleasing everyone' is weakness. But there are those few who will make a stand for their beliefs, like Tiananmen Square in China." Despite President Clinton's saxophone playing and Madonna's MTV campaign urging younger people to vote, few did. One 25-year-old volunteered to help during the last Democratic convention, but her objective was to meet people, not fulfill a civic duty.

Organizations, even the White House, will continue to seek talent, and talent will come with a price. By the year 2000, there is an anticipated labor shortage—seven workers for every 10 jobs. Hints of the future are evident today. While HR organizations peddle "recruitment and retention" seminars, headhunters forage through resumes, only to bleakly report to their clients that "all the good ones are taken." This dearth of workers should prove to be Xer's advantage—especially the star performers. Generation X, predict business soothsayers, will influence the work place more than the three generations preceding it.

How? Generation X includes more African-Americans, Hispanics and Asians. They are potent advocates for diversity. Xers don't poke a toe into technology and shudder—they plunge ahead, and technology, like the Internet, is exploding. If Boomers had strength in numbers, Xers have strength in scarcity. Those born in the mid-'70s represent the smallest pool of entry workers in six decades. With older Boomers retiring earlier, even more positions will be vacated. Since there are fewer of them, Generation X may successfully bend the work force to their will. Look to these possibilities: shorter work weeks, flexible hours, expanded job boundaries and greater personal development.

Then again, such a sunny interpretation of the future is a 360-degree spin from another perspective. The delineation of Boomers versus Busters depends on who you're talking to. An October 1993 *Fortune* magazine article advises to "throw out the textbook definitions that identify boomers and busters." Bill Strauss and Neil Howe, authors of *Generations* and the *13 Gen,* call the generation born between 1961 and 1981, "13ers," denoting their status as the 13th generation since the founding of the republic. Says Strauss, in that same *Fortune* article, "Our shorthand is that boomers are too young to remember Roosevelt dying while 13ers are too young to remember Kennedy's assassination." 13ers outnumber Boomers and have dim prospects—as Boomers get richer, 13ers poorer, for one.

Auren, a Berkeley, Calif., student, cautions against definitions or generalizations. "The problem is that there are very few spokespeople for us. There are millions of Xers with thousands of different personality types. One message will never reach them all."

Leigh is a 28-year-old technical writer and former programmer, now steering her career toward multimedia. Her story echoes Xer themes, yet she bristles at the term. "When I hear 'Generation X,' I think of dirty flannel shirts, MTV and Mountain Dew commercials. I'm not a part of that. I'm very aware of the job market, and do not feel any allegiance to one employer. I know that if I get laid off tomorrow, I have skills to get a new job quickly or become an independent consultant. If my current position does not provide an opportunity to learn, use the latest technology, or attend training, I will have no problem leaving. A lot of my MBA friends have turned down the high-powered, big-paying management consulting or investment banking jobs. They're taking jobs that offer the easier lifestyle."

Xers believe in life after work. Money's okay. Titles are pretty innocuous. Freedom—now; freedom to the Xer is everything. Daniel posted an "X" essay at his web site and suggests their casual philosophy will never fit inside a Fifth Avenue suit. "I think young people would feel less comfortable at IBM than the local computer store," he says. "People my age want to earn a living, not sell out their principles."

Xers are primarily offspring of Boomers. They refuse to become their parents, a timeless thread in human civilization. Yet, the two may be more alike than dissimilar. If Boomers yearn for status, isn't the Xer need for attention essentially the same? Both seek answers but seldom look inward. Xer grandparents, the parents of Boomers, endured hardships with quiet resolve. They survived the depression, fought World War II and rebuilt Europe. They certainly didn't have the luxuries their successors do. Perhaps with choices comes endless speculation—and self-absorption. "Go into a shop where five shirts are on the shelf, and the decision is easy," says one partner of a large consulting firm. "Go into another store where there are 200 shirts, and after you choose, you'll always second-guess yourself."

The fallout from today's corporate unrest is unknown. We are bystanders at the merry-go-round. We see the swirl of colors, but we don't know when it will stop. Social transformations, such as women going to work en masse, were double-edged, affecting the office and the homefront, and in ways we could not have imagined. Downsizing, globalization, competition and technology kept Boomers busy enough. Now come the impudent Xers, who seem as uncompromising as they are technically brilliant.

We grow older and thankfully, more mellow. Will Xers mirror the Boomers of today when they're 40? "Probably," says Michael, the almost-30 programmer. He grins and shakes his head. "No—we'll definitely be more like them. We'll think our children are too spoiled and have life too easy."

## Retaining Xers

One career advisor calls her young clients "hummingbirds" because they flutter from job to job. Generation X likes "doers," not talkers, when it comes to companies. Here are tips on how to keep them:

### Ask and Listen

Ask how they feel. It shows your respect. Inquire how to improve the project. Caring about their opinions gets them involved. In Generation X surveys, the best boss is "someone who listens to me." One Xer elaborates: "We feel that being a loyal boss is just as important as being a loyal employee. Accept our views as our own, not as anti-management." Support Xers outside the job too. If they have personal problems, offer to talk it over.

### Don't Coddle

Rigid management styles or smother tactics drive Xers away. Don't hand-hold or hover. Xers prize their independence. And condescension will raise anyone's hackles—especially the Xer's. Instead, help them set goals. They'll take it from there.

### Hates Routines, Loves Challenges

If your company is steeped in paperwork and processes, your Xer employees will become frustrated. They don't talk. They do. Jobs that provide a little adventure attract the Xer, whether it is solving a pesky problem or discovering a faster way to do something. They need work that engages them. Mundane tasks are boring.

### Train and Nurture

Mentor Xers, and provide personal growth programs. Meet with Xers daily, don't send a written report. Give them positive feedback. Recognize them. Training is a big motivator. They believe in strengthening their skills, especially mastering new technology. It makes them more marketable.

### Specify Expectations

Some Xers will test their supervisors to see what they can get away with. Everyone had a starting point, and had mentors who helped inspire them. Teach responsibility. Teach by example. Responsibility helps fuel an individual's sense of purpose. Accomplishment is gratifying.

### Make Work Fun

Xers love social events like sales events, holiday parties, family picnics and softball teams. Personal touches like birthday parties help lift morale and cultivate team spirit.

### Play Now, Pay Later?

Companies ought to invent fresh ways to reach their Xer employees. Benefit statements often get tossed by Xers. "I don't think we're looking at retirement," said a 28-year old technical consultant. "Most Xers don't stay very long with a company to have a large 401k. And with social security becoming non-existent, we could be struggling at an old age."

## Alex, 27

*Technical Analyst*

Alex belongs on a beach, stretched out on soft sand, his fingers tapping on a wireless laptop. A handsome African-American, Alex's wide smile and breeziness are straight out of Hollywood. He recites box-office statistics and hoots over last night's "Friends" TV episode. On weeknights, he and a cadre of young consultants bar-hop. Alex's salary approaches six figures and his new gig is with a high-tech monolith. He is affable yet speaks his mind. He also has blown off a breakfast meeting or two. Still, he is given more responsibility. "Alex can handle anything," says one of the team leads on the project. "He's smart and he catches on fast. He can switch from programming to testing to documentation. That's why we call him a wild card." Alex shrugs at the compliment. Work for a Fortune 500 firm? Maybe, he tells you. Maybe not.

## Shannon, 31

### Marketing Consultant

Shannon languished in a manager position where her writing skills were wasted. The woman she supervised was nearly 10 years older. They were cubicle neighbors, which annoyed Shannon. "If I'd had an office, that would have established who was boss." When Shannon turned 30, she was promoted. Now, she travels internationally and orchestrates global events. Shannon's a tireless member of "Executives Under 35." As lieutenant to one of the most powerful people in her firm, she is cementing an invincible business network. Two years ago, Shannon's performance evaluation was a disaster. Her supervisor didn't like her. Today he's in the same office, but under different circumstances. Shannon laughs. "Now he seems a little afraid of me."

## Melinda, 26

### Switching to Social Work

Five phone calls later, Melinda tosses the head-set on her desk. She glances at the religious say-

---

## Getting to X

Bruce Tulgan, 28, author of *Managing Generation X: Bring Out the Best in Young Talent*, counsels the communicator on how to reach Xers:

*How can the corporate communicator reach the Generation X audience?*

Let's say you're the editor of an employee newsletter.

Be real. Get the information out. Keep the message brief, straight and simple; keep the lines open and clear. Communicate relevant information that is key to personal success, growth and development.

*Why are companies like Microsoft so skilled at attracting and keeping the best GenX employees? About 80 percent of their employees are under 40.*

They operate in an exciting entrepreneurial environment. What matters is not where you've been, who you know or what you've done—but what can you do right now. If it works, you do it and they sell it. They also know what Xers want: marketable skills, relationships with decision makers, creative challenges. This gives Xers the chance to collect proof of ability to add value (tangible results with your name on it), growing spheres of responsibility, the chance for creative expression, control over their own schedules. Teams focused on clear goals, where everybody has a clear role, and leadership is facilitative—and more.

*Why do Boomer bosses fail to connect with their Generation X employees?*

Management failures happen at any age. Here are the more frequent ones: poor time management, which includes face-to-face time, holding on to intermediate results with slow turnaround time. Micromanagement is another bad sign. Fear-based, or abusive management, will always result in high turnover. Bosses who don't give enough feedback, credit or rewards fail to connect with employees. Watch out for unwelcoming corporate cultures, where the individual is undervalued. You'll usually find too many layers of management at those places, poor communication and closed-door policies.

Bruce Tulgan is founder of Rainmaker, a Connecticut-based firm.

---

ings adorning her cube. Helping others is gratifying, which is a large chunk of her customer service job, but she's searching for more. After graduating from college, Melinda was courted by the big six accounting firms. She left after two years of consulting, then started with a high-tech company. Melinda quickly learned her forte isn't paperwork, politics or technical wizardry. It's people. If a coworker is pushed around, Melinda becomes the crusader. Her outspokenness has gotten her into trouble, and she isn't apologetic. Restless and discouraged,

Melinda longs to carve her initials somewhere. So, at nights, while her husband baby-sits their cats and dogs, she pursues a master's in sociology. Melinda is also completing an internship. There, she's befriended another social worker. He's chasing the bigger bucks and prestige of the corporate world. "It's strange, he wants to get in, I want out." Melinda's eyes are pensive. "But I want a soul when I grow older."

 **Article Review Form at end of book.**

# WiseGuide Wrap-Up

- Although the importance of leadership is almost universally recognized and accepted, an exact definition of the concept has been more elusive. The most widely shared definition of leadership is that it is an interpersonal influence process.

- Emotional maturity and social skills, which together comprise emotional intelligence, are complimentary to IQ and technical skills in terms of managerial effectiveness.

- The effect of monetary compensation on employee motivation is a frequently debated topic in business. Like almost any managerial concept, the efficacy of formal reward on motivation depends on the context. In the case of a monetary reward, the connection between the reward and performance, and the receiver's perception of how and why the reward is proffered, are critical to the reward's efficacy.

- Authentic and rich communication is an important component of interpersonal relationships, and as such, can facilitate managerial effectiveness. Communication processes are multifaceted and must consider the context of the values and preferences of both the sender and receiver.

## R.E.A.L. Sites

This list provides a print preview of typical **Coursewise** R.E.A.L. sites. (There are over 100 such sites at the **Courselinks**™ site.) The danger in printing URLs is that web sites can change overnight. As we went to press, these sites were functional using the URLs provided. If you come across one that isn't, please let us know via email to: webmaster@coursewise.com. Use your Passport to access the most current list of R.E.A.L. sites at the **Courselinks** site.

**Site name:** Mckinsey Quarterly
**URL:** http://www.mckinseyquarterly.com/home.htm
**Why is it R.E.A.L.?** At this site are summaries of articles on management from a leading management consulting firm.
**Key topics:** motivation, future management trends, research reports
**Try this:** Read and summarize an interview with a successful manager.

**Site name:** Wharton: Center for Leadership and Change Management
**URL:** http://www-management.wharton.upenn.edu/leadership/
**Why is it R.E.A.L.?** This web page is sponsored by the Wharton School of the University of Pennsylvania and its Center for Leadership and Change Management.
**Key topics:** leadership, motivation, change management
**Try this:** Locate and comment on an article concerning the management of teams.

**Site name:** Managing Your Boss
**URL:** http://www.srg.co.uk/mgboss.html
**Why is it R.E.A.L.?** This site provides advice on how to manage one's superior, such as being a good listener and asking supportive (instead of argumentative) questions.
**Key topic:** nature of management
**Try this:** Can you use information at this site to manage your professor?

# section 7

## Learning Objectives

- Describe the advantages and disadvantages of the use of self-managed teams to improve organizational productivity.

- Explain the role of top-level management in setting organizational purpose and keeping organizations on track.

- Explain how employee perceptions of managerial actions impact motivation and productivity.

*Control* is a word that often evokes a negative reaction, particularly when used in regard to relationships with others. However, an essential function of management is to maintain control over enterprise activities and to direct efforts and resources toward the achievement of predetermined goals and objectives. An axiom of contemporary management is that workers are likely to prefer personal discretion and to resent autocratic or authoritarian leadership. So once again, tension and competing values affect managerial work. On the one hand is a management imperative to maintain control over what is accomplished in the manager's domain of responsibility; on the other hand is the awareness that the employees the manager directs prefer more flexible arrangements. The readings in this section offer several perspectives on how managers resolve this dilemma and deal with the omnipresence of change in organizational life.

To their dismay, some managers find that the more they try to specifically control organizations, the less control they seem to have. A particularly autocratic manager in one organization had a legendary obsession with control. He was particularly tough on his employees, spending an inordinate amount of time patrolling the break area to identify those who stayed longer than the prescribed time. The workers had a habit of lining up in front of the time clock, hoping to be the first to punch out at the end of the day and thus win the race to the parking lot, a practice that infuriated the manager. At one point, a supervisor who worked for the manager described the sorts of skills he was developing in this organizational culture as being exactly the same as those needed by prison guards. Want to take a guess as to the overall efficiency and productivity of the organization?

In a sort of managerial jujitsu, some organizations have experimented with utilizing less management as a way of achieving more orientation toward goals and objectives. Reading 30 is a case study of Xerox's effort to let small groups and teams manage themselves, rather than report to a traditional managerial hierarchy of shift leaders, first-line supervisors, and managers. The reading does a nice job of identifying the keys to success learned from that experience.

Reading 31 is about a senior manager, Craig Barrett, of Intel Corporation, the giant computer chip manufacturer. Barrett is at the helm of an organization in an industry that is constantly buffeted by considerable, fast-paced change. Reading 32 recounts the life of Sam Walton, a man who worked from a very modest beginning to establish the retailing colossus that bears his name. This reading demonstrates how some people achieve success by having a particularly acute sense of what will happen next in society and commerce. As you read Readings

31 and 32, consider how individuals like Barrett and Walton deal with change and the need to control large organizations.

Reading 33 describes the work arrangements at L.L. Bean and is somewhat similar to Reading 30 in that it discusses a new form of work organization intended to decrease the traditional supervisory arrangements through self-directed teams that rely on the initiative, goodwill, and intelligence of workers. Reading 34 is a *Harvard Business Review* case study in which readers are asked to describe what action they believe a manager should take when faced with layoffs. What would you do?

## ? Questions ? ?

**Reading 30.** In general, what factors account for the success of self-managed teams?

**Reading 31.** How does "management by flying/walking around" facilitate effectiveness?

**Reading 32.** What accounts for the entrepreneurial success of executives like Sam Walton? What sorts of managerial skills will be necessary to replicate this sort of success in the future?

**Reading 33.** How can or should total quality management initiatives be directed toward the human resources of an organization?

**Reading 34.** What are the key considerations for managing employee sentiment in organizations undergoing rapid and destabilizing change?

In general, what factors account for the success of self-managed teams?

# Case Study:

# Critical Success Factors for Creating Superb Self-Managing Teams at Xerox

Which has the greater impact on team performance, team design or effective coaching? The answer may surprise you.

## Ruth Wageman

*Ruth Wageman is an associate professor of organizational behavior in the Management of Organizations Division at Columbia University Graduate School of Business. Her teaching interests include design and leadership of self-managing teams, reward-system design for groups, human motivation, and structural and individual influences on group and interpersonal behavior. Her consulting experience includes creating and conducting workshops to help managers design and lead teams and also design and implement reward systems for group-based organizations. Her recent research has appeared in such journals as* Administrative Science Quarterly *and* Journal of Organizational Behavior. *Dr. Wageman received her B.A. from Columbia College and her Ph.D. in organizational behavior from the Harvard Joint Doctoral Program.*

Self-managing teams are fast becoming the management practice of choice for organizations that wish to become more flexible,

push decisionmaking to the front lines, and fully use employees' intellectual and creative capacities. Indeed, claims for the astounding potential of teamwork in general and self-managing teams in particular are abundant and increasing. Partisans of teamwork claim that organizations need teams to compete, and the proliferation of manufacturing teams, cross-functional teams, quality teams, and the like suggests that managers are listening.

The central principle behind self-managing teams is that the teams themselves, rather than managers, take responsibility for their work, monitor their own performance, and alter their performance strategies as needed to solve problems and adapt to changing conditions. This way of running an organization's day-to-day activities is said to:

- enhance the company's performance, because those closest to the customer and best able to respond to customer demands have the authority to meet those demands;

- enhance organizational learning and adaptability, because members of self-managing teams have the latitude to experiment with their work and to develop strategies that are uniquely suited to tasks; and

- enhance employees' commitment to the organization, because self-managing teams offer wider participation in and ownership of important organizational decisions.

Clearly, self-managing teams have the potential to make a multifaceted contribution to an organization's competitiveness.

## Why, Then, Mixed Results?

What sounds straightforward in principle—a change in authority—turns out to be troublesome in practice. While numerous examples of the gains to performance, learning, and commitment attributed to self-managing teams are offered in evidence of their value, an increasing number of organizations are becoming disenchanted with the idea. Managers observe slow and sometimes nonexistent progress in team members' efforts to take on responsibility for decisions that previously belonged to managers. They note that many teams continue to operate much as they always have: Members divide their work and do it independently, showing little inclination to join in a collective effort to improve their work strategies, take responsibility for difficult decisions, or solve problems.

These dysfunctions are not surprising when one considers that, in many U.S. companies, teamwork is an "unnatural act." These organizations have long histories of hierarchical decision-making cemented with a work ethic based on individual achievement. Given this culture and context, team members will balk at the idea of relying on one another to get work done.

For all their claimed promise, then, many self-managing teams never contribute to organization performance and adaptability—because they never operate as intended. This raises a critical question for many organizations: How can managers get teams to take on self-management and ensure that those teams will perform superbly—especially if this means bucking a long history of manager-directed, individualistic work?

## Case in Point: Customer Service Teams at Xerox

This is precisely the question that faced the Xerox Corporation's Customer Service organization. "Working solo" was part of this unit's culture. In fact, the customer service engineers (CSEs) were hired, in part, because of their ability to work alone, independently, and without supervision.

For many years, each individual CSE handled specific territories and customer accounts. This changed when the unit's senior management created interdependent self-managing teams, each composed of multiple CSEs who would share responsibility for the team's collective customers. Moreover, the groups would be responsible for more than simply fixing equipment—they would design maintenance procedures for their many kinds of machines, analyze and monitor the machines' performance levels, manage the costs of their work, and solve the problems created by unpredictable customer needs.

In many cases, management intended the groups to go even further in the decisions they made: Teams would select their own members, provide peer feedback, and assist in the design of support systems. The Xerox teams provide the main point of contact between the company and its customers—and their effectiveness is critical to the company's ultimate success.

How well do these self-managed service teams actually function? In general, the results are quite positive. But a closer look shows that the teams vary in the degree to which they have embraced self-management and matured into the proactive problem-solving units they were intended to be. Consider two examples, selected from our observations of the Xerox teams.

One team of veteran CSEs approached their machine maintenance responsibilities in a way that was distinctively different from the other groups. When our researchers asked what was going on, a team member explained that they were running an experiment. The team was attempting to increase the time certain copier parts lasted by cleaning related machine areas more frequently. Each team member was trying this process on several machines and recording the length of time that the parts lasted. If the experiment proved successful, they could make substantial savings in parts expenses.

This same team conducted a team meeting after work hours, giving our researchers an opportunity to see its problemsolving dynamics in action. A team member who had been absent earlier in the day explained that he was actually on vacation and had come in just for the meeting. We asked if this happened often. "When we need to," he replied. "We're in charge of our own schedules, so we have to make our vacation plans work with no decrease in care for our customers. All of us have come in on vacation days at some time or another when the call rate got too high for the rest of the team to handle."

We observed a second team, also composed of veteran CSEs, as it reviewed performance data at a group meeting. This team's leader (first-line manager) presented graphical data indicating problems with machine reliability—customers often had to call back to fix repeated problems. What was the team going to do about it? He put this question on the table, then left the meeting, expecting that the group would analyze and solve the problem.

Once the leader had gone, however, the conversation took a different tack. Some team members focused on problems with the data: "It's more than a month old. Who knows if that's even accurate anymore?" Others laid the problem at the feet of their customers: "Some of these call-backs are for trivial problems, and at least one of those machines was abused." Still others chose not to participate in the conversation: "Those aren't my customers."

While these critiques of the data and the customers may have been accurate, the conversation avoided any focus on what could be done—even on how to get better data or how to manage their customers better to prevent machine abuse.

While both teams had responsibility for managing their own work, the degree to which real self-management was expressed in their actual behavior varied dramatically. Members of teams that are genuinely managing themselves show three basic characteristics in the way they approach their work:

- They take personal responsibility for the outcomes of their team's work.

- They monitor their own work performance, actively seeking data about how well they are performing.

- They alter their performance strategies as needed, creating suitable solutions to work problems.

All these signs were visible in the first team discussed above, and all were absent in the second.

## A Question of Leverage: Design or Coaching?

How can leaders help their teams become more like the first team? Where should they concentrate their resources and energy to help guide their teams toward effective, proactive self-management? A fast-growing body of advice centers on two basic influences: (1) how the team is set up and supported, and (2) how the team's leader (or coach) behaves in his or her day-to-day interactions with the team.

Although some research addresses team design features such as team composition and organizational reward systems, a much larger body of writings focuses on the second influence—leader behavior vis-a-vis the team. Many consulting practices, skill-assessment instruments, and training courses address how the role of the manager/leader needs to change from directing and controlling the work to coaching the team as it decides how best to get its work done.

Just how important is high-quality coaching relative to high-quality team design? To find out, we conducted an in-depth examination of 43 self-managing teams in the Xerox service organization. The researchers looked at both the basic design features of the teams and the day-to-day actions of team leaders to see which of these had the greater impact on effective team self-management. The study sought to answer the following question: "If we have limited resources (such as time and money), what critical few factors should we focus on to increase the chances our self-managing teams will be superb?"

## A Close Look at the Differences

To launch the research, we first asked Xerox managers to identify teams that were either superb or ineffective. Superb teams (a) consistently met the needs of their customers, (b) appeared to be operating with increasing effectiveness over time, and (c) were made up of members who were engaged in and satisfied with their work. Ineffective teams (a) frequently failed to meet customer needs, (b) appeared to be operating increasingly poorly over time, and (c) were made up of members who were alienated from or dissatisfied with their work.

The researchers then assessed a wide variety of team features to determine which most strongly differentiated between the superb and the ineffective. Each self-managing team participated in a two-hour interview, describing their history, their work, and the context in which they operated. Their first-line managers provided extensive descriptions of how these teams were set up and supported. Finally, each team member completed an extensive survey describing the team, its interactions, and its environment.

Team self-management was measured by assessing such behaviors as the degree to which the team monitored its own performance and acted to improve its work strategies without waiting for direction.

Researchers also measured a range of coaching behaviors, some of which were expected to promote self-management, others to undermine it. Appropriate coaching included sending cues that the team was responsible for its own performance, providing timely feedback and information, and helping the team develop problem-solving strategies. Ineffective coaching included intervening in the team's day-to-day work and providing solutions to team problems.

Design factors covered a wide range of features, including team composition, team size, the design of the task, the design of the reward system, and many others. (See Exhibit 1 for a list of the full range of potential influences assessed.)

These measures allowed a direct test of the following question: Which makes a bigger difference in team self-management and performance—how well leaders coach their teams, or how well the teams are designed and supported?

## Critical Ingredients for Team Self-Management

We asked 43 team leaders (the first-line managers) to draw on their considerable experience and predict how our research would answer this question. Almost without exception, they chose coaching as the critical differentiating factor—and they were wrong.

The quality of a team's design, our data showed, actually had a larger effect on its level of self-management than coaching—by a wide margin. Well-designed teams show far stronger signs of self-managing than poorly designed teams. While high-quality coaching does influence how well a team manages itself, it does so to a much smaller degree.

For team leaders, a most important finding to note is the joint effect of design and coaching. Exhibit 2 shows how quality of

---

**Exhibit 1**  Potential Influences on Team Self-Management Measured in the Research

### Design Features

1. Clear, engaging direction
2. Task interdependence
3. Authority to manage the work
4. Performance goals
5. Skill diversity of team members
6. Demographic diversity of team members
7. Team size
8. Length of time the team has had stable membership
9. Group rewards
10. Information resources
11. Availability of training
12. Basic material resources

### Coaching Behaviors

*Potential positive influences:*

1. Providing reinforcers and other cues that the group is responsible for managing itself
2. Appropriate problem-solving consultation
3. Dealing with interpersonal problems in the team through team-process consultation
4. Attending team meetings*
5. Providing organization-related data*

*Potential negative influences:*

1. Signaling that individuals (or the leader/manager) were responsible for the team's work
2. Intervening in the task
3. Identifying the team's problems
4. Overriding group decisions**

---

*Because all leaders engaged in this behavior, it was impossible to determine whether it influenced team behavior.

**Because very few leaders engaged in this behavior, it was impossible to determine whether it influenced team effectiveness.

---

design and coaching work together to influence team self-management. The first diagram shows the influence of high-quality coaching on well-designed vs. poorly designed teams. Note that good coaching had a far more powerful effect on well-designed teams than on poorly designed ones. The implication is that teams whose leaders are good coaches are better self-managers only when the team structures are well designed.

Teams that had many of the critical design features in place became even more self-managing when their leaders provided effective coaching—for example, helping the team build its problem-solving repertoire. Poorly designed teams hardly responded at all to good coaching. Leaders who tried to help a poorly designed team had almost no impact on the team's ability to self-manage, despite the fact that the leaders followed the principles of effective coaching.

Moreover, ineffective coaching had a much more detrimental effect on poorly designed teams than on well-designed teams. At the same time, coaching errors (such as intervening in the team's work and overriding decisions) had very little negative impact on well-designed teams. These teams were robust enough to remain highly self-managing in spite of a leader's blunders— whereas poorly designed teams were hindered by such errors. (The second panel in Exhibit 2 shows the influence of poor coaching on well-designed vs. poorly designed teams.)

These findings suggest that the first step in creating effective

Exhibit 2

How Team Design and Quality of Coaching Affect Team Self-Management

**High-quality coaching**

| | Team design | |
| --- | --- | --- |
| | High quality | Poor quality |
| Little | Moderate to high self-management | Low self-management |
| A great deal | Very high self-management | Low self-management |

**Poor-quality coaching**

| | Team design | |
| --- | --- | --- |
| | High quality | Poor quality |
| Little | Moderate to high self-management | Low self-management |
| A great deal | Moderate to high self-management | Very low self-management |

self-managing teams is to get the team designed right. Only then does it make sense to tackle the hands-on coaching and counseling that are part of a leader's day-to-day interactions with the team. To have the greatest possible influence, then, a team leader needs:

1. knowledge of the design factors that most strongly influence the effectiveness of self-managing teams;

2. the diagnostic skills to tell which factors are present and which are absent; and

3. the ability to act—to put the missing factors in place.

The following discussion addresses each of these three issues. We first focus on the seven critical success factors that the study revealed had the most impact. To address the second issue, we present a set of diagnostic questions to help assess whether a particular factor is in place for a team. To address the third area, the discussion of critical factors includes examples of actions leaders took to put high quality design factors in place.

## Critical Success Factors

Seven features emerged as the ones most likely to be seen in su-

perb teams and not in ineffective teams. Collectively, they were strongly related to a wide range of performance measures such as customer satisfaction, speed of response to customer calls, and expense management.

Moreover, each factor is something that team leaders can influence. That is, first-line managers can determine whether or not their teams have each supportive feature and can take action to get the missing ingredients in place. The seven success factors are discussed in descending order of importance.

## Factor 1: Clear, Engaging Direction

Superb teams, far more than ineffective ones, have a clear and engaging direction—a sense of why the group exists and what it is trying to accomplish. One team, for example, stated its mission as follows: "This team exists to keep customers so pleased with Xerox that they will remain with Xerox; and the team aims to do so in a way that uses Xerox resources as efficiently as possible." This statement of direction is exemplary for the following reasons:

1. It is clear and simple. That is, it contains only a few objectives.

But those objectives can orient the team and allow its members to make intelligent trade-offs. Faced with a decision regarding whether a course of action is sensible, the statement invites the team to ask "Would this action please the customer, and would it do so without excessive cost to Xerox?"

2. It specifies the ends, but not the means. That is, it is clear about the team's purpose but does not say how the team should get there. Research has shown that this is the best way to enhance team motivation—a leader should be clear about where the team is going and let the team choose the path.

Two common errors in setting direction emerged from the study: (1) failing to set any direction at all and (2) setting a direction that is all about means—the how—but doesn't specify ends—the why. The first error occurs when leaders assume "we all know what we're here for" and launch the team without a discussion of its basic purpose. The second error occurs when there is excessive specification of how a team should operate. This undermines members' motivation to manage themselves.

## Factor 2: A Real Team Task

A self-managing team requires work that is designed to be done by a team. That is, basic elements of the work should require members to work together to complete significant tasks. Spending time together as a whole team is critical—especially in organizations where members have little experience with teamwork.

In the Xerox customer service teams, the basic task elements included sharing responsibility for all its customers (vs. having customers assigned to specific individuals), managing expenses, designing basic work practices, and solving problems. Groups with real team tasks do all these things collectively. That is, they have no individual territories—rather, members respond to calls from any of the team's customers (often consulting about which member should handle a particular call). They design their work practices collectively and monitor members' compliance with those practices; they meet every week or two; they are fully cross-trained and are thus able to help each other at any time; and they are given a group budget, with only group-level information about expenses—that is, they manage the parts budget as a group.

Two common task design errors are (1) creating a "team-in-name-only"; or worse, (2) designing a task that only occasionally requires a real team. The first error involves designating some group of individuals a team without changing the nature of the work. Previous research has shown that such teams perform relatively well, but only because they continue to operate precisely as they had before—as a loose collection of individuals. They learn little from each other, cooperate infrequently, and make few decisions collectively.

The second design error—creating a task that sometimes requires significant team activity, sometimes significant individual activity—results in what can be called a "hybrid" task. In this study, a typical hybrid task design asked the team to handle one set of activities as a team (for ex-

ample, members designed their work practices as a collective, met occasionally, and managed expenses for the group as a whole) and another set of tasks individually (for example, members had specific customers and product specialties).

Hybrid task designs create difficulties for teams because they send mixed signals to the group about whether or not this really is a team. The pull in both directions—to operate alone and to operate as a team—leaves these groups floundering, as some members attend more to their solo tasks than to collective activities. Moreover, hybrid designs prevent a group from investing significant time in learning how to operate effectively as a team. And when members work together only periodically, they discover that much of their "together" time is more difficult and less effective than their "solo" time. In the end, both team members and their leaders may be convinced that teamwork is not such a good idea after all.

This issue is a particular problem for organizations in which members are relatively inexperienced at teamwork—as many U.S. companies are. Self-managing teams need a task that is defined as a team task, that is measured as a team task, and that requires the members to spend a great deal of time accomplishing something together. A task designed this way creates the opportunity—indeed, the necessity—of learning how to operate effectively as a unit.

## Factor 3: Rewards for Team Excellence

This study, as well as previous research, shows that team rewards (not individual or mixed rewards)

are strongly associated with superior team self-management. In our study, teams were considered to have team rewards if at least 80 percent of the available rewards were distributed equally among team members. The exceptions to this were: (1) small rewards from the leader that are given to individual team members for actions that support the team and (2) rewards given to the team as a whole but distributed differentially by team members themselves.

The use of mixed rewards—about half provided to individuals and half to the team—emerged as the most common error in reward system design. Leaders tend to provide mixed rewards for the same reason they create "hybrid" tasks—they assume that it is best to introduce team members gradually to the idea of being fully dependent on each other. Like hybrid tasks, mixed rewards send mixed signals to the team and undermine its ability to operate as an effective unit.

This success factor is often a major challenge for front-line managers interested in getting the design right for their teams. It often requires exercising upward influence in the organization to redesign established reward systems. This has been an uncomfortable process in many organizations, especially in cases where employees have participated in designing the former individual merit system. In these cases, getting group rewards in place means a leader must exercise authority over the teams themselves and create an appropriate team-based reward structure. Some lingering discomfort remains in many companies—among managers and employees alike—about "group-only" rewards. But, contrary to what many managers believe, rewards that are about 50/50 individual/group are associated with the lowest team performance.

## Factor 4: Basic Material Resources

These are the physical materials the team needs: the tools, appropriate meeting space, access to computing services, and other resources that make it possible for the team to work in a timely, proactive, and effective fashion. Teams that had such resources readily available strongly outperformed teams that did not. My observations suggest that leaders are sometimes reluctant to provide resources to struggling teams, under the premise that "they haven't learned to manage them yet." But this very lack of resources may be among the factors demoralizing the team and preventing it from embracing self-management.

Some leaders dealt with their reluctance to hand over resources to struggling teams by engaging the teams in a discussion of resources they really needed to perform well. They then negotiated an agreement in which the teams committed to tackling particular performance problems in exchange for additional resources. Such practices helped the teams see more clearly what they needed to do—and assured them that they would have the basic materials necessary to solve their work problems.

## Factor 5: Authority to Manage the Work

Authority to manage the work means that the team—and not the leader—has decision rights over basic work strategies. We asked teams and their leaders to tell us who—the leader, the team, or some combination—made decisions about basic day-to-day tasks. In this study, such tasks might include deciding which customer call to take next, how to allocate tasks to team members, how to schedule their time when members were away at training, and how to solve customer problems. These are decisions about the work itself—how the basic tasks are accomplished. Teams with the prerogative to make these decisions themselves, without interference from their leader, strongly outperformed those that did not.

While many of these decisions might "officially" belong to the team, some leaders frequently intervened—for example, by monitoring call rates during the day or asking a team member to take a particular call. These interventions compromise a team's sense of ownership of the work. Moreover, when things go wrong, they can easily attribute the cause to their leaders rather than to themselves. Leaders' ambivalence about the team's authority erodes the very purpose of having self-managed teams.

By contrast, the leaders of the more effective teams explicitly addressed the teams' authority and the boundaries around it. And they made it clear that they were available for consultation—but that the ultimate decisionmaking authority for solving work problems belonged to the team.

What about decisions regarding distribution of rewards, team involvement in performance appraisal, and changes in team membership? Should the team decide these issues as well? Actually, these are decisions about the context in which the team operates—different from decisions about managing the work itself. The study discovered that leaders tend to empower teams with this kind of decisionmaking once they have matured into high-performance units capable of making solid decisions about the work itself.

## Factor 6: Team Goals

This critical success factor refers to whether the team has performance goals that are congruent with the organization's objectives. Unlike the team's statement of its overall purpose, goals are specific (often quantified) descriptions of work the team is to accomplish within a specific time frame. In this study, we classified a team as having such goals if members could articulate what they wanted to accomplish as a team by some clear deadline: "maintaining 100 percent customer satisfaction this year," or "improving our customer satisfaction performance by 2.5 percent and our parts expense performance by 5 percent this year."

In some cases, the leader set these goals, and in some cases, the team itself did. For a goal to enhance performance, it had to be congruent with the team's overall direction, challenging, and completed by a specified deadline. For example, one team said that its goal was to become the best-performing team in the district by the end of the year; another identified "overachieving the performance targets of the district by the end of the second quarter" as its goal.

## Factor 7: Team Norms That Promote Strategic Thinking

Norms are the informal rules that guide team members' behavior. Our findings showed that norms that promoted strategic thinking about work issues were related to team effectiveness. Self-managing teams, unlike manager-led teams, require an outward focus on the part of team members—they must be aware of their environment, able to detect problems, and accustomed to developing novel ways of working.

This kind of forward thinking may not come naturally to teams, especially if members shoulder greater responsibility than they ever had before. But group norms that promote proactive strategic thinking are very important for effective team self-management.

Superb teams encourage members to (1) experiment with new ways to work more effectively, (2) seek best practices from other teams and other parts of the organization, (3) take action to solve problems without waiting for direction, and (4) discuss differences in what each member has to contribute to the work. These are all ways in which the team encourages a proactive stance toward problems and increases its responsiveness to changing demands.

Norms emerge naturally in teams, regardless of whether a leader attempts to guide their development. However, norms that are left to emerge on their own often do not support strategic planning. Leaders can—and should—help appropriate norms develop. One way to do this, as demonstrated by the Xerox managers, is to recognize and reinforce strategic thinking early in the team's life. If, for example, a team notes a trend in customers' needs and brainstorms approaches to that opportunity, the leader can reinforce that behavior through praise and rewards. Modeling long-term planning and rewarding teams that think strategically about their work increased the chances that the members themselves would support and encourage such behavior within the group.

Another distinction of note emerges from the comparison of well-designed and poorly designed teams. In the former, such norms were more likely to emerge naturally, and they were even more likely to take root when a leader explicitly encouraged them. The implication is that when a leader gets the other six critical success factors in place, norms that support active problemsolving and strategic thinking tend to take hold more quickly and to be more carefully maintained by team members. Tackling the other six factors first greatly increased the chances that a leader was successful in building appropriate team norms.

## On Coaching Well

For many team leaders, the struggle to learn how to coach effectively has been a difficult one. It requires new behaviors that differ widely from their old habits of directing and coordinating work. Such habits are difficult to unlearn. For these leaders, the study findings on team design should come as good news: Once their teams are designed well, leaders have the latitude to experiment with their own behavior and learn how to coach effectively. If their teams are set up right, a leader's coaching errors will not harm the teams much. And as leaders develop their coaching skills, they will see much more evidence of their effectiveness.

We collected behavioral descriptions from teams and their leaders regarding how the leader spent his or her time in day-to-day interactions with the team. We used these data to assess which kinds of common coaching behaviors were positively or negatively related to effective team self-management. Among the leader behaviors that helped a team were:

- providing rewards and other signals that the team is responsible for managing itself (e.g., rewarding the team for solving a problem; spending more time in interaction with the group as a whole, rather than with individuals); and

- broadening the team's repertoire of problem-solving skills (e.g., teaching the team how to use a problem-solving process; facilitating problem-solving discussions without imposing one's own view of a solution).

These behaviors underscored the team's responsibility for its own outcomes, motivated the team to tackle problems as a group, and enhanced members' basic self-management skills.

Among the coaching behaviors that undermined a team were:

- signaling that individuals (or the manager/leader) were responsible for managing the team (e.g., by spending more time with individuals than with

**Exhibit 3** Critical Success Factors: Diagnostic Questions for Team Leaders

**1. Clear direction**

Can team members articulate a clear direction, shared by all members, of the basic purpose that the team exists to achieve?

**2. A real team task**

Is the team assigned collective responsibility for all the team's customers and major outputs?

Is the team required to make collective decisions about work strategies (rather than leaving it to individuals)?

Are members cross-trained, able to help each other?

Does the team get team-level data and feedback about its performance?

Is the team required to meet frequently, and does it do so?

**3. Team rewards**

Counting all reward dollars available, are more than 80 percent available to teams only, and not to individuals?

**4. Basic material resources**

Does the team have its own meeting space?

Can the team easily get basic materials needed for the work?

**5. Authority to manage the work**

Does the team have the authority to decide the following (without first receiving special authorization)?

- How to meet client demands
- Which actions to take, and when
- Whether to change their work strategies when they deem necessary

**6. Team goals**

Can the team articulate specific goals?

Do these goals stretch their performance?

Have they specified a time by which they intend to accomplish these goals?

**7. Strategy norms**

Do team members encourage each other to detect problems without the leader's intervention?

Do members openly discuss differences in what members have to contribute to the team?

Do members encourage experimentation with new ways of operating?

Does the team actively seek to learn from other teams?

---

the team; by running team meetings rather than coaching the team on how to run its own meetings effectively); and

- intervening in the task in ways that undermined the team's authority (e.g., monitoring team actions and assigning a team member a particular responsibility; dealing directly with a team's customer without involving the team; and overriding a team decision—even if it seemed to be a poor one).

Coaching behaviors do influence whether the team takes responsibility for its work and monitors and manages its own performance. The most critical thing to remember about coaching is that, as we saw above, high-quality coaching had much more positive influence on teams that already had the majority of the critical success factors in place.

## The Role of the Leader

Why were leaders so convinced that their day-to-day coaching was the key to effective self-management? Perhaps it is because their ongoing interactions

with teams are highly visible. By contrast, team design is invisible—part of the background. But, as we have seen, those background elements are of critical importance.

Do leaders matter? The findings of this study might be taken to imply that leaders don't matter much. A better interpretation is that our emphasis on a leader's day-to-day coaching is misplaced. After all, setting up a team right in the first place and ensuring that it has the needed resources are critical leadership functions. The elements of team design discussed here are all features that a leader or first-line manager can and should influence.

Exhibit 3 presents a guide to help leaders determine where their leadership is most needed to get their teams set up right. The guide can serve as a diagnostic tool to determine which of the critical success factors need most attention.

## On Leadership and Timing

Leaders do have an important role in the life of teams—but that role differs at various stages in the team's life. It is useful to look back at the critical success factors to see how the leader's role changes as he or she takes action to get all the pieces in place.

**Role 1: Designer** (critical success factors one through five). This role is most critical when the team is first launched. The leader's action at this stage is to set a direction for the performing unit, design a team task and a team reward system, make sure the team has the basic material resources it needs to do the work, and establish the team's authority over and its responsibility for its performance strategies. These actions serve to get a team started in the right direction and with the right supports for high-quality performance.

**Role 2: Midwife** (critical success factors six and seven). This role becomes important after the team is launched; it is best played at natural break-points in the team's work. In this role, the leader works with the team to establish appropriate performance goals. Goals represent measurable aims that specify how a team will take on its work in ways that fulfill its overall direction. Consequently, the critical factors related to task and direction must be firmly in place.

The leader also helps establish norms about strategic thinking, thus influencing how the team uses its resources and authority. In shaping these norms, the leader is helping the team develop work strategies that use the team's decisionmaking power over how it operates. This keeps the team moving in an upward direction—toward growth and excellence.

**Role 3: Coach.** Finally, the coaching role takes over—and continues throughout the life of the team. With the critical success factors in place, the team is now positioned to take full advantage of high-quality coaching. This means that the time and energy a leader invests in day-to-day coaching will be resources well used, not wasted effort. Moreover, because well-designed teams are robust enough to bounce back from inappropriate leader actions, the leader now has the latitude to unlearn old managerial habits and take the time that is needed to learn effective team coaching skills.

## Conclusion

The seven critical success factors matter for anyone leading a team—from front-line managers leading shop-floor teams to senior managers launching problem-solving groups. Indeed, the messages here may be especially critical for senior managers. Putting the success factors in place may require organization-wide changes—in reward systems, in work design, in resources available to teams. Because it is middle and senior managers who have the most opportunity and authority to change these design features, it is particularly critical that they be aware of what teams require throughout the organization. Putting these factors in place gives the organization the greatest possible chance of getting the creativity, flexibility, and responsiveness that are the whole point of building self-managing teams.

## Selected Bibliography

For a helpful treatment of the major ways in which managers fail to set up their teams right, see the concluding chapter on "tripwires" in J. Richard Hackman (ed.), *Groups That Work and Those That Don't* (San Francisco: Jossey-Bass, 1990).

And for an extended discussion of team design and its implications for leaders, see J. Richard Hackman's "The Design of Work Teams" in J. W. Lorsch (ed.), *Handbook of Organizational Behavior* (Englewood Cliffs, N.J.: Prentice-Hall, 1987).

For a study that shows the consequences of failing to attend to team task design, see Susan Cohen and Gerald Ledford's 1994 research, "The Effectiveness of Self-Managing Teams: A Quasi-Experiment," published in *Human Relations,* Vol. 47, pp. 13–43.

For a thorough examination of effective team leader coaching for self-managing teams, see the work of Charles Manz and Henry Sims, including their 1984 piece, "Searching for the 'Unleader': Organizational Member Views on Leading Self-Managed Groups," published in *Human Relations,* Vol. 37, pp. 409–424; and their 1987 work, "Leading Workers to Lead Themselves: The External Leadership of Self-Managing Work Teams" published in *Administrative Science Quarterly,* Vol. 32, pp. 106–128.

 **Article Review Form at end of book.**

How does "management by flying/walking around" facilitate effectiveness?

# The New Man inside Intel

## Brent Schlender

Talk about a tough act to follow. Craig Barrett, a laconic metallurgist who soon will become the fourth CEO in the 30-year history of Intel, follows in the overlarge footsteps of three semiconductor industry demigods. First there was the late Robert Noyce, one of the inventors of the integrated circuit; then came Gordon Moore, who gave his name to the chip industry's key business principle; then, perhaps most daunting, Andy Grove, Mr. High-Output Management himself, a.k.a. *Time* magazine's 1997 Man of the Year. Asked how he stacks up alongside his doughty predecessors, Barrett pauses for a moment and deadpans, "I'm taller."

It's a typical Barrett comment—terse, understated, and disarming. But in his unassuming way, this 6-foot 2-inch former Stanford University professor has already put his own mark on Intel and, for that matter, on the American semiconductor industry at large. That's because it was he, in the middle and late 1980s, who more than anyone else was responsible for halting the Japanese juggernaut, namely by plotting the transformation of

Intel's then-mediocre chip-manufacturing operations into the world's most efficient and sophisticated. Without that factory prowess, Intel couldn't have parlayed its stewardship of the computer industry's most crucial component—the microprocessor—into a powerful and profitable virtual monopoly.

So successful has Intel become in the 1990s—a period during which annual revenues have grown eightfold, to more than $25 billion, and return on assets has doubled amid an $18.3 billion capital-spending spree—that it's easy to forget just how dire the situation was back in 1986, when Noyce, Moore, and Grove asked Barrett to figure out why Japanese giants like Hitachi, NEC, and Toshiba were so much more proficient at making chips. While many in the U.S. were complaining that the Japanese were dumping product below cost, it was an undeniable fact that they could pound out silicon faster and better than anyone. In fact, Intel by that time had become so battered that it withdrew altogether from making memory chips—once its mainstay business—and laid off nearly a third of its employees, just so it could afford to stay in business.

Barrett, who earlier in his career had been in charge of Intel's quality-assurance program, took to the problem with the obsessiveness of a detective and the desperation of a graduate student. He shook down American chipmaking equipment vendors for detailed descriptions of how Japanese fabs (chip plants) used their gear. He asked big chip customers what they saw on their visits to their Japanese suppliers, toured the plants of Intel's own Japanese partners, and studied every scrap of public and academic information about how competitors designed and managed their operations. Then he came back and overhauled Intel's manufacturing process from the ground up and devised a means to quickly replicate new fabrication techniques at all of Intel's far-flung plants.

"If there's a key to how we changed, it was that we outlawed one excuse from our vocabulary—complexity," says Barrett. "By refusing to hide behind the fact that each generation of chip was more complex, we were able to set expectations throughout the company to get better by every measure, each turn of the screw."

Through it all he developed the practice of what might be called "management by flying around." Seemingly immune to jet lag, Ironman Barrett has made it a point to visit each of Intel's dozens of manufacturing facilities around the world once a year. (He calls the whirlwind tours "death marches.") And even though he has held a corporate-level job for 15 years, he has maintained home base in Phoenix, where Intel has its largest manufacturing complex, rather than at headquarters in Silicon Valley. Grove jokes that Barrett "has enough frequent-flier miles to buy America West Airlines."

Grove started his tenure as CEO just as Intel backed out of the memory chip business. Barrett is taking over at another pivotal point in the company's history. For the first time since the mid-1980s, Intel's momentum seems to be flagging: Its first-quarter revenues actually dropped 7% from last year. Compounding the challenge is the fact that PC product cycles aren't driven so much by increases in microprocessor power anymore, but by decreases in microprocessor costs. Even though it clearly still dominates, Intel is feeling real pressure from competitors like Advanced Micro Devices and National Semicon-ductor, whose Pentium-compatible processors are making inroads in the burgeoning market for sub-$1,000 PCs.

"For PC customers, the question has become: 'Do I need to spend $2,000 for a computer 50 times more powerful than what I need, or $1,000 for one 25 times what I need?' The answer is B," says T.J. Rodgers, CEO of Cypress Semiconductor and a friend of Barrett's. "That's not good for

Intel. In the old days when the typical PC cost $2,000, $400 of that price would be silicon, and Intel would get $300 of it. Now all the silicon inside amounts to $160, and Intel gets that much less. Still, Barrett is precisely the right guy to run the ship if price pressure is going to happen."

That's because the same skills that ratcheted Intel into a monopoly-wielding manufacturing ace will serve the company well as the marketplace for microprocessors becomes more a cost competition than a volume game. Barrett won't be focused on building up capacity, however. He recently announced that Intel's capital spending will slow. Instead, he will bring his expertise to bear on making Intel's existing fabs even more productive and efficient. Says Grove: "After ten years of steady growth we have probably accumulated our share of bad habits and excesses and inefficiencies. In the face of a less benign environment, to move forward is going to be a tough task."

So Barrett will have to ensure that Intel is more efficient than any of its newly threatening microprocessor competitors, and at the same time identify new kinds of business to get the company growing again. As Moore suggests, "We've had a phenomenal growth period, but it has been very dependent upon a single-product area. In the future we'll need to put more emphasis on broadening what we do. The trouble is that one product area has been so successful that everything else sort of pales by comparison. I never imagined we would get to the point where we would say, 'Shucks, that's just a billion-dollar business opportunity,' but here we are."

While Barrett concedes he's more inclined to "get down on

my hands and knees looking for dust under the machines while Andy thinks the grand thoughts," he does have some ideas of where Intel will find renewed growth. Look for him to put more emphasis on special chips that help PCs handle digital photography and video. He has also been pushing Intel hard into networking gear, especially for smaller businesses. And he's keen to make Intel a player in electronic commerce, by teaming up with SAP to provide Internet transaction-processing services—that's right, services—to help manufacturers of all kinds better manage their supply chains and inventories. Says Barrett: "We're pretty good at planning and logistics, so why not try to sell what we know?"

That's not to say he isn't sanguine about the prospects for the PC industry, and by extension the microprocessor. "Today there are 200 million PCs out there in the world, and it won't be so long before there will be a billion," he says. "Many of them will be outside the U.S., and most of them will be connected. Our biggest job is to figure out what the opportunities will be once they're all out there."

Barrett may be unproven as a business strategist, but he has an ace in the hole: Andy Grove, who will stay on as chairman and who will no doubt weigh in on how Intel will broaden its business. Says Barrett: "Intel has always been guided by a collective personality, first with Bob and Gordon, then with Gordon and Andy, and now with Andy, Gordon, and me."

 **Article Review Form at end of book.**

What accounts for the entrepreneurial success of executives like Sam Walton? What sorts of managerial skills will be necessary to replicate this sort of success in the future?

# Discounting Dynamo— Sam Walton

Wal-Mart brought low prices to small cities, but its creator also changed the way Big Business is run.

## John Huey

*John Huey, managing editor of* Fortune, *co-wrote* Sam Walton: Made in America.

No one better personified the vitality of the American Dream in the second half of the 20th century than Sam Walton. A scrappy, sharp-eyed bantam rooster of a boy, Walton grew up in the Depression dust bowl of Oklahoma and Missouri, where he showed early signs of powerful ambition: Eagle Scout at an improbably young age and quarterback of the Missouri state-champion high school football team. He earned money to help his struggling family by throwing newspapers and selling milk from the cow. After graduating from the University of Missouri, he served in the Army during World War II. Then, like millions of others, he returned home in 1945 to earn a living and raise a family in an uncertain peacetime economy.

Over the decades that followed, the way America worked and lived changed profoundly,

and Walton found himself at the center of much of that change. He possessed a gift for anticipating where things were headed, and he probably understood the implications of the social and demographic currents that were sweeping the country—especially outside its cities—better than anyone else in business. That acumen hastened his rise from humble proprietor of a variety store in the little Delta cotton town of Newport, Ark., to largest retailer in the world and richest man in America.

When Walton died in 1992, with a family net worth approaching $25 billion, he left behind a broad and important legacy in American business as well as a corporate monument. Wal-Mart stores is the No. 4 company in the Fortune 500, with annual sales of close to $120 billion, ranking behind only General Motors, Ford and Exxon.

At the risk of oversimplifying a rather complex business phenomenon, it can be said that the easiest way to grasp the

essence of what Sam Walton meant to America is to read his ad slogan emblazoned on all those Wal-Mart trucks you see barreling down highways around the country: WE SELL FOR LESS, ALWAYS. Walton did not invent discount retailing, just as Henry Ford didn't invent the automobile. But just as Ford and his cars revolutionized America and its industrial model, Walton's extraordinary pursuit of discounting revolutionized the country and its service economy. Walton didn't merely alter the way much of America shopped; he changed the philosophy of much of American business, instigating the shift of power from manufacturer to consumer that has become prevalent in industry after industry.

Though it's hard to believe today, discount retailing was a controversial concept when it began to gain ground in the '50s at stores such as Ann & Hope, which opened in a reclaimed mill in Cumberland, R.I. Traditional retailers hated it, and so did manufacturers; it threatened their control of the marketplace. Most states had restrictions on the practice.

When the business began to emerge in the early '60s, Walton was a fairly rich merchant in his 40s, operating some 15 variety stores spread mostly around Arkansas, Missouri and Oklahoma. They were traditional small-town stores with relatively high price markups.

Walton was an active student of retailing—all family vacations included store visits—so by the time a barber named Herb Gibson from Berryville, Ark., began operating discount stores outside towns where Sam ran variety stores, Walton saw what was coming. On July 2, 1962, at the age of 44, he opened his first Wal-Mart store, in Rogers, Ark. That same year, S. S. Kresge launched K Mart, F.W. Woolworth started Woolco and Dayton Hudson began its Target chain. Discounting had hit America in a big way. At that time, Walton was too far off the beaten path to attract the attention of competitors or suppliers, much less Wall Street.

Once committed to discounting, Walton began a crusade that lasted the rest of his life: to drive costs out of the merchandising system wherever they lay—in the stores, in the manufacturers' profit margins and with the middleman—all in the service of driving prices down, down, down.

Using that formula, which cut his margins to the bone, it was imperative that Wal-Mart grow sales at a relentless pace. It did, of course, and Walton hit the road to open stores wherever he saw opportunity. He would buzz towns in his low-flying airplane studying the lay of the land. When he had triangulated the proper intersection between a few

small towns, he would touch down, buy a piece of farmland at that intersection and order up another Wal-Mart store, which his troops could roll out like a rug.

As the chain began to take off, Walton made major adjustments to manage the growth—again always seeming to see ahead. As early as 1966, when he had 20 stores, he attended an IBM school in upstate New York. His goal: to hire the smartest guy in the class to come down to Bentonville, Ark., and computerize his operations. He realized that he could not grow at the pace he desired without computerizing merchandise controls. He was right, of course, and Wal-Mart went on to become the icon of just-in-time inventory control and sophisticated logistics—the ultimate user of information as a competitive advantage. Today Wal-Mart's computer database is second only to the Pentagon's in capacity, and though he is rarely remembered that way, Walton may have been the first true information-age CEO.

To his great delight, Walton spent much of his career largely unnoticed by the public or the press. In fact, hardly anyone had ever heard of him when, in 1985, *Forbes* magazine determined that his 39% ownership of Wal-Mart's stock made him the richest man in America. After that, the first wave of attention focused on Walton as populist retailer: his preference for pickup trucks over limos and for the company of bird dogs over that of investment bankers. His extraordinary charisma had motivated hundreds of thousands of employees to believe in what Wal-Mart could accomplish, and many of them had ridden the company's stock to wealth. It was the American Dream.

As Wal-Mart's influence grew, however, and passed that of com-

petitors K Mart and Sears, Walton began to be villainized by some, especially beleaguered small-town merchants. They rallied a nostalgic national press, which—from its perch in Manhattan—waxed eloquent on the lost graces of small-town America, blaming that loss squarely on Sam Walton.

Walton viewed all these arguments as utter foolishness. He had been a small-town merchant. And he had seen the future. He had chosen to eat rather than be eaten. And anyway, he believed that small-town merchants could compete—if they would make major changes to adapt. As it turned out, of course, the consumer voted heavily with Walton. He gave America what it really wanted—low prices every day.

There is no argument offered here that Sam Walton didn't clutter the landscape of the American countryside or that he didn't force a lot of people to change the way they made a living. But he merely hastened such changes. The forces of progess he represented were inevitable. His empowering management techniques were copied by businesses far beyond his own industry; his harnessing of information technology to cut costs quickly traveled upstream to all kinds of companies; and his pioneering retailing concepts paved the way for a new breed of "category killer" retailer—the Home Depots, Barnes & Nobles and Blockbusters of the world. This wave of low-overhead, low-inventory selling continues to accelerate. The Internet, in fact, is its latest iteration. One can only wonder what a young cyber Sam would set out to accomplish if he were just getting started.

 **Article Review Form at end of book.**

How can or should total quality management initiatives be directed toward the human resources of an organization?

# At L.L. Bean, Quality Starts with People

As a TQM process overhauled this mail-order company's operations, HR managed the change.

## Dawn Anfuso

From its humble beginnings in 1912, L.L. Bean has made customer service its No. 1 priority. It made good on guarantees to its first customers: holders of hunting licenses in Maine to whom the company mailed fliers offering mail-order merchandise. Throughout the years, employees have gone above-and-beyond to carry on this tradition, giving the Freeport, Maine-based company a reputation for quality service. For example, when a customer in New York didn't receive his canoe in time for a weekend trip, an L.L. Bean sales representative strapped one on his car and drove it to the purchaser.

That incident certainly proved that the company is committed to giving its customers quality service. However, it also prompted management to wonder: Why wasn't the canoe delivered on time in the first place? Seeking answers to that question led L.L. Bean executives to a painful discovery. They learned that although its employees had the mindset for delivering quality service, they didn't have the power to execute it. Nor could they prevent problems before they occurred because they didn't have the knowledge of processes elsewhere in the company that affect the situation.

To remedy the problem, L.L. Bean engaged in a total quality management (TQM) system. Rather than focusing on process improvement as most companies do when embarking on such an initiative, however, L.L. Bean focused on employee development. Its definition of total quality explains why: "Total quality involves managing an enterprise to maximize customer satisfaction in the most efficient and effective way possible by totally involving people in improving the way work is done."

Its TQM system has been successful. Now in its fifth year, it has challenged every assumption and has helped the company redesign most processes. The company has boosted profits and

### Managing Change

**Organization**
L. L. Bean Inc.

**Industry**
Mail-order and retail

**Headquarters**
Freeport, Maine

**Employees**
Approximately 3,500 (varies seasonally)

**President & CEO**
Leon Gorman

**VP Total Quality & HR**
Robert Peixotto

**Operations**
In addition to its mail-order operations, L. L. Bean operates one retail store in Freeport, Maine, and four factory outlet stores—two in Maine and two in New Hampshire.

increased customer satisfaction. In addition, conformance has improved, safety has been enhanced and there has been a reduction in backlogs.

The company owes this success to the way the process was managed. And because the process focused on people development, it was managed predominantly by HR. Number one on its list of elements that contributed to a successful turnaround is people involvement. Number two and three are the development of a new role for managers and a system for communicating that role. At the time the company engaged in the TQM process in 1989, it had a traditional hierarchical system in which decisions were made at the top. Managers were mostly technical experts who spent little time managing people. To create an environment conducive to employee empowerment required changing these managers from doers to coaches and developers.

Other elements that L.L. Bean credits as the success factors of its TQM process are a clearly stated definition of total quality and communication of this definition to its staff; the development of an assessment/improvement process that's aligned with its quality measures; a revised accountability and reward system to recognize quality performance; and an enhanced internal-customer focus.

 **Article Review Form at end of book.**

What are the key considerations for managing employee sentiment in organizations undergoing rapid and destabilizing change?

# After the Layoffs, What Next?

Sales and stock prices are soaring at Delarks department stores, but morale among the survivors has hit bottom.

## Suzy Wetlaufer

"Periwinkle, definitely periwinkle." Claire Ladd's insistent voice filled the room, but it was greeted with dead silence.

"Did you hear me, Harry? I said periwinkle. It's the color of the fall season. And Harry, no suits this year. We're seeing all separates out of Milan, Paris, and Seventh Avenue. The woman's suit is dead."

Harry Denton shook his head and stared blankly at the woman across his desk. He knew he should be paying attention to her. After all, Claire Ladd represented a major apparel distributor for Delarks, the Chicago-based department-store chain of which he was CEO. But ever since Denton had read that morning's *Women's Wear Daily*, he had been unable to concentrate on anything but the headline stripped across the top of the second page: "Delarks Merchandising Chief Defects—Will Others Follow?"

Ladd walked around Denton's desk and gently shook him by the shoulders. In the 20-odd years they had known each other, starting when they were both "rack runners" in New York's bustling garment district, their relationship had always been honest—and even familial. "Snap out of it, Harry!" she laughed. "I'm not hawking periwinkle sweater sets for my health. Are we going to place orders here today or not?" When there was no immediate response, Ladd leaned closer, looking at Denton quizzically. "I mean, Harry," she said, "I was expecting a big order from you—everyone says Delarks is soaring again. You saved the chain. You're a hero on Wall Street. And when I was walking through the Springfield store last week, the place was filled with customers. It was packed—not like the old days, when you could set off a cannon in there and no one would notice. And Harry, the customers: they were buying. We like that."

Denton sighed. He liked it too. In fact, he loved it, as did the company's board of directors. Just that Monday, they had informed him that his contract had been renewed for two more years, with an increased salary and more stock options. They were delighted with his performance—and with Delarks. In just one year, Denton had transformed Delarks from a boring, outdated chain that catered to "aging dowager princesses," as Denton called them, into a fun, chic shopping emporium for the Midwest's growing population of affluent female baby boomers. The 28-store chain, with shops in small and mid size cities such as Bismarck, North Dakota, and Peoria, Illinois, had been on the verge of bankruptcy when Harry was lured away from his job running a national chain's flagship store in Manhattan. Now Delarks's success was the talk of the retail industry, in large part due to a leap in revenues to $400 million and the accompanying 20% surge in the chain's stock price. But the truth was, success wasn't tasting as sweet as Denton had hoped it would.

The problem, Denton knew, was that Delarks's transformation had involved quite a bit of bloodshed in the form of layoffs. Turnarounds always do; Denton had made that clear to his direct reports in his first week on the job. His strategy included refurbishing dowdy-looking stores and slashing overhead to meet the huge remodeling costs. And the strategy emphasized the need for a highly trained sales force that could execute "link selling," in which shoppers who enter the store looking for one product end up leaving with five, and feeling happy about it to boot. Link selling meant that "deadwood"—a term he never used publicly, of course—would have to be cleared out to make room for a new breed of sophisticated, energized sales associates.

In other words, Denton told himself, layoffs had been inevitable. Especially at a company like Delarks, which had for years been run by an old-fashioned, even patriarchal, group of managers led by the founder's son. Even after Delarks went public in 1988 and hired some new senior managers, the chain boasted salaries and benefits that were out of line for the industry, as well as a no-layoff policy.

Denton was well aware of that policy when he made the decision to cut Delarks's employment rolls by 20%, about 3,000 people in all. Some of the layoffs were less painful than others. For instance, most people understood that the chain's-in-store restaurants had to be shut down. Gone were the days when women had time for a leisurely lunch as they shopped. The restaurants were rarely busy; closing them eliminated about 400 jobs. The consolidation of several half-empty distribution centers was also widely accepted by the organization. But people seemed to take the firing of several hundred longtime sales-women very hard. Denton had predicted such a reaction, but he knew he had no choice: many of the old-timers were the lowest producers. And they had neither the abilities required for link selling nor a feel for the new kind of merchandise Delarks was offering: urban, modern, and trendy.

The pink slips had gone out on a Friday morning before lunch. That was the way Denton had always done it; indeed, it was the way he had always seen it done in the industry. It gave people time to clean out their desks and say their goodbyes before the end of the day. It also gave the survivors a weekend to cool off before returning to work. Denton wasn't coldhearted about the process, but having lived through about a dozen downsizings in his career, he believed there was really no "kinder, gentler" way to fire people. The best approach was to do it quickly and in one fell swoop, and to make sure that everyone received a fair severance package. In fact, Denton believed he had gone beyond fair. The laid-off employees had been given two months pay and free outplacement services for one month, practically an unheard-of deal in the retail industry.

Still, the reaction had been severe. Not so much from the fired people; most of them went quietly. But the survivors were angry, and even the new staff Denton had brought in with him were upset. Many thought he should have held meetings before the layoffs to warn people they were coming. But he had rejected that idea. His view was that when a company is in deep financial trouble and a new CEO is brought in to save it, everyone knows that layoffs are next. Why make matters worse by rubbing their noses in it?

But now Denton was nervous. The wounds opened by the layoffs were not healing. In the newspaper article about Rachel Meyer's defection, the reporter had speculated that the move by Delarks's head of merchandising was connected to the downsizing initiative. The company was a morass of bad feelings, the article suggested, although Meyer had said "no comment" when asked directly about morale at the company.

An anonymous source quoted in the article had been more forthcoming. "There's no trust at Delarks," the source had said. "People feel like senior management isn't honest with its people. They just want to fix up the company fast and mop up the damage later." Denton felt stung. Who had said that? Was it someone from inside? Denton felt he had been honest, although maybe in the rush of executing the turnaround he hadn't done enough to prove it.

"This company is a mess, Claire," Denton blurted out. "I feel like everything I've built in the last year is collapsing around me."

"What—you've got to be kidding!"

Denton pulled the newspaper out of his desk drawer and showed it to her. "Rachel Meyer is leaving," he said, "and she's walking right across the street to Blake and Company. That's bad on its own, but what if she takes other people with her? What if she takes Liz Garcia?"

Ladd frowned. Garcia was Delarks's director of sales-associate training and one of the main reasons for the chain's turnaround. Denton had brought her with him from New York, and she had performed just as expected, giving Delarks's sales associates the savvy, direction, and skills they needed to connect with the company's new clientele. Her contribution was critical, especially because Denton had switched the salespeople's compensation system from one based on salary to one based on commission.

"You can't lose Liz," Ladd said quietly. "Harry, I'm going to get out of here so you can take care of the business that really matters now. Can we meet in a week?"

Denton nodded. "Thanks, Claire," he said. "Maybe I'll have stopped the bleeding by then."

But by the next day, the bleeding was worse. Garcia was still on board. But Thomas Wazinsky, Delarks's head of HR, told Denton that rumors were flying: four or five other senior people were supposedly on their way out, including the head of the profitable store in Wichita, Kansas. And there was also talk that "legions" of salespeople were packing up to leave the company.

"Is this just talk?" Denton pressed Wazinsky. "Have you received any official resignations?"

"No—no letters," Wazinsky allowed. "But Harry, you've got to realize, people are terribly unhappy. Morale is really low."

"That's not what you told me when we paid $20,000 for that employee attitude survey!" Denton snapped. "It didn't say people were ready to quit in droves." Three months earlier, Wazinsky had hired a small, local consulting firm to take the pulse of the company's employees. The results showed that pockets of employees were disaffected but that most were satisfied with the chain's new strategy. The consulting firm said that the results were typical for a company going through a downsizing, and even a bit more positive than usual. But it also recommended that Denton get out into the organization soon, both to reassure people that there would be no more lay-

offs and to explain the ones that had been necessary.

Denton had taken part of the advice. He did visit about half of the stores, and he did explain why Delarks had laid people off but he refused to promise that there would be no more layoffs. In a turnaround situation, Denton knew, you have to leave your options open. And in fact, Denton had been right not to make assurances. Four weeks after his visits to the field, he decided to shut the chain's worst-performing store, in Madison, Wisconsin, eliminating another 200 jobs. After that, Denton felt relatively sure that the downsizing of Delarks was over, but again, he thought it would be unwise to make that news public. Too risky.

Now Denton was reconsidering: the time may have come to tell people that no more layoffs were impending. He tried the idea out on Wazinsky.

"I doubt people will believe you," he replied. Wazinsky was one of the few executives left over from the old regime. A native of Minnesota, he had been with the chain nearly 30 years, his entire career. Denton felt as though Wazinsky had never warmed to him and at times had even wondered if he should let him go. But he had decided a few months ago that Wazinsky, on balance, was a very valuable resource: he was keyed in to the organization in a way that Denton was not. It sometimes seemed, in fact, as if Wazinsky knew every single employee in the company on a first-name basis.

"Harry, can I be straight with you?" Wazinsky asked. "Of course. Aren't you always?" Wazinsky shrugged. "I might as well go for broke here, since I think my days are numbered—"

"Are you quitting?" Harry cut him off.

"No," Wazinsky said, "but I bet you're thinking of firing me."

An awkward silence filled the CEO's office.

"You're not going to be fired, I promise you that," Denton said finally. He meant it, and as he said the words, he was struck by how much trouble he was in if even Wazinsky didn't trust him. After all, the two of them spoke every day, often about the most confidential details of the turnaround strategy. The one exception had been the closing of the Madison store. Denton hadn't told anyone about that in advance except for members of the board, for fear of the news leaking to the press before the employees heard officially.

"I guess I should have told you beforehand about Madison," Denton acknowledged.

"Madison was a big screwup, if you don't mind my saying," Wazinsky replied with a rueful smile. "Yes, you should have told me—and you should have told Sylvia O'Donnell, the store manager. She should not have gotten her letter along with everyone else. People aren't going to forget that." Wazinsky paused, then went on. "I mean, Harry, there are stories going all around this company about the day Madison closed. They say people ran into Sylvia's office after the announcement and found her sitting there in shock, shaking her head and saying, 'I had no idea,' over and over again."

"I was just trying to make sure people didn't find out through the press or the grapevine," Denton quietly protested.

"Well, whatever you were trying to do doesn't matter now," said Wazinsky. "It backfired."

"So now what?" Denton asked with a short laugh. "I mean, it's crazy, isn't it? Sales are up, and I just got our last quarter's results a few days ago. We're going to have solid profits by year's end. But if the rumors are true, our great big success is going to shrink in a hurry."

The two men stared at each other, lost in thought. Then both started to talk at once. They were struck by the same plan: to hold a series of "town meetings" at every store in the chain, in which Denton would talk straight with the employees. He would promise no more layoffs, apologize for the ways those in the past had been handled, and set the tone for the company's future. "We need to clear the air," Denton said. "People should be celebrating around here, not complaining."

The first town meeting was called for two days later in one of the chain's largest stores, in St. Paul, Minnesota. All 600 employees were invited to attend the session, which was held in the conference room of a hotel in downtown St. Paul, near the store. As he surveyed the crowd before going on stage, it looked to Denton as if all 600 employees were there. He couldn't help but notice that the room was remarkably quiet. There was tension in the air.

Denton was tense, too. At the airport in Chicago earlier that day, Wazinsky had approached him with a pained look. "Harry, I just listened to a voice mail from Liz," he said. "She wants to meet with you as soon as possible."

"How bad is it?" Denton demanded. "Is she leaving?"

"Well, she says she can't stand working in a place where everyone hates coming to work. My guess is she's considering joining Rachel across the street."

Now, several hours later, Denton tried to block out his concerns about Liz and summon up

his confidence. He cleared his throat and began speaking. "Delarks is a retail chain to be proud of again," he said, "thanks to you. In the past 18 months, there have been many changes in the way Delarks does business. What we asked of you wasn't easy—far from it—but you rose to the challenge and made success happen."

Denton had expected applause at that line, but there wasn't any. He moved on to the hard part: the layoffs. "I'll be honest with you," he began, "I probably should have handled the downsizing differently—"

Here, he was cut off by applause, raucous and prolonged. He waited until it died down, and continued. "Layoffs are never easy. I'm not even sure there is a 'right' way to do them. But I take full responsibility for doing them in a way that felt wrong to a lot of you."

Again, the room broke into loud applause. But Denton could tell the applause wasn't a positive release of energy: people looked angry. He decided to cut his losses and move right into the question and answer period.

He didn't recognize the first person to approach the microphone—a middle-aged man in a plaid flannel shirt. Denton figured he was someone from the stockroom.

"Delarks may be making a lot of money now, Mr. Denton," he said pointedly, "but it's not a family anymore. It doesn't feel right. You and your folks from New York are always hiding up there on the eighteenth floor. You don't care anything about the people who are earning your big salaries for you."

Again, cheers.

The man continued, "You just fired people like Mae Collier

without any warning. Just up and fired her. That woman gave her whole life to Delarks. She was like a mother to a lot of us, especially the girls on the sales floor. You treated her like a hired hand. That's not right. You broke the heart of the store that day."

Denton had no idea who Mae Collier was, and the truth probably showed on his face. She had been a saleswoman, obviously, and most likely one who had low sales per square foot. But beyond that . . .

"Is Mae coming back?" the man at the microphone interrupted Denton's thoughts.

Denton hadn't expected this. He knew he would have to handle tough questions about how he had managed the downsizing. He had even expected that he would have to grovel about how he had botched the Madison closing. But to be questioned about an individual employee like this Mae Collier—that was not something he had prepared for.

He stalled for a moment, but he knew there was no point trying to placate the crowd with some sort of fudged half-truth. When he spoke, his answer was simple. "No," he said, "Mae Collier is not coming back. None of the employees who were let go are coming back. Delarks is a different store now, and we need to let go of the past and focus on the future, and our future is very bright."

Another member of the audience pushed her way to the microphone. "People are hurting, Mr. Denton," she almost shouted. "You can't talk about the future with us until you make up for the past."

"That's what I'm trying to do right now," he shot back, exasperated. "What do you think I'm standing up here for?"

No one answered directly, but the crowd was rumbling unhappily. Denton was about to speak when Wazinsky appeared at his shoulder and pulled him back from the podium. "Don't dig yourself in any deeper," he whispered. "Wrap it up. Say you're sorry and let's get out of here."

Denton turned back to the crowd, ready to close the meeting with an appeal: give me a chance, he wanted to say. But, looking out, he could see people were already filing toward the door. No one would listen to him anyway. He shut off his microphone and followed Wazinsky to a back exit of the hotel.

HBR's cases present common managerial dilemmas and offer concrete solutions from experts. As written, they are hypothetical, and the names used are fictitious. We invite you to write to Case Suggestions, *Harvard Business Review*, 60 Harvard Way, Boston, MA 02163, and describe the issues you would like to see addressed.

What should Delarks do to repair the damage caused by a mismanaged downsizing?

Five experts offer advice on how to revive morale at the successful but troubled company.

**Bob Peixotto is vice president for total quality and human resources at L.L. Bean in Freeport, Maine.**

Harry Denton is increasingly isolated from the company he has chosen to lead. He has put strategy before people, when his people should have been an integral part of the strategy. In his quest for a bold turnaround, he has broken trust at every turn. Thomas Wazinsky speaks for the entire company when he confides, "I think my days are numbered. I

bet you're thinking of firing me." Faced with fear and distrust and the imminent defections of top-level people, Denton needs to do the following:

Stabilize key people. He must carefully assess his senior staff, deciding how much he trusts each person and determining the value that each brings to the company. Then he should sit down with them privately and acknowledge his mistakes and what he has learned. He should express his confidence in them, his desire to have each person on his team, and his vision for Delarks's future—including what's in it for them. Finally, he should ask for each person's commitment. Straight talk, heartfelt expressions of confidence, and a picture of an engaging future are more powerful motivators than any retention bonus.

Appoint a "change cosponsor." Delarks has undergone a drastic restructuring. A CEO can rarely lead a change of such magnitude alone. Denton needs help. He should ask Wazinsky to cosponsor the company's change efforts.

As one of the few executives remaining from the old regime, Wazinsky seems to have unique credibility with the company's employees. If he is seen embracing the changes at Delarks, the whole effort will be viewed in a new light by the frontline people. But Denton will first have to heal the breach in trust that he opened up when he failed to tell Wazinsky about his plan to close the Madison store.

Clarify the change message. Although the downsizing is over with, Denton and his senior team need to develop a brief, compelling message that includes three elements: the case for

change, a view of the future, and a commitment to what will not change. Everyone in the management team should know the message well and repeat it often.

The people at Delarks need to understand the case for change: how the industry changed and why the company needed to respond. Denton may want to go beyond the message, in fact, to launch an education program that would enrich people's understanding of the business, demonstrate commitment to their development, and show trust by sharing information. By creating business-savvy employees, the program would also make future efforts to change easier.

The view of the future should describe the key elements of the change: the refurbishing of stores, the repositioning of the product line, link selling, and the new compensation system for sales associates. It should make clear the desired outcome of the changes, and it must be based on values that the people at Delarks can embrace.

Finally, Denton needs to spend some time alone thinking about what will not change. He's already rejected Delarks's former customers as "aging dowager princesses" and its longtime employees as "deadwood." One can bet that these "private" confidences have spread widely enough to become legendary. Denton needs to find something about Delarks's past that he can personally appreciate and publicly revere, something he can use as a cornerstone for the company's future. Delarks's people need to know that Denton values their past efforts.

Communicate, communicate, communicate. Communication must be constant, candid, and two-way. Denton has been assuming that people understand his intentions. But, because of the company's long-standing policy against layoffs, they were not anticipating the downsizing. And many may not have recognized the company's deep financial troubles or the way the marketplace was changing. A 20% surge in the stock price has not been nearly as important to people deep in the organization as the trust, long-term relationships, and predictability that used to exist. Denton needs to develop listening posts to stay in touch with his organization. At L.L. Bean, for example, we sample reactions to potential changes from a specially selected panel of employees.

Denton should also resume the town meetings. In 1995, following a voluntary reduction in the workforce at Bean, company president Leon Gorman conducted 27 town meetings over a two-week period. Nearly a third of each meeting was reserved for questions from the audience. This was the richest part of each meeting. It let frontline people vent their feelings and know that they had been heard.

Invest in the survivors. Delarks must create a way to help the sales force change. New performance expectations need to be clear and linked to the business case. The company has a golden opportunity to signal real trust in its frontline people by asking them to help define the competencies required for link selling. Top employees can be tapped as trainer-coaches to help their peers. Denton is likely to be surprised by the emergence of a group of energized leaders of change.

Drive out fear and build in trust. Denton should remove as much uncertainty as possible by declaring layoffs a last resort and by being clear about how decisions affecting individuals and stores will be made. People should understand that layoffs are not random acts and that their strong performance and support for the company's new directions can limit their vulnerability.

At the same time, it doesn't make strategic sense for Denton to assure people that there will never again be layoffs. No one would believe him. The only promises the company's leaders should be making are short-term tangible ones that can be kept.

Keep the spirit of change alive. Communication should not be limited to a onetime town-meeting blitz. Delarks's leaders need to repeat frequently the key points about the change effort. Frontline people need continual opportunities to vent their feelings. New information about the company's direction should be delivered to employees regularly. Such updates can occur at team meetings and should focus on measurable goals and clear milestones; and questions should be welcome. As progress, small wins, and new behaviors are celebrated, a renewed sense of energy and momentum will carry Delarks to higher levels of prosperity.

**Jim Emshoff is CEO of IndeCap Enterprises, a consulting firm based in Lake Forest, Illinois.**

I'm surprised that Denton has been so successful in improving Delarks's performance. Generally, a company whose staff is unraveling wouldn't experience this kind of turnaround.

That does not mean I think Denton is some sort of miracle manager. To restore his employees' trust and rebuild morale, he has serious work to do. But let me be very clear about what he should not do: under no circumstances should Denton backpedal or pretend to "start over" with his current staff. He should definitely not hold another town meeting or any other event in which Delarks's employees are encouraged to rehash the bloodletting they have just lived through.

Why not? Because whether or not any of the employees realize it, they have all been through the toughest part of the restructuring. Denton has already convinced the employees, old and new, that if Delarks hadn't changed, it would be bankrupt. That's why he has a shiny new sales force in place. That's why he has successfully changed the merchandise and the way the stores are operated. And that's why, in an amazingly short time, Wall Street is taking notice. Saying to employees, "Trust me—when we get through this, we're going to have a stronger company," is difficult. Many senior managers fail to get this point across in turnarounds. Denton, somehow, has succeeded.

No, this is not the time to look back. Instead, Denton must begin to capitalize, in a very tangible way, on the solid foundation he has built. Specifically, he should focus on three things.

First, capitalize on the company's financial strength. The company's stock price—and its sales—are up. The stock may be rising on the early part of an S curve; it may shoot up even more rapidly in the near future. Denton needs to share that success with his senior management team by giving them a large stock-option award, phased in over five years. He needs to make sure that they have an incentive to remain with the company through thick and thin.

He should also open up an option or stock-grant program for all Delarks employees. People need to understand that the changes at Delarks are not just skin deep—that the company is no longer the old-school, paternalistic place it once was. And the way to do that is to let them into the organization's heart. Denton should want his employees to understand exactly what the restructuring was all about; he should want them to be looking at the financial pages in their newspapers and doing the math. The sales staff, the stock clerks, and the sanitary workers should see how a stock uptick means they will have that much more money for their retirement or for their children's college tuitions.

The sales associates need particular attention. If the commission program was designed properly, they should be taking in much more money than they did under Delarks's salary system. But Denton must make sure that the salespeople are drawing the right conclusions. They should understand that the commission program is a real, positive change resulting from the restructuring.

Second, rebuild a cohesive senior management team. Build, in fact, might be a better term; it's not clear that Denton ever had a proper leadership team to begin with.

Denton is a loner, that much is certain. His way of keeping people in the dark has been largely responsible for all the free-floating anxiety in the organization. The fact is, you can't work as a loner when you hold the top job in any organization. This seems to be Denton's first leadership position, and anyone in a new job needs time to learn

and adjust. Even so, Denton must change the way he manages.

He should start by focusing on Liz Garcia. After all, she came with him to this company. She had faith in him at some point—enough to leave another job—and she has been successful at Delarks. Denton should bring her in and say, "Look, we've crossed phase one of this thing, now the fun can begin. I want you to take the lead in building the next-generation plan for the sales associates. I'm making you responsible for tweaking the commission program to encourage cooperation among the salespeople. I'm here to help, and so is Wazinsky." And Denton should ask her some challenging questions. Can we rehire some of the old sales associates and retrain them in the new system? Do you think virtually all the stores' customers are new? Should the company segment its sales force? Have we missed other opportunities to turn the staff into a team? These assignments should remotivate Garcia, what she needs is an opportunity to move from being a trainer to becoming an integral part of the company's senior-leadership team. I would be surprised if, after receiving Denton's proposal, she didn't decide to stay at Delarks.

When Garcia is back on board, Denton should turn to the rest of the senior managers. Holding an off-site session dedicated to sharing the senior group's knowledge about Delarks and defining the innovations needed to take the company to the next level would set things right quickly. I would strongly recommend that Denton hire a facilitator to help him run the session. He doesn't need a repeat of the town meeting. But the senior management team probably will be no larger than 15 people, and he can

use the meeting to bring them together. The way he announces the stock option plan, for example, can help bond the group.

The key will be letting his managers know that he understands how Delarks fits in with their careers and with their lives in general, and that their experience should be both challenging and enjoyable. And he should impress upon them that he wants them to become the agents of a new culture that travels down through the organization.

Third, create a permanent communication process for all Delarks employees. When I was CEO of Diner's Club, we had a successful program, and my suggestions stem from that. Denton should start a program called Take Stock in Delarks. If he follows my first recommendation, all Delarks employees will be stockholders and thus will be doubly interested in the company. To capitalize on that interest, he should issue a quarterly report on progress and challenges and then use the reports as a vehicle to generate discussions in individual stores. Subsequently, he can report on what he has learned and any employee ideas he has implemented, thus strengthening the connection between management and staff. Denton might also consider hosting an annual meeting or celebration as part of the program.

It will probably be a couple of years before the program takes hold—that is, before employees believe that the program isn't a gimmick. But if Denton takes my first two suggestions to heart, resolves to keep his focus on the future, and stops playing the lone ranger, morale should improve to the point that it mirrors those amazing turnaround numbers.

Richard Manning is the former editor of the *Boston Business Journal* and *New England Business* magazine. He is now a writer, editor, and consultant north of Boston.

Denton needs to start all over again where he should have started in the first place: with his employees. And he needs to start with a display of honesty and forthrightness that so far has been incredibly lacking on his part.

The first thing he has to do is stop the bleeding. He has to send out a companywide memo that says two things: the layoffs are over, period, and I'll soon be visiting all 28 stores to meet with all the company's employees. If a copy of the memo ends up on page one of the next day's *Chicago Tribune*, well, that's simply a risk that Denton will have to take. His main problem has been isolation, after all, and anything that will bring him closer to his workforce will redound to the company's benefit. Even a press leak.

Denton needs to explain to his people in the memo that from the outset he had the equation upside down. The memo might look something like this:

"I felt that the way to turn the company around lay along the course of improving infrastructure, improving the product, and improving merchandising. And I was wrong in that assumption, because the assumption ignored the development of the company's most important assets: its employees.

"I realized this suddenly over the last few days when I learned that the head of merchandising was leaving, the head of HR was totally demoralized, and the chief of sales-associate training was poised to jump. I'd become so enmeshed in the balance sheet that I thought I could take the pulse of the company's most important assets by commissioning something as preposterous as an employee attitude survey. Such surveys are nothing but an invitation to dissemble, shrug, and flatter, and they often have no bearing on reality.

"What I have ignored all along is that in any corporation, large or small, the most important assets all wear shoes. They walk if you tell them to—as I've told 3,000 to do in the past year—or they walk if they're scared for their jobs. No steel mill, no law firm, no clothing retailer will be able to prosper if the assets that wear shoes are not managed the same way a prudent manager manages merchandising, infrastructure, and other parts of the business.

"This has been my greatest failing so far. In admitting that, I am putting my rear where I know everyone else's been all along: on the line. I should have been in Peoria and Bismarck and Madison talking with employees at the very outset, but I was not. I've been relying on outside consultants and managing in the splendid isolation of the eighteenth floor. And I've just come to the terrible realization that no matter what I do with the ledgers, if the company's assets decide to vote with their feet, there will be no company left. Dresses don't sell dresses. People sell dresses. People unload trucks. People stock stockrooms. People work cash registers.

"I've been blissfully ignorant of those truths for the past year, and it's my fault that morale is low and that people are talking about leaving in droves. To get things back to where they should be, Thomas Wazinsky, our head of HR, will organize employee feedback circles at each of the stores. The purpose of the circles will be to come up with ideas about how to make the company work better and to let employees know they have a real say in how the company operates. Store managers will present the circles' findings at monthly meetings at headquarters in Chicago.

" 'Meaningful work,' to quote William Butler Yeats, 'is not the filling of a pail but the lighting of a fire.' I want Delarks people to know they can light fires at the company."

Gun Denhart is the founder and chair of Hanna Andersson Corporation, a children's clothing direct-mail company in Portland, Oregon.

I don't believe that all is lost for Denton. At least not yet. But if he is to save Delarks, he must act fast, and his first priority must be rebuilding his employees' trust— in him and in the company.

First, I would suggest that he try again to meet with small groups of employees throughout the organization. He must be honest with them. No manager can promise a completely rosy future, and so he can't guarantee that there will never be another layoff at Delarks. But he should tell them that if the need ever arises again—if Delarks finds itself in a position in which downsizing is the only way to ensure survival—the situation will be handled much, much differently. And he should promise that employees will be kept up-to-date on the company's performance so that they will never again be blindsided.

It might be a good idea if Denton began these meetings with an apology. And at some point in the meeting, perhaps after he has assured people that there will be no more layoffs in the current restructuring, he should give them a chance to talk. People need to show their emotions, and Denton should let them do so without getting defensive. He should just listen until everyone who wants to speak has had a say.

I realize that that will be very difficult for him. He does not strike me as the kind of person who is sensitive in that way—who knows when to talk and when to listen. But perhaps he can prepare a bit beforehand—by role-playing with someone, for example—or at least make sure that his HR director is by his side at the meetings to raise a warning finger if he begins to get defensive or to talk over his employees.

Denton must understand, before hosting these meetings, that people are going to be very angry and that given the opportunity, in a safe forum, they will vent their true feelings. But he must also understand that anger is not going to be the only emotion fueling the storm. The employees who remain at Delarks are probably feeling quite a bit of guilt as well. After all, some of their closest friends—people with lifelong careers at the company—are now looking for work, while they still collect their pay. He must be ready to acknowledge that guilt and to take on some of it as his own.

When a meeting is over, Denton should hand out a letter to each employee that confirms his apology and his assurance that such a mismanaged downsizing will never again occur. That Denton means what he says and is ready to stand by his word must be made very real to everyone who attends.

The meetings are just a start. To follow through on his promises, Denton must change his management style. Specifically, that means visiting his stores on a regular basis. Getting to know employees' names and histories. Keeping people informed about the state of the business. Delarks employees should know if the stores are doing well or poorly. They should know why, and they should have a way to tell Denton what works at Delarks and what does not. In other words, they must be active participants in Denton's strategy for success, not just tools.

Denton's new management style must also include a commitment to communication—in both directions—with his senior management team. It is unconscionable that he did not inform his HR director or the manager in Madison that he was going to shut down that store. Denton has a great problem with trust. He has to realize that none of his employees will ever trust him unless he begins to trust them.

At least Denton realizes that something is dreadfully wrong at Delarks, and he wants to make things right. To that end, I would recommend that he contact Business for Social Responsibility, an organization based in San Francisco whose mission is to help managers achieve commercial success while maintaining the highest possible respect for people, the community, and the environment. With that help, and with some hard work, he may be able to salvage what was once a strong, positive company culture.

**Saul Gellerman is a management psychologist in Irving, Texas, and the former dean of the Graduate School of Management at the University of Dallas.**

I'd fault Delarks's board of directors more than Denton for what looks like an impending disaster. Denton is a former store manager with no prior experience as a CEO. Without an informed mentor—someone who can ask tough questions and demand thoughtful answers—an inexperienced CEO can turn into a loose cannon, as Denton did.

There's no evidence of oversight by the board on Denton's decisions. It was content to look at the numbers, never inquiring whether they were sustainable or what the costs and risks of achieving them were. In brief, the board's governance was superficial and helped create this looming fiasco.

That said, the immediate question is, What's best for Delarks now?

In the short run, nothing is going to change the fact that Delarks lacks an effective leader. Denton lost much of his credibility when he axed the entire Madison store without warning. That shock made the isolated gripes of the disaffected few suddenly seem all too valid to the previously silent majority. It left the survivors anxious and cynical. After the Madison massacre, they probably lived in dread of Fridays. And after the St. Paul meeting, where Denton did more preaching than listening, they most likely lost all faith in the CEO.

The company still needs Denton's strategic guidance, but it needs someone else to implement his strategy on a day-to-day basis. In brief, Delarks needs someone to front for Denton, someone the frontline troops will believe.

The only senior executive in the case who could play that role convincingly is the head of HR, Wazinsky. His job title should be changed to executive vice president. But Denton should make this appointment with his eyes open, because Wazinsky—although he may have the respect of Delarks's employees—was not a strong HR director.

First, he settled for an amateurish employee-attitude survey. His consultants focused on a side issue—how morale at Delarks compared with that of other downsizing firms—and never got down to the key question: What issues were driving the "disaffection" that burst out of its "pockets" like a virus when Denton made his big blunder and closed the Madison store?

Second, there is no evidence that Wazinsky warned Denton that Delarks would be wide open to an age discrimination suit if he based mass layoffs on anything but performance. Firing "several hundred longtime saleswomen" like Mae Collier could come back to haunt Denton in ways that he fails to recognize.

Nevertheless, the appointment of Wazinsky would at least temporarily calm a very troubled organization. The message Wazinsky should try to convey is that while the good old days are gone forever, the company will cling to its original core values—decency and respect for each employee—even as it sheds some outdated values—the guaranteed job security and disregard for change that characterized the old Delarks.

Keeping Denton behind the scenes is a first step, but not the last. To rescue Denton's career at Delarks, the board's chair would have to intervene. Specifically, he or she would have to insist that Denton agree to cooperate with a consultant of the chair's choosing. In other words, Denton would have to want to fight on at Delarks so much that he would be willing to work with an outsider to learn a new management style.

If Denton does not agree to this course of action, the board would be better off owning up to its mistake. It should buy out his contract and shop around for a more thoughtful CEO. Of course, that implies major disruptions on the board itself. But that's the price of looking only at results and ignoring how they were achieved.

Fortunately, Denton already seems open to change. He's upset and knows that he's in trouble, both of which are good signs. They mean he's beginning to face the possibility that his own decisions are at the root of his difficulties.

One final point. Whenever you contemplate firing people, whether you're letting a single individual go or carrying out a massive downsizing, the most important consideration is always this: How will your decision affect the survivors? If morale plummets, you could lose your best people and get only the minimum effort from those left behind. In short, no economic gains for a lot of psychological pain.

 **Article Review Form at end of book.**

# WiseGuide Wrap-Up

- It is difficult, if not impossible, for managers to directly and completely control even the simplest organization. Sometimes, the best way to maintain control of organizational activities is to create organizational structures and cultures that help to make the organization self-controlling through procedures or the shared sentiment of employees.

- Often, the most potent managerial forces are the perceptions that employees have of the organization's top leadership. People want to be proud of their leaders and to work for organizations they perceive as having fair policies, fairly carried out.

- How people perceive organizational policies, especially in regard to fairness, is critical for all organizations, particularly those undergoing change that may be disadvantageous to some organization members.

## R.E.A.L. Sites

This list provides a print preview of typical **Coursewise** R.E.A.L. sites. (There are over 100 such sites at the **Courselinks**™ site.) The danger in printing URLs is that web sites can change overnight. As we went to press, these sites were functional using the URLs provided. If you come across one that isn't, please let us know via email to: webmaster@coursewise.com. Use your Passport to access the most current list of R.E.A.L. sites at the **Courselinks** site.

**Site name:** Andersen Consulting
**URL:** http://www.ac.com/
**Why is it R.E.A.L.?** At this site are detailed descriptions of this international consulting firm's business areas and clients. Extensive career information and features about management and information technology also are provided.
**Key topics:** research reports, future management trends
**Try this:** Find and summarize an article about the use of self-managed work teams.

**Site name:** Employee Ownership Research Library
**URL:** http://www.fed.org/library/index.html
**Why is it R.E.A.L.?** This site from the Federation for Enterprise Development is dedicated to championing the issue of employee ownership.
**Key topics:** research reports, organizational control
**Try this:** What information at this site indicates that employee ownership facilitates organizational productivity?

**Site name:** American Society for Training and Development
**URL:** http://www.astd.org
**Why is it R.E.A.L.?** The American Society for Training and Development is a member organization dedicated to providing information and resources to facilitate effective organizational training and development activities.
**Key topics:** management of change, organizational development, training and development
**Try this:** Identify a training technique that you could use with a campus organization.

**Site name:** Wall Street Research Net
**URL:** http://www.wsrn.com/
**Why is it R.E.A.L.?** This site provides excellent up-to-date information on publicly held companies.
**Key topics:** nature of management, organizational culture
**Try this:** Identify a company that is enjoying success in the stock market, and research the organizational culture of that company.

# section

8

## Learning Objectives

- Describe the ways in which management is likely to change in the twenty-first century.

- Explain the current impact of technology on managerial practices and how it is likely to change in the future.

- Describe personal practices that will contribute to managerial effectiveness.

- Describe the likely changes in future organizational life and how these changes will impact management practice.

# Managing in the Twenty-First Century

A few years ago, my wife and I took a wonderful rafting trip with some friends down the Colorado River. Preparing for the trip, we looked over a number of brochures from guide services and outfitters, each of which seemed to include a picture of a group of people holding on for dear life as their raft went through a tumultuous rapid. When we finally got to the river, we discovered that while some of the rapids are impressive, they constitute only a small percentage of the river's journey through the magnificent Grand Canyon. Once you make it through the white water, you are shot out into a relatively peaceful and quiescent river and simply float along, enjoying the majestic scenery.

A trip down the Colorado is something like the world of management— moments of relative calm mixed with moments of turmoil and tumult, never being completely sure what is waiting around the next bend. When in the rapids, we are surrounded by tremendous forces, not all of which we can clearly see, all coming at us with incredible speed and complexity. They simultaneously threaten to destroy us or—if through skill and luck we navigate them successfully—to propel us forward to a less tumultuous future.

I was sharing this idea with a group of experienced managers, and one of the more waggish members of my audience opined from the back row, "Yeah, but they have been messing with the rapids and have pushed them all a lot closer together." Frankly, I'm not so sure that the past was as quiescent as we sometimes recall it. However, in reflecting on this individual's comments, I suppose he may be right. We tend to view the current world as more demanding and challenging than the world we or others experienced in the past. However, there is no doubt that the current and future demands on managers and management are considerable and will require new and creative responses.

Management guru and theorist Peter Vaill describes the world of contemporary managers as one of "permanent white water." The imperative for individuals, managers, and organizations is to learn to deal with constant and unrelenting change. Although we cannot know the future with any certainty, we do know that it will be distinctly different from the past. The readings in this section provide a variety of perspectives on these future demands and how we can prepare ourselves and our organizations for those challenges.

This final section begins with commentary from the father of modern management theory, Peter Drucker. In Reading 35, he reflects on the foundations of management and the challenges the future holds for those in positions of responsibility in the world. In Reading 36, Dan Johnson explores the nature and consequences of the "Third Wave," having seen commerce evolve from a concentration on agriculture, to the

Industrial Revolution—the era Alvin Toffler called the second wave—to a current concentration on services and knowledge workers.

In Reading 37, John A. Byrne further speculates on the nature of the corporation of the future. Reading 38, from *Management Review,* offers personal advice to managers working in the maelstrom of future organizational life. In Reading 39, Erick Schonfeld offers perspectives on the impact of technology on managers and management.

My sincerest hope is that these perspectives will be of value to you as you navigate the "permanent white water" of whatever management position you hold in the future.

## Questions

**Reading 35.** What are the key characteristics of successful organizations of the future?

**Reading 36.** What are some key environmental issues that will impact management and determine managerial success in the future?

**Reading 37.** How will organizational culture impact and determine organizational success in organizations of the future?

**Reading 38.** What will be the importance of individual decision making in the future, and how will it impact managerial effectiveness?

**Reading 39.** To what extent will goods be typically customized in the future, and what managerial skills will be needed to provide them?

What are the key characteristics of successful organizations of the future?

# Peter Drucker

**Patricia A. Galagan and
Stephen H. Rhinesmith**

*Patricia A. Galagan is editor-in-chief of*
Training & Development. *Stephen H.
Rhinesmith is president of Rhinesmith
& Associates.*

A figure walks onstage to accept an award for a lifetime of achievement. Eight thousand people jump to their feet and fill the vast hall with noisy tribute. A swarm of fans rush the stage with cameras. The noise rolls on and on and finally fades like summer thunder.

No, the furor wasn't for Tom Cruise or any rock star. This celebrity is Peter Drucker, leading candidate for being the most influential observer in modern business history. At 89, Drucker is a living icon for generations of managers and their teachers. An awestruck young spectator says, "I feel like I've just seen Elvis."

That a man of ideas—a writer, teacher, and mentor—would excite so much admiration gives one hope for the state of heroism in our time. It's not just that he has published 30 books and mentored some of the most famous business leaders in the world, or that his ideas permeate the practice of modern manage-

ment around the globe. It's that it all adds up to such sustained accomplishment. In an age of evanescent fame and fleeting brilliance, Drucker is a genuine, made-to-last hero.

Though he walks with the help of a cane, sensibly tagged with his return address, and must deal with the inconvenience of tuning a pair of hearing aids, Drucker has the lively mien of a younger man. White, wispy hair rises off a high forehead as if charged by the mental energy within. He has the courtly demeanor of his upbringing in pre-World War I Austria, but it's layered over with a sense of humor and a frankness that is quite American. He understands American culture so well that Henry Luce hired him to complete *Fortune* magazine's 10th-anniversary issue. English is the language Drucker writes in, teaches in, and probably thinks in, but he still speaks it with some indelible German consonants. "Ve sneak out," he said as he and his wife were leaving a reception a bit early.

He is a romantic who insists on kissing his wife goodbye before she heads out on an errand, and yet he can be feisty and gruff in defense of a cherished idea,

marshaling such phrases as "I insist" and "I forbid."

It's Drucker's writing that reveals his genius, not just for observation and insight, but also for clear and original thinking beautifully expressed. He is to management what Steven Jay Gould is to natural science, Isaac Asimov to astronomy, and John McPhee to geology.

Drucker is also a life-long teacher, first at Sarah Lawrence, then at Bennington, and for the past 20 years at the Claremont Graduate School. His model for teaching, according to a chapter in his autobiographical *Adventures of a Bystander*, was a pair of spinster sisters who ran a small school for young children in Austria before World War I. Miss Elsa, clad in shiny black bombazine and high-button shoes, and Miss Sophy, draped in pastel chiffon scarves, taught the boy Peter the essence of good teaching: to give sparing but deserved praise and ask challenging questions. That he never mastered legible handwriting nor the manufacture of a three-legged milking stool did not prevent the precocious Drucker from being promoted early to secondary school or from being "incurably infected" to teach. In 50-some years of teaching humanities, social sciences, religion, philosophy, literature, history, government, management, economics, and statistics he has "not found a subject yet that is not sparkling with interest." Miss Sophy gave him "respect for the task" and Miss Elsa "a work discipline and the knowledge of how one organizes for performance."

Drucker claims to have happened onto his role as the fountainhead of the discipline of management by sheerest serendipity. "This was largely luck; I happened to be there first." That, of course, overlooks the fact that in 1943, he saw the catalytic ideas in the management practices of General Motors—the only company that would permit him to observe upclose—and that he translated those insights into one of the most popular and seminal management books of all time, *Concept of a Corporation.* It was the first book to treat a business corporation as a political and social institution. Though economists scorned it for its absence of insight into pricing theory and the like, managers fell on it like starving dogs on prime sirloin.

One of Drucker's most original ideas was the "self-governing plant community," by which he means the assumption of managerial responsibility by individual employees, work teams, and employee groups over such areas as the structure of jobs, the performance of major tasks, and the management of "community affairs," meaning such things as shift and vacation schedules, safety, and benefits. When Drucker first proposed the self-governing plant community in the 1940s, it was a heretical challenge to managerial authority. As you will learn in our interview, he is distressed that the notion of employee responsibility has been

corrupted by the mindless granting of empowerment, something he terms an abomination.

Drucker continues to see what others overlook and to champion ideas that will probably not get their due until he is enjoying a more celestial perspective on the world. He already has an intellectual legacy that includes such ideas as the decentralization of large organizations, management by objectives, and the role of the knowledge worker. His prediction that the continuing education of adults is the next growth industry is already coming to pass. The lessons he draws from not-for-profits haven't come to a boil yet nor have his observations about demographic change ("populations are shrinking, not growing"), but he has the patience of a profoundly insightful man who has seen his vision come to be many times. To quote the American poet Robert Frost: "We dance round in a ring and suppose, but the Secret sits in the center and knows."

**Galagan:** You've described the difficulty of increasing the productivity of knowledge workers and the impossibility of supervising them in the sense of telling them how to do their work. Given that, what should a management curriculum be teaching today? What are you teaching your management students that you weren't teaching them a decade ago?

**Drucker:** I am no longer teaching subjects I focused on barely 10 years ago: I am teaching subjects I merely touched 10 years ago. I no longer teach the management of people at work, which was one of my most important courses, because I no longer think that learning how to manage other people, especially subordinates, is the most important thing for execu-

tives to learn. I am teaching, above all, how to manage oneself.

The course I just finished teaching is on the knowledge worker. It deals with what you have to know about yourself—how you have to learn, how to place yourself, how to take charge of your own work and your own career, how to make yourself productive, and so on.

Another major course I teach now, but didn't teach at all 10 years ago, is the productivity of the knowledge worker.

And another area I am focusing on is how to manage relationships in which you are not in command—alliances, partnerships, contracts, outsourcing. Such relationships are the way the world economy is going.

And finally, I am teaching a course on the information that executives need. This course does not focus on the computer and data processing, which so far I believe have resulted in executives having less information than they used to, rather than more. Instead, it focuses on the information they need and how to get it. It focuses especially on how to organize the supply of a type of information that is totally absent today for executives—information about the world outside the company. By that I mean such information as the economic chain of which your business is a small part, the market, the environment, the society, the world economy. These are all areas on which our modern technology gives absolutely no information, and yet in which both the costs and the results are for business.

**Galagan:** You've written about management and leadership, but much more about the former. How do you define the difference between them, and which one do you think is more important for success in the knowledge economy?

**Drucker:** This is largely a misunderstanding. I have written a great deal about leadership, starting with my earliest management book, *Concept of the Corporation,* which came out in 1946. In *The Practice of Management,* written in 1954, there is a whole chapter called "The Spirit of an Organization" that deals primarily with leadership. And I wrote the very first book on leadership in organizations, *The Effective Executive,* which came out in 1966 and is still a best-seller. And since then, I have published quite a bit on leadership.

I know something that today's writers on leadership mostly do not know or want to know. I come out of political science and, therefore, I know what every political scientist has known since Aristotle 2,400 years ago: Leadership has to be grounded in a Constitution. Otherwise, it quickly becomes irresponsibility. The people who knew that best were the founding fathers of the American Republic, and especially the authors of *The Federalist Papers*—which is still by far the best book on leadership.

Leadership grounded in charisma, which is what so many writers today want to advocate, inevitably becomes misleadership. I am amazed that today's prominent writers on leadership do not seem to realize that the three most charismatic leaders in all recorded history were named Hitler, Stalin, and Mao. I do not believe that there are three men who did more evil and more harm.

Leadership has to be grounded in responsibility. It has to be grounded in a Constitution. It has to be grounded in accountability. Otherwise, it will lead to tyranny. When I look at the last 30 to 50 years—I've been around that long—without exception, the charismatic leaders—whether in business, government, or religion—have ended in failure and disgrace. And they have left a legacy of mismanagement and chaos.

The test of any leader is not what he or she accomplishes. It is what happens when they leave the scene. It is the succession that is the test. If the enterprise collapses the moment these wonderful, charismatic leaders leave, that is not leadership. That is—very bluntly—deception.

I have written, I would say, as much about leadership as most of today's prominent experts on the subject, but I have always stressed that leadership is responsibility. Leadership is accountability. Leadership is doing—to use the title of one of my most popular articles and one that is quoted again and again.

And as for separating management from leadership, that is nonsense—as much nonsense as separating management from entrepreneurship. Those are part and parcel of the same job. They are different to be sure, but only as different as the right hand from the left or the nose from the mouth. They belong to the same body.

**Galagan:** In the decades that you've been observing organizations and work, you've seen many things that others missed but that came to pass and have a major impact, such as the rise of knowledge work and the social role of organizations. What are you seeing now that you think most people are missing?

**Drucker:** The one thing I see that most people are missing, and not only in business, is the tremendous implication of demographic change.

When I was born almost 90 years ago, practically everybody—95 percent of all people, even in the most highly developed countries—made their living by working with their hands and largely doing unskilled, untrained, repetitive work. They were farm workers, domestic servants, underlings in small shops; a minority worked in factories. Today, in developed countries, the proportion of the workforce that makes a living by working with its hands is down to one-fifth. No such demographic change has ever happened before, let alone in a short century.

When I was born, less than one-third of the human race lived in cities. Even in the most highly developed countries, city dwellers were still a minority. Today, there are very few countries where the great majority does not live in cities. Again, that is an unprecedented change.

And finally, the biggest change of them all is the change in age structure. I am not talking about the increase of older people, which by now everyone knows—although when I first began to talk about this 40 years ago, nobody did. The really important change for the next 30 years in developed countries is the very fast decrease in the number of young people.

The birth rate in every developed country except the United States is well below the reproduction rate of 2.2 live births per woman of reproductive age. In southern Europe—Portugal, Spain, southern France, Italy, and

Greece—the birth rate is down to one live birth per woman. In Germany and Japan, it is 1.4. Only in the United States is the rate still adequate, and that is only because of the tremendous wave of immigration from countries where the birth rates are still very high. The U.S. birth rate will go down around the year 2010. In Europe, the younger population is already shrinking fast. In Japan, it is beginning to shrink. This decrease in the number of young people not only aggravates the problem of supporting older people but also creates a totally new social, political, and economic environment.

And that, by the way, explains why the productivity of people with advanced education will increasingly become the one and only major criteria in international economics.

**Galagan:** You take a global view of management, yet there are many cultural, political, and economic factors that work against a global management model. Do you believe that an effective global management model is emerging and, if so, what are its most common characteristics?

**Drucker:** Yes, there is a global management model emerging; and, no, there is no global management model emerging. The tasks, the tools, and the problems are becoming the same everywhere, so you have to organize yourself for doing the same tasks—but with different conventions.

Japanese management does exactly what American or German management does, but we all know that in important aspects Japanese management does things differently. The same is true of the rapidly emerging overseas Chinese. We used to joke that the Japanese succeeded in con-

verting the modern corporation into a family. The overseas Chinese are busily converting the family into a modern corporation. And they are quite successful.

I hate to use the word *culture*. I think it is a word one should avoid. It has far too many meanings and not one of them is clear. Still, from country to country, culture is so different, meaning is so different.

The other day, I heard a very distinguished friend of mine, who was an ambassador to Japan, talk about his frustration in working with the Japanese bureaucracy. What he really complained about was that he never got a straight "no" from them. They would say, "maybe." But everybody who knows Japan knows that means "no."

If he had been an ambassador to France, he would have complained just as much about the bureaucracy. French bureaucracy doesn't say "no" either: It loses the file again and again, and that means "no." And we, in the United States, appoint a committee. That also means "no."

One has to learn how to say "no." The secret of good management is learning how to say "no" much more often than "yes." But different cultures, different conventions, and different managers say "no" differently. And, in that sense, the same is true of relationships, titles, and so on.

Yes, there is global management emerging simply because the tasks are the same. To run an automobile factory in Malaysia is no different than to run one in Nagoya, Japan, or in Detroit. Training people in these countries is almost exactly alike, if the training is any good. But relationships are very different between worker and supervisor, supervisor and superintendent, and be-

tween the factory and the company, even though the management tasks are exactly the same.

**Galagan:** You've written that "the task of management in the knowledge-based organization is not to make everybody a boss. It is to make everybody a contributor." Could you elaborate on the perils of empowerment and tells us how managers can avoid them?

**Drucker:** I have never used the word *empowerment* and never will. I consider it a despicable word. I have always talked of responsibility and only of responsibility. Only if there is responsibility can there be authority—that too is the first lesson of political science. If an organization is based on power, it makes no difference whether the power is at the top or at the bottom. It is an abomination and an offense, and so I will only talk of responsibility. One must push responsibility as far down as one possibly can. That leads to authority.

And so I demand—I am not saying I recommend—I demand in every organization in which I have anything to say that managers start with these questions: What contribution can this institution hold you accountable for? What results should you be responsible for? And then ask, "What authority do you then need?" That is the way to build a performing institution.

The models are plentiful. It is the model that the Catholic Church used to restructure itself in the 13th century when it was in total shambles. It is the model on which the United States Marine Corps operates, and the model on which the American Constitution was built. It is the model for every company I know that is truly well-managed. I only wish there were more.

# My Days with Peter Drucker

*By Stephen H. Rhinesmith*

It was a rainy Sunday in New York in June 1974. I was looking through the *New York Times Book Review,* and there was a review of Peter Drucker's new work, simply titled *Management.* It was a very favorable review. I don't remember the details, but what I do remember are two sentences: "Peter Drucker believes strongly in nonprofit organizations and feels their management is critical to the future. He therefore offers pro-bono consultation to a number of organizations."

At the time, I was in my third year as president of the American Field Service International Student Exchange Program. AFS is a worldwide organization that each year sends more than 10,000 students abroad to live with families in one of 60 countries. The OPEC oil crisis had just hit in the fall of 1973, and I was struggling to contain international transportation costs as well as find new ways to recruit host families around the world. I wondered out loud whether Drucker would be interested in helping me. My wife, who overheard my query, said, "Of course, why don't you write and ask him?"

I did—and it was one of the most important letters of my life. Within a week, I received a phone call, with this wonderfully gravelly voice on the other end: "This is Peter Drucker. I have read your letter. I know AFS, and I would be happy to talk with you. Come and see me." That was it—Peter doesn't talk much on the phone.

I flew to California within a couple of weeks and went to his home in Claremont around 9 in the morning. Peter answered the door, invited me in, and asked me to tell him about AFS. We talked for the morning; had lunch with his wife, Doris; went for a walk in the afternoon; and when I finally left in the early evening, we had been talking for 10 hours. I remember feeling intellectually exhausted, but I wondered what I had learned. It seemed as if I had done all of the talking. Peter had taken no notes, and I had not much on my own notepad because he had given me very few answers to my questions. I was a little disappointed at having spent such a long time with one of the world's great minds and that I seemed to have nothing to show for it.

A week later, I received a letter. It was nine pages, single-spaced, and had been typed by Drucker himself! It had taken him two days to write it, and it contained a detailed analysis of our discussion, with absolutely brilliant insight into the issues I had raised. It was obvious that Peter had spent the day doing what consultants should do—listening. Without taking a note, he had absorbed my life and my organization.

He raised in his letter to me his classic question: "What business are you in?" He observed that the business I was in was not international student exchange but "family finding." The students were what we put into families, but it was the families who were really our customers. He was right, and I spent some years working on that proposition.

But what really reveals Peter Drucker is the end of the letter. Let me quote:

"My dear Mr. Rhinesmith, I happen to believe that a professional relationship is not proper unless money changes hands. I consider our relationship a professional one, though I also hope that, as in every good professional relationship, it will contain a good, warm, close personal relationship. I am not willing to take money from AFS International Scholarships—under no circumstances. I am thus forced by my professional propriety to enclose a donation to AFS to be used by you wherever you feel that the need is the greatest."

It was vintage Peter Drucker—ethical, clear, philanthropic, and supportive. It was also the beginning of a six-year relationship, in which we saw one another several times a year to talk about the "state of the world." We always met at his home and took walks. He also started advising me on my career. That led to discussions about my future in nonprofit versus for-profit organizations. Peter eventually counseled me to become president of the American Management Association—an organization that he had supported for many years. He felt it would be a perfect combination of training and development, international operations, and nonprofit leadership. I was interested, but timing became a factor and, while waiting to hear from AMA, I received an offer to become president of Holland America Cruise Lines. It was an opportunity to practice in the real, for-profit world. I took the job; Peter was very disappointed with me. I had a difficult time there and was eventually terminated.

In an act of synchronicity, however, the day I was fired I received a call from the United States Information Agency asking me to come to Washington to provide some advice on international student exchanges. That led, over several years, to my appointment as Special Ambassador to the Soviet Union for President Reagan to coordinate his U.S. Soviet Exchange Initiative. From there, I became involved in globalization and the American Society for Training & Development. On June 2, 1998, Peter and I were re-united at the ASTD International Conference in San Francisco when he received ASTD's Lifetime Achievement Award and I received the Gordon Bliss Award.

Throughout these extraordinary times, my days with Peter have remained with me. It was a rare privilege to see not only how his mind works, but also how his integrity, commitment, and passion to providing insight on the human condition have produced one of the greatest bodies of management literature in history. These are days that I shall always cherish.

And Peter Drucker is a man whom we all should cherish—always.

 **Article Review Form at end of book.**

What are some key environmental issues that will impact management and determine managerial success in the future?

# Catching the Third Wave:

## How to Succeed in Business When It's Changing at the Speed of Light

**Dan Johnson**

Tomorrow's economy is developing from an information revolution that futurist Alvin Toffler termed the Third Wave. Just as the Second Wave, the Industrial Revolution, transformed the lives of the eighteenth-century agrarians, the Third Wave is re-making the world and the future.

"In the past ten years or so, much of the established world order has crumbled," write management consultants Jeremy Hope and Tony Hope in their new book, *Competing in the Third Wave* [Harvard Business School Press, 1997]. "We are currently in the dislocation phase between the second and third-wave economies."

Suddenly, companies born and raised in the second-wave economy are struggling to overcome profound shock, trying to learn new skills, and searching for third-wave opportunities all at once. Managers face a host of new business realities, including:

- A rapidly accelerating high-tech sector driving a third-wave economy of constant change.

- The rise of world markets and the global nature of money and information.

- The fall of government monopolies and the breakup of conglomerates.

- A dramatic reduction of inventory levels as technology allows companies to manufacture products on demand.

- The emergence of knowledge as the key economic resource.

- Changing patterns of employment that include an explosion of outsourcing and new alliances.

The authors suggest a number of ways that managers can learn to ride the third wave successfully.

Finding and keeping loyal and profitable customers is essential. The route to long-term success is to find loyal customers who represent a close strategic fit with the company and are also likely to be profitable. Rather than trying to meet the needs of a larger group of people, third-wave managers work to attract and keep the right customers. Loyalty-based strategies yield spectacular results for some companies.

MBNA, a credit card company, targets specific affinity groups whose members have above-average earnings: sports clubs, universities, and associations. The company produces

Originally published in the March 1998 issue of *The Futurist.* Published with permission from the World Future Society, 7910 Woodmont Avenue, Bethesda, MD 20814.

Visas and Mastercards for 4,300 such groups, usually with personal logos. MBNA's strategy is hitting the bull's-eye: The average balance held by its cardholders is three times the national average.

Technology is creating unprecedented opportunities to build a loyal consumer base by customizing products. Levi-Strauss offers its Personal Pair outlets for women who want a perfectly fitting pair of jeans. A computer picks out exactly the right size and sends the woman's specifications to the factory. For an added $10 fee, her made-to-measure jeans arrive a few days later.

Third-wave organizations realize the power that resides in the minds of their best people, embedded in systems, databases, and competencies. Successful managers learn how to acquire, define, and use knowledge to build long-term capabilities.

Chaparral Steel is a working prototype of a knowledge-based organization. The company has set world records for producing safe, low-cost, high-quality steel.

The company invests heavily in education, training, and formal apprenticeship programs.

"Expertise must be in the hands of the people who make the product," says CEO Gordon Forward. Along with strong incentive and education systems, Chaparral maintains an openness to outside ideas and a tolerance for failure that help to keep innovative thinking alive.

 **Article Review Form at end of book.**

How will organizational culture impact and determine organizational success in organizations of the future?

# The Corporation of the Future

Cisco is a good model. It reads the market well, responds quickly. And it knows how to harness high tech.

## John A. Byrne

*San Jose, Calif.*

The once unthinkable decline of many of the world's largest corporations has become all too common in recent years. Strategic blunders and oversights by management have pulled down such powerful and mighty giants as AT&T, Eastman Kodak, and General Motors.

Yet there is a less visible but even more critical danger: the inability to adapt to the speed and turbulence of technological change. After massive high-tech investments, management is only beginning to make the organizational changes needed to transform information technology into the potent competitive weapon that it will need to be in the 21st century.

Few companies have grasped the far-reaching importance of the new technology for management better than Cisco Systems Inc. The San Jose (Calif.) company has become the global leader in networking for the Internet, with annual revenues of more than $8 billion. It's also a Wall Street darling, with a market cap approaching $100 billion.

Cisco could well provide one of the best road maps to a new model of management. Partly because it makes the tools to build the powerful networks that link businesses to their customers and suppliers, Cisco itself has been at the forefront of using technology to transform management practices.

## Near-Religious

But it's not only the company's innovative use of technology that wins favorable reviews. It's also the company's mind-set and culture, its willingness to team up with outsiders to acquire and retain intellectual assets, its near-religious focus on the customer, and its progressive human resource policies. "Cisco is the quintessential outside-in company" says James F. Moore, chairman of consultants GeoPartners Research Inc. "They have mastered how to source talent, products, and momentum from outside their own walls. That's a powerful advantage."

This corporate adolescent—founded in 1984 by a group of computer scientists from Stanford University—is headed by a leader, John T. Chambers, who cut his teeth at successful companies that stumbled. At both IBM and Wang Laboratories Inc., the soft-spoken West Virginian got a firsthand glimpse of how arrogance and reluctance to change caused severe pain and dislocation.

Those experiences, including a traumatic time when he survived five layoffs in 15 months at Wang—before resigning in 1990—colored his view of what a healthy organization should be. "It taught me how a company should be built in the first place and how to do things dramatically different the next time," says Chambers, 48, who joined Cisco in 1991 and became CEO in 1995. "Laying off people was the toughest thing I ever did. I'll move heaven and earth to avoid doing that again."

To hear Chambers tell it, his people and his organization are "in the sweet spot"—where technology and the future meet to transform not only business but all of life. His vision is simple: "We can change the way people live and work, play and learn." It is an idealistic phrase that falls out of his mouth repeatedly and unabashedly. It is also an inspiring and motivating declaration for each of Cisco's 13,000-plus employees.

Chambers aims to be the Jack Welch of the new millennium. Like General Electric Co.'s Chairman Welch, he has decided he wants to be No. 1 or No. 2 in every market, a condition that already exists in 14 of the 15 markets in which Cisco competes. Beyond that strategic goal, Chambers believes that the new rules of competition demand organizations built on change, not stability; organized around networks, not a rigid hierarchy; based on interdependencies of partners, not self-sufficiency; and constructed on technological advantage, not old-fashioned bricks and mortar.

The network structure has vast implications for managing in the next century. GM's Saturn Div. and Dell Computer Corp. have shown how the network can eliminate inventory, by connecting with partners that deliver goods only when they are needed. In the new model that Chambers is creating at Cisco, however, the network is pervasive, central to nearly everything.

It seamlessly links Cisco to its customers, prospects, business partners, suppliers, and employees. This year, Cisco will sell more than $5 billion worth of goods—more than half its total—over the Internet, nearly three times the Internet sales booked by pioneer Dell. So successful has Cisco been in selling complex, expensive equipment over the Net that last year Cisco alone accounted for one-third of all electronic commerce.

Seven out of 10 customer requests for technical support are filled electronically—at satisfaction rates that eclipse those in-volving human interaction. Using the network for tech support allows Cisco to save more money than its nearest competitor spends on research and development. "It has saved me 1,000 engineers," gushes Chambers. "I take those 1,000 engineers, and instead of putting them into support, I put them into building new products. That gives you a gigantic competitive advantage."

The network also is the glue for the internal workings of the company. It swiftly connects Cisco with its web of partners, making the constellation of suppliers, contract manufacturers, and assemblers look like one company—Cisco—to the outside world. Via the company's intranet, outside contractors directly monitor orders from Cisco customers and ship the assembled hardware to buyers later in the day—often without Cisco even touching the box. By outsourcing production of 70% of its products, Cisco has quadrupled output without building new plants and has cut the time it takes to get a new product to market by two-thirds, to just six months.

## "Personal Touch"

The network also is Cisco's primary tool for recruiting talent, with half of all applications for jobs coming over the Net. When an employee wants information about a company event or health benefits, or needs to track an expense report, the network is the place to go at Cisco. The upshot: More than 1.7 million pages of information are accessible by employees who use the Cisco network thousands of times every day. "We are," says Chambers, "the best example of how the Internet is going to change everything."

Technology aids and abets this business model, but it does not completely displace human interaction. "The network works better when you've already had a personal touch," insists Chambers. That's why he does quarterly meetings with employees at a nearby convention center, why all employees in the month of their birth are invited to one of his $1\frac{1}{2}$-hour "birthday breakfasts," and why he works harder than most to encourage open and direct communication with all of Cisco's leaders.

Chambers also believes in partnering with other businesses. Plenty of companies forge links with others, but Cisco has a track record of making them work. "Partnerships are key to the new world strategies of the 21st century," says Donald J. Listwin, a Cisco senior vice-president. "Partners collapse time because they allow you to take on more things and bring them together quicker."

A good example is Cisco's partnership with Microsoft Corp., which last year resulted in a new technology to make networks more intelligent. The software lets networks know immediately a user's identity and location and to respond differently to each one. The partnership allows both companies to expand this market together more rapidly. "From initial discussion to technology, it took 18 months to get the product out," says Listwin. "It would have taken us four years to get to where we are [without such a partnership], and it's not clear we had the competence to get there alone."

Another theme—often heard but seldom exercised by corporate leaders—is the central importance of the customer. Nothing causes Chambers more restless nights than worry over how to serve customers better. That's why he spends as much as 55% of his time with customers and why he receives every night, 365 nights a year, voice mail updates on as many as 15 key clients.

## "Arrogant"

In this new model, strategic direction is not formed by an insular group of top executives, but by the company's leading customers. It's an outside-in approach, as opposed to an inside-out. The customer is the strategy. "There is nothing more arrogant than telling a customer: 'Here is what you need to know,'" says Chambers. "Most of the time, you are not going to be right." Rather, Cisco's leading-edge customers are seen as partners in forming the company strategy. Example: After Boeing Co. and Ford Motor Co. informed Chambers that their future network needs were unlikely to be satisfied by Cisco, Chambers went out to make his first acquisition to solve the problem. That deal, to acquire local-area-network switchmaker Crescendo Communications in 1993, put the company into a sector of the industry that now accounts for $2.8 billion in annual revenue.

Even such tactical moves as acquisitions and mergers are seen differently by a new-world company. Rather than acquire merely to speed growth or swell market share, Cisco routinely employs acquisitions to capture intellectual assets and next-generation products. "Most people forget that in a high-tech acquisition, you really are acquiring only people," says Chambers. "That's why so many of them fail. At what we pay, at $500,000 to $2 million an

employee, we are not acquiring current market share. We are acquiring futures."

While most companies immediately cut costs and people from newly acquired outfits, Cisco adheres to what it calls the "Mario rule"—named after Senior Vice-President Mario Mazzola, who had been CEO of Crescendo when it was bought by Cisco. Before any employee in a newly acquired company can be terminated, both Chambers and the former CEO must give their consent. "It tells new employees that Cisco wants them, that Cisco cares about them, and that we're not just another big company," says Daniel Scheinman, vice-president for legal and government affairs. "It buys the trust of the people . . . and their passion is worth a lot more than any of the downside legal protection."

In talent-hungry Silicon Valley, Cisco measures the success of every acquisition first by employee retention, then by new product development, and finally return on investment. The company has been phenomenally successful at holding on to the intellectual assets it buys: Overall turnover among acquired employees is just 6% a year, two percentage points lower than Cisco's overall employee churn. The company works hard to embrace employees acquired in deals, often giving top talent key jobs in the new organization. Three of Cisco's main businesses are led by former CEOs of acquired companies.

## Good Fit

Every acquisition, moreover, must meet Cisco guidelines. For years, Chambers watched IBM and other high-tech outfits acquire and then slowly smother

any number of entrepreneurial companies. What he learned was that you never buy a company whose values and culture are much different from your own. Nor do you buy a company that is too far away from your central base of operations. The latter makes a cultural fit less likely and severely limits the speed a company needs to compete in the new economy.

Chambers also believes that each deal must boast both short-term and long-term wins for customers, shareholders, and employees. "If there are no results in three to six months, people begin to question the acquisition," says Charles H. Giancarlo, vice-president for global alliances. "If you have good short-term wins, it's a virtuous cycle."

Through it all, the emphasis is on doing it faster, cheaper, and better—an integral part of success in the new economy. At Cisco, wages are less important than ownership. Some 40% of the stock options at the company are held by "individual contributors" who on average boast more than $150,000 in option gains. Egalitarianism is critical to successful teamwork and to morale. "You never ask your team to do something you wouldn't do yourself," says Chambers, who flies coach and has no reserved parking space at headquarters.

There are other leaders, of course, besides Chambers, who hope to create an organization that may very well revolutionize the fundamental business models of major global companies. But he's surely in the "sweet spot," helping to write the new rules for managing.

 **Article Review Form at end of book.**

What will be the importance of individual decision making in the future, and how will it impact managerial effectiveness?

# Position Yourself to "Get a Life" in the 21st Century

## Perry Pascarella

*Perry Pascarella is the former editor in chief of* IndustryWeek. *His latest book is* Leveraging People and Profit: The Hard Work of Soft Management *(Butterworth-Heinemann, 1998).*

"If it ain't broke don't fix it." That was a common attitude in American business during the 1980s. But stability has broken down, and today's managers must constantly be in a fixing-and-changing mode.

"We forget that business in this country is very different than it was a few years ago. The whole global marketplace is brand new. The whole competitive issue is brand new," Gerald Celente, a leading trends forecaster, reminds us.

Whether it's the cause or the result of other changes, the breakdown of institutional authority—church, government, business, you name it—is a major new reality. Along with that, our systems of law, healthcare, education and so forth are disintegrating. It's no longer a question of "Is it broke?" It's a matter of "Who will fix it and how?"

As Gerald writes in his book, *Trends 2000* (Warner Books, 1997), "The world is out of con-

trol. But your resolution is: No matter what the state of the world, I will take control of my own life." In other words, each of us—rather than our cultural institutions—will do the fixing.

Gerald highlighted the importance of individual action when we discussed his book. "More of the responsibility is going to be put on the people making individual decisions, but [it will be] directed toward the collective good," he says. "You will have the freedom to be who you want to be, but not in a narcissistic manner of 'I want, I need, this is mine.'"

## Trends to Watch

Gerald makes his predictions as director of the Trends Research Institute, a consortium of scholars, scientists, artists, writers and businesspeople that reviews the media to link events and trends. Using a process called "Globalnomics," they view all things as connected and ask which areas are affected by any given development.

A popular saying in their office is: "Opportunity misses those who view the world only through the eyes of their profession." Business managers, for example,

often don't know about all the developments outside their areas of interest that are affecting them.

Many corporations are finding that trends research is essential, and more and more of them want to learn how to do it, Gerald finds. Some are beginning to develop change-management boards and teams. "It's funny, though; they want to know how to do it, but they think it's something you do in your spare time. What they still don't understand is that it's not like you perform heart surgery and play the banjo at the same time. It's a full-time job," he says.

Studying the news, detecting trends and relating developments to each other isn't brain surgery, but it isn't banjo playing either. It's a matter of observation and deep analysis. Unfortunately, it seems that people in the business world don't have time to think today. No matter how much they talk about managing change, they slip back into a status quo attitude.

Some individuals are thinking, however. "Forced into freedom, millions of people on every level started finding ways to take control of their lives and do what they had always wanted to do," Gerald writes in his book as if looking back at the present from the year 2000.

He believes the most important trend of the new millennium—the driving force behind a global Renaissance—will be this focus on freedom, along with the opportunity to exercise individual creativity. In terms of jobs or careers, people will seek work that both brings them personal enjoyment and helps others in some way. The break from the status quo will be led by some of the baby boomers; they will be joined by others who have either lost their jobs or choose to trade in high-paying, high-stress, high-power positions for lives that provide more leisure and family time, more satisfaction and more control.

Beyond the focus on freedom, Gerald expects the following trends to help shape the new millennium:

- *Voluntary simplicity.* Echoing some thinking that emerged in the 1970s, he sees a growing movement toward "voluntary simplicity," a philosophy that encompasses moderation, self-discipline, care of the mind and body and spiritual growth.

  This trend does not imply that we're all going to live in the desert, the forecaster points out. "It means that you're going to buy what you need, and what you're going to need are high-quality products." He links the maturing of this trend to the maturing of the U.S. population. In 1970, the average age in the United States was 28. It will be 36 by 2000 and 40 in 2010. This maturing process will show up in the types of foods and entertainment we choose and the quality of products we buy.

- *Home-based tribes.* As people fashion new lives for themselves, more of their time will be centered in the home—home business, home farming, home study. Individuals will reach out from that center and become increasingly community-minded. Again, speaking as one looking back from the year 2000, Gerald writes, "To the technotribal 'We Generation,' community interests took precedence over selfish interests; harmonious habitat took precedence over economic development."

  People will do their thing in small towns, both old and new. Gerald predicts that those at the vanguard will see "the American dream not as fame and fortune but as being their own boss." As he notes, those downsized out of jobs, young retirees and those escaping big-city and suburban life will either form new communities or take over and transform traditional small towns and villages. As a result, interest in exurban commercial and residential real estate will be on the rise for at least the next 25 years.

- *A greater focus on health.* Those of us looking for better futures and for business opportunities should investigate the health arena. Gerald presents some frightening information on current levels of dirty water, food and air and nuclear radiation.

  But today's health concerns are nothing compared with those he foresees in the years ahead. "The health/fitness/nutrition trend, in its infancy and early childhood in the '80s and '90s, will go into an accelerated growth stage at the turn of the century," he writes.

  Gerald states, "The trend for 'clean' food is in the early stages of its life cycle. It will accelerate rapidly and will continue to grow beyond the foreseeable future." That growth will trigger a ripple effect along the food chain—farmers, chemical and fertilizer manufacturers, haulers, packagers, processors and distributors. Fast-food health restaurants will be a hot industry.

- *More "micros."* The microbrewery, the microbakery and other microbusinesses will grow in number as long as mergers and acquisitions continue to increase. Like boulders filling a hole, giant companies leave a lot of space between them.

  There will be plenty of room for small businesses, particularly in areas related to emotional, physical and

**The Thinker:** Gerald Celente, founder and director, Trends Research Institute

**Home Base:** Rhinebeck, N.Y.

**Latest Book:** *Trends 2000: How to Prepare for and Profit from the Changes of the 21st Century* (Warner Books, 1997)

**Key Ideas:**
- Freedom and the ability to exercise individual creativity will be the driving forces behind a global Renaissance.
- You are more likely to search for the "right livelihood"—a job that provides you enjoyment and, in some way, helps others.
- The trend toward "voluntary simplicity" means you will buy only what you need, but what you will need are high-quality products.

spiritual health. But don't today's microbusinesses already serve primarily upscale folks? True, but that number will continue to rise as people realize that less is more. "They are going to buy less quantity, higher quality," Gerald believes.

At first, Gerald's picture of the future struck me as frightening or at least disappointing. It will be a time of scaling back. But that was when I thought in terms of the status quo: How can I preserve what I've got? Now, when I look ahead to what I can make of and for myself, as well as for oth-ers, the future sparkles with opportunity and becomes a time of scaling upward.

**Article Review Form at end of book.**

To what extent will goods be typically customized in the future, and what managerial skills will be needed to provide them?

# The Customized, Digitized, Have-It-Your-Way Economy

Mass customization will change the way products are made—forever.

## Erick Schonfeld

A silent revolution is stirring in the way things are made and services are delivered. Companies with millions of customers are starting to build products designed just for you. You can, of course, buy a Dell computer assembled to your exact specifications. And you can buy a pair of Levi's cut to fit your body. But you can also buy pills with the exact blend of vitamins, minerals, and herbs that you like, glasses molded to fit your face precisely, CDs with music tracks that you choose, cosmetics mixed to match your skin tone, textbooks whose chapters are picked out by your professor, a loan structured to meet your financial profile, or a night at a hotel where every employee knows your favorite wine. And if your child does not like any of Mattel's 125 different Barbie dolls, she will soon be able to design her own.

Welcome to the world of mass customization, where mass-market goods and services are uniquely tailored to the needs of the individuals who buy them. Companies as diverse as BMW, Dell Computer, Levi Strauss, Mattel, McGraw-Hill, Wells Fargo, and a slew of leading Web businesses are adopting mass customization to maintain or obtain a competitive edge. Many are just beginning to dabble, but the direction in which they are headed is clear. Mass customization is more than just a manufacturing process, logistics system, or marketing strategy. It could well be the organizing principle of business in the next century, just as mass production was the organizing principle in this one.

The two philosophies couldn't clash more. Mass producers dictate a one-to-many relationship, while mass customizers require continual dialogue with customers. Mass production is cost-efficient. But mass customization is a flexible manufacturing technique that can slash inventory. And mass customization has two huge advantages over mass production: It is at the service of the customer, and it makes full use of cutting-edge technology.

A whole list of technological advances that make customization possible is finally in place. Computer-controlled factory equipment and industrial robots make it easier to quickly readjust assembly lines. The proliferation of bar-code scanners makes it possible to track virtually every part and product. Databases now store trillions of bytes of information, including individual customers' predilections for everything from cottage cheese to suede boots. Digital printers make it a cinch to change product packaging on the fly. Logistics and supply-chain management software tightly coordinates manufacturing and distribution.

And then there's the Internet, which ties these disparate pieces together. Says Joseph Pine, author of the pioneering book Mass Customization: "Anything you can digitize, you can customize." The Net makes it easy for companies to move data from an online order form to the factory floor. The Net makes it easy for manufacturing types to communicate with marketers. Most of all, the Net makes it easy for a company to conduct an ongoing, one-to-one dialogue with each of its customers, to learn about and respond to their exact preferences. Conversely, the Net is also often the best way for a customer to learn which company has the most to offer him—if he's not happy with one company's wares, nearly perfect information about a competitor's is just a mouse click away. Combine that with mass customization, and the nature of a company's relationship with its customers is forever changed. Much of the leverage that once belonged to companies now belongs to customers.

If a company can't customize, it's got a problem. The Industrial Age model of making things cheaper by making them the same will not hold. Competitors can copy product innovations faster than ever. Meanwhile, consumers demand more choices. Marketing guru Regis McKenna declares, "Choice has become a higher value than brand in America." The largest market shares for soda, beer, and software do not belong to Coca-Cola, Anheuser-Busch, or Microsoft. They belong to a category called Other. Now companies are trying to produce a unique Other for each of us. It is the logical culmination of markets' being chopped into finer and finer segments.

After all, the ultimate niche is a market of one.

The best—and most famous—example of mass customization is Dell Computer, which has a direct relationship with customers and builds only PCs that have actually been ordered. Everyone from Compaq to IBM is struggling to copy Dell's model. And for good reason. Dell passed IBM last quarter to claim the No. 2 spot in PC market share (behind Compaq). While other computer manufacturers struggle for profits, Dell keeps reporting record numbers; in its most recent quarter the company's sales were up 54%, while earnings soared 62%. No wonder Michael Dell has become the poster boy of the new economy. As Pine says, "The closest person we have to Henry Ford is Michael Dell."

Dell's triumph is not so much technological as it is organizational. Dell keeps margins up by keeping inventory down. The company builds computers from modular components that are always readily available. But Dell doesn't want to store tons of parts: Computer components decline in value at a rate of about 1% a week, faster than just about any product other than sushi or losing lottery tickets. So the key to the system is ensuring that the right parts and products are delivered to the right place at the right time.

To do this, Dell employs sophisticated logistics software, some developed internally, some made by i2 Technologies. The software takes info gathered from customers and steers it to the parts of the organization that need it. When an order comes in, the data collected are quickly parsed out—to suppliers that need to rush over a shipment of hard drives, say, or to the factory

floor, where assemblers put parts together in the customer's desired configuration. "Our goal," says vice chairman Kevin Rollins, "is to know exactly what the customer wants when they want it, so we will have no waste."

The company has been propelled by this thinking ever since Michael Dell started selling PCs from his college dorm room in 1983. The Web makes the process virtually seamless, by allowing the company to easily collect customized, digitized data that are ready for delivery to the people who need them. The result is an entire organization driven by orders placed by individual customers, an organization that does more Web-based commerce than almost anyone else. Dell's future doesn't depend on faster chips or modems—it depends on greater mastery of mass customization, of streamlining the flow of quality information.

It's not much of a surprise that a leading tech company like Dell is using software and the Net in such innovative ways. What's startling is the extent to which companies in other industries are embracing mass customization. Take Mattel. Starting by October, girls will be able to log on to barbie.com and design their own friend of Barbie's. They will be able to choose the doll's skin tone, eye color, hairdo, hair color, clothes, accessories, and name (6,000 permutations will be available initially). The girls will even fill out a questionnaire that asks about the doll's likes and dislikes. When the Barbie pal arrives in the mail, the girls will find their doll's name on the package, along with a computer-generated paragraph about her personality.

Offering such a product without the Net would be next to impossible. Mattel does make specific versions of Barbie for customers such as Toys "R" Us, and the company customizes cheerleader Barbies for universities. But this will be the first time Mattel produces Barbie dolls in lots of one. Like Dell, Mattel must use high-end manufacturing and logistics software to ensure that the order data on its Website are distributed to the parts of the company that need them. The only real concern is whether Mattel's systems can handle the expected demand in a timely fashion. Right now, marketing VP Anne Parducci is shooting for delivery of the dolls within six weeks—a bit much considering that that is how long it takes to get a custom-ordered BMW.

Nevertheless, Parducci is pumped. "Personalization is a dream we have had for several years," she says. Parducci thinks the custom Barbies could become one of next year's hottest toys. Then, says Parducci, "we are going to build a database of children's names, to develop a one-to-one relationship with these girls." That may sound creepy, but part of mass customization is treating your customers, even preteens, as adults. By allowing the girls to define beauty in their own terms, Mattel is in theory helping them feel good about themselves even as it collects personal data. That's quite a step for a company that has stamped out its own stereotypes of beauty for decades, but Parducci's market testing shows that girls' enthusiasm for being a fashion designer or creating a personality is "through the roof."

Levi Strauss also likes giving customers the chance to play fashion designer. For the past four years it has made measure-to-fit women's jeans under the Personal Pair banner. In October,

Levi's will relaunch an expanded version called Original Spin, which will offer more options and will feature men's jeans as well.

With the help of a sales associate, customers will create the jeans they want by picking from six colors, three basic models, five different leg openings, and two types of fly. Then their waist, butt, and inseam will be measured. They will try on a plain pair of test-drive jeans to make sure they like the fit before the order is punched into a Web-based terminal linked to the stitching machines in the factory. Customers can even give the jeans a name—say, Rebel, for a pair of black ones. Two to three weeks later the jeans arrive in the mail; a bar-code tag sealed to the pocket lining stores the measurements for simple reordering.

Today a fully stocked Levi's store carries approximately 130 ready-to-wear pairs of jeans for any given waist and inseam. With Personal Pair, that number jumped to 430 choices. And with Original Spin, it will leap again, to about 750. Sanjay Choudhuri, Levi's director of mass customization, isn't in a hurry to add more choices. "It is critical to carefully pick the choices that you offer," says Choudhuri. "An unlimited amount will create inefficiencies at the plant." Dell Computer's Rollins agrees: "We want to offer fewer components all the time." To these two, mass customization isn't about infinite choices but about offering a healthy number of standard parts that can be mixed and matched in thousands of ways. That gives customers the illusion of boundless choice while keeping the complexity of the manufacturing process manageable.

Levi's charges a slight premium for custom jeans, but what

Choudhuri really likes about the process is that Levi's can become your "jeans adviser." Selling off-the-shelf jeans ends a relationship; the customer walks out of the store as anonymous as anyone else on the street. Customizing jeans starts a relationship; the customer likes the fit, is ready for reorders, and forks over his name and address in case Levi's wants to send him promotional offers. And customers who design their own jeans make the perfect focus group; Levi's can apply what it learns from them to the jeans it mass-produces for the rest of us.

If Levi's experiment pays off, other apparel makers will follow its lead. In the not-so-distant future people may simply walk into body-scanning booths where they will be bathed with patterns of white light that will determine their exact three-dimensional structure. A not-for-profit company called [TC]2, funded by a consortium of companies including Levi's, is developing just such a technology. Last year some MIT business students proposed a similar idea for a custom-made bra company dubbed Perfect Underwear.

Morpheus Technologies, a wacky startup in Portland, Me., hopes to set up studios equipped with body scanners. Founder Parker Poole III wants to "digitize people and connect their measurement data to their credit cards." Someone with the foresight to be scanned by Morpheus could then call up Eddie Bauer, say, give his credit card number, and order a robe that matches his dimensions. His digital self could also be sent to Brooks Brothers for a suit. Gone will be the days of attentive men kneeling on the floor with pins in their mouths. Progress does have its price.

Thirty years ago auto manufacturers were, effectively, mass customizers. People would spend hours in the office of a car dealer, picking through pages of options. But that ended when car companies tried to improve manufacturing efficiency by offering little more than a few standard options packages. BMW wants to turn back the clock. About 60% of the cars it sells in Europe are built to order, vs. just 15% in the U.S. Europeans seem willing to wait three to four months for a vehicle, while most Americans won't wait longer than four weeks.

Now the company wants to make better use of its customer database to get more Americans to custom-order. BMW dealers save about $450 in inventory costs on every such order. Reinhard Fischer, head of logistics for BMW of North America, says, "The big battle is to take cost out of the distribution chain. The best way to do that is to build in just the things a consumer wants."

Since most BMWs in the U.S. are leased, the company knows when customers will need a new car. Some dealers now call customers a few months before their leases are up to see whether they'd like to custom-order their next car. Soon, however, customers will be able to configure their own car online and send that info to a dealer. Fischer can even see a day when the Website will offer data about vehicles sailing on ships from Germany, so that people can see whether a car matching their preferences is already on the way. That does, of course, raise the question, Why not send the requests directly to BMW, circumventing dealers altogether? Says Fischer: "We don't want to eliminate their role, but maybe they should have a 7% margin, not 16%." Ouch.

Such dilemmas are inevitable, given that mass customization streamlines the order process. What's more, mass customization is about creating products—be they PCs, jeans, cars, eyeglasses, loans, or even industrial soap— that match your needs better than anything a traditional middleman can possibly order for you.

LensCrafters, for instance, has made quick, in-store production of customized lenses common. But Tokyo-based Paris Miki takes the process a step further. Using special software, it designs lenses and a frame that conform both to the shape of a customer's face and to whether he wants, say, casual frames, a sports pair, sunglasses, or more formal specs. The customer can check out on a monitor various choices superimposed over a scanned image of his face. Once he chooses the pair he likes, the lenses are ground and the rimless frames attached.

While we tend to think of automation as a process that eliminates the need for human interaction, mass customization makes the relationship with customers more important than ever. ChemStation in Dayton has about 1,700 industrial-soap formulas— for car washes, factories, landfills, railroads, airlines, and mines. The company analyzes items that are to be cleaned (recent ones in its labs include flutes and goose down) or visits its customers' premises to analyze their dirt. After the analysis, the company brews up a special batch of cleanser. The soap is then placed on the customer's property in reusable containers ChemStation monitors and keeps full. For most customers, teaching another company their cleansing needs is not worth the effort. About 95% of ChemStation's clients never leave.

Hotels that want you to keep coming back are using software to personalize your experience. All Ritz-Carlton hotels, for instance, are linked to a database filled with the quirks and preferences of half-a-million guests. Any bellhop or desk clerk can find out whether you are allergic to feathers, what your favorite newspaper is, or how many extra towels you like.

Wells Fargo, the largest provider of Internet banking, already allows customers to apply for a home-equity loan over the Net and get a three-second decision on a loan structured specifically for them. A lot of behind-the-scenes technology makes this possible, including real-time links to credit bureaus, databases with checking-account histories and property values, and software that can do cash-flow analysis. With a few pieces of customized information from the loan seeker, the software whips into action to make a quick decision.

The bank also uses similar software in its small-business lending unit. According to vice chairman Terri Dial, Wells Fargo used to turn away lots of qualified small businesses—the loans were too small for Wells to justify the time spent on credit analysis. But now the company can collect a few key details from applicants, customize a loan, and approve or deny credit in four hours—down from the four days the process used to take. In some categories that Wells once virtually ignored, loan approvals are up as much as 50%. Says Dial: "You either invest in the technology or get out of that line of business."

She'd better keep investing. Combine the software that enables customization with the ubiquity of the Web, and you get a situation that threatens Wells' very existence. If consumers grow accustomed to designing their own products, will they trust brand-name manufacturers and service providers or will they turn to a new kind of middleman? Frank Shlier, a director of research at the Gartner Group in Stamford, Conn., sees disintermediaries emerging all over the Net to help people sift through the thousands of choices presented to them. In financial services, he suggests, there is "a new role for a trusted adviser, maybe someone who doesn't own any banks."

Shlier's middleman sounds a lot like Intuit, which lets visitors to its quicken.com Website apply for and purchase mortgages from a variety of lenders, fill out their taxes, or set up a portfolio to track their stocks, bonds, and mutual funds. Tapan Bhat, the exec who oversees quicken.com, says, "The Web is probably the medium most attuned to customization, yet so many sites are centered on the company instead of on the individual." What would lure someone to Levi's if she could instead visit a clothing Website that stored her digital dimensions and ordered custom-fit jeans from the manufacturer with the best price and fit? Elaborates Pehong Chen, CEO of Internet software outfit BroadVision: "The Nirvana is that you are so close to your customers, you can satisfy all their needs. Even if you don't make the item yourself, you own the relationship."

Amazon.com has three million relationships. It sells books online and now is moving into music (with videos probably next). Every time someone buys a book on its Website, Amazon.com learns her tastes and suggests other titles she might enjoy. The more Amazon.com learns, the better it serves its customers; the better it serves its customers, the more loyal they become. About 60% are repeat buyers.

The Web is a supermall of mass customizers. You can drop music tracks on your own CDs (cductive.com); choose from over a billion options of printed art, mats, and frames (artuframe. com); get stock picks geared to your goals (personalwealth.com); or make your own vitamins (acumins.com). And you can get all kinds of tailored data; NewsEdge, for example, will send a customized newspaper to your PC.

These companies want to keep customers happy by giving them a product that cannot be compared to a competitor's. Acumin, for instance, blends vitamins, herbs, and minerals per customers' instructions, compressing up to 95 ingredients into three to five pills. If a customer wants to start taking a new supplement, all Acumin needs to do is add it to the blend.

Acumin's products address what Pine calls customer sacrifice—the compromise we all make when we can't get exactly the product we want. CEO Brad Oberwager started the company two years ago, when his sister, who was undergoing a special cancer radiation treatment, couldn't find a multivitamin without iodine. (Her doctor had told her to avoid iodine.) "If someone would create a vitamin just for me, I would buy it," she told her brother. So he did.

The Web will make that kind of response the norm. Sure, there are any number of ways for consumers to provide a company with information about their preferences—they can call, they can write, or, heck, they can even walk into the brick-and-mortar store. But the Web changes everything—the information arrives in a digitized form ready for broadcast. Says i2 CEO Sanjiv Sidhu, "The Internet is bringing society into a culture of speed that has not really existed before." As new middlemen customize orders for the masses, differentiating one company from its competitors will become tougher than ever. Responding to price cuts or quality improvements will continue to be important, but the key differentiator may be how quickly a company can serve a customer. Says Artuframe.com CEO Bill Lederer: "Mass customization is novel today. It will be common tomorrow." If he is right, the Web will wind up creating a strange competitive landscape, where companies temporarily connect to satisfy one customer's desires, then disband, then reconnect with other enterprises to satisfy a different order from a different customer.

That's the vision anyway. For now, companies are struggling to take the first steps toward mass customization. The ones that are already there have been working on the process for years. Matthew Sigman is an executive at R.R. Donnelley & Sons, whose digital publishing business prints textbooks customized by individual college professors. "The challenge," Sigman warns, "is that if you are making units of one, your margin for error is zero." Custom-fit jeans do come with a money-back guarantee. Levi's can't afford for you not to like them.

 **Article Review Form at end of book.**

# WiseGuide Wrap-Up

- Although no one can know the future with any certainty, the one thing that does seem incontrovertibly true is that it will be characterized by rapid and occasionally destabilizing change.

- An environment of change provides both threats and opportunities, and those managers and organizations that are best able to anticipate and to cope with change are likely to benefit.

- Twenty-first century managers will be critical to organizational success and will require a mix of technical and interpersonal skills.

## R.E.A.L. Sites

This list provides a print preview of typical **Coursewise** R.E.A.L. sites. (There are over 100 such sites at the **Courselinks**™ site.) The danger in printing URLs is that web sites can change overnight. As we went to press, these sites were functional using the URLs provided. If you come across one that isn't, please let us know via email to: webmaster@coursewise.com. Use your Passport to access the most current list of R.E.A.L. sites at the **Courselinks** site.

**Site name:** Xerox Research Centre Europe
**URL:** http://www.rxrc.xerox.com/home.html
**Why is it R.E.A.L.?** This site provides reports on projects undertaken as well as research, investigations, the work practices, and organizational contexts of settings organized around the use of computer technology, especially document technology. The fieldwork methods involve "ethnographic" studies of work sites and organizations.
**Key topics:** technology and management, future management trends
**Try this:** Read the article on multilingual technology found at this site, and make some predictions on the implications for management.

**Site name:** Harvard Business School Faculty Research Computing Center
**URL:** http://www.hbs.edu/research/
**Why is it R.E.A.L.?** This site provides reports on research projects at Harvard Business School, which modestly describes itself as "the world's leading business school." You will need Adobe's Acrobat Reader to view or print the files.
**Key topics:** technology and management, research reports
**Try this:** Summarize the results of a research report available on this site.

**Site name:** Michael Finley's "Future Shoes"
**URL:** http://www.skypoint.com/~mfinley/
**Why is it R.E.A.L.?** This site offers an unusual perspective on organizations and how they fail to work as expected.
**Key topics:** future of management, technology and management
**Try this:** Find an interesting perspective on the future that you feel is relevant to management.

**Site name:** Rockford Consulting Group
**URL:** http://ourworld.compuserve.com/homepages/RockfordConsultingGroup/
**Why is it R.E.A.L.?** This site outlines a high-involvement technique that equips planners and small business owners with a tool for creating vision statements that provide strategic direction.
**Key topic:** future management trends
**Try this:** Locate and summarize an article on managerial performance in the future.

# Index

**Note:** Names and page numbers in **bold** type indicate authors and their articles.

# Putting It in *Perspectives*
## -Review Form-

Your name:_____     Date: _____

Reading title: _____

**Summarize:** Provide a one-sentence summary of this reading: _____

_____

_____

_____

**Follow the Thinking:** How does the author back the main premise of the reading? Are the facts/opinions appropriately supported by research or available data? Is the author's thinking logical?

_____

_____

_____

_____

_____

_____

**Develop a Context** (answer one or both questions): How does this reading contrast or complement your professor's lecture treatment of the subject matter? How does this reading compare to your textbook's coverage?

_____

_____

_____

_____

_____

_____

**Question Authority:** Explain why you agree/disagree with the author's main premise.

_____

_____

_____

_____

_____

_____

**COPY ME!** Copy this form as needed. This form is also available at http://www.coursewise.com
Click on: *Perspectives*.